Environmental Psychology

second edition

Environmental Psychology

second edition

Norman W. Heimstra
University of South Dakota

Leslie H. McFarling

Brooks / Cole Publishing Company
Monterey, California
A Division of Wadsworth Publishing Company, Inc.

Consulting Editor: Edward L. Walker, University of Michigan

Printed in the United States of America

10 9 8 7 6 5 4 3 2 1

Library of Congress Cataloging in Publication Data

Heimstra, Norman W.
      Environmental psychology.

      Bibliography: p. 259.
      Includes index.
      1. Environmental psychology.   I. McFarling,
Leslie H., joint author.   II. Title.
BF353.H37   1978   155.9   78-913
ISBN 0-8185-0266-5

Acquisition Editor: *William H. Hicks*
Manuscript Editor: *Grace Holloway*
Production Editor: *Marilu Uland*
Interior Design: *Jamie S. Brooks*
Cover Design: *Katherine Minerva*
Typesetting: *Computer Typesetting Services, Glendale, California*

PREFACE

In the preface to the first edition of *Environmental Psychology*, we pointed out the growing concern for the quality of the physical environment and the interest not only in the ways in which humans affect their environment but also in the manner in which the physical environment influences human behavior. Interest in people/environment relationships remains at a high level, and researchers in a number of disciplines continue to study these relationships. The purpose of this second edition, as of the first edition, is to present an overview of the basic concepts and major research concerns in the field of environmental psychology.

We have made an effort to make this book readable for students in a number of different disciplines, who, in many instances, may have only a minimal background in psychology. Topics dealt with in this book should prove of interest to students in such diverse fields as psychology, sociology, urban planning, environmental studies, architecture, design, engineering, and other fields—in brief, to anyone concerned with the ways in which human behavior may be modified and shaped by the physical environment.

The second edition of *Environmental Psychology* has been considerably expanded, although we have not attempted to develop an encyclopedia of studies but, rather, have selected areas of research that represent major concerns in the field. There is some question as to what topics should be covered in a book dealing with environmental psychology, and what to include and what to delete often presented us with difficult decisions. However, we have selected those topics that we believe are most relevant to environmental psychologists.

In this second edition, we have added considerable new material. At the suggestion of a number of users of the first edition, we have devoted an entire chapter to research methods in environmental psychology. We have also added a chapter on social behavior and the physical environment and have covered in some detail the topics of privacy, territoriality, personal space, and crowding. Materials retained from the first edition have been updated, with discussions of recent studies and, in some cases, new topics, such as energy and the built environment, have been added. In general, we have followed the first edition approach of discussing the physical environment in terms of the built and natural environment and of the relationships that exist between these environments and human behavior.

There are a number of individuals who contributed in various ways to this book. Our experience with the Brooks/Cole publishing team—particularly William Hicks, Marilu Uland, and Jamie Brooks—was once again rewarding, and we wish to express to them our appreciation. We also appreciated and benefited from the reviews of the manuscript that were undertaken by Irwin Altman of The University of Utah, Mike Copp of Orange Coast College, Arthur H. Patterson of The Pennsylvania State University, Paul Paulus of the University of Texas at Arlington, Warren R. Street of Central Washington State College, Eric Sundstrom of the University of Tennessee, and Herbert Weaver of the University of Hawaii. Jeff Phillips, of the Human Factors Laboratory of the University of South Dakota, provided useful comments and contributions to Chapter 6. Finally, we are particularly grateful to Rosie Phillips for her contributions; her ability to maintain her patience and good humor throughout the typings and retypings that were necessary is sincerely appreciated.

Norman W. Heimstra
Leslie H. McFarling

CONTENTS

CHAPTER 1

INTRODUCTION

Perhaps at no other time in history have people been more aware of the environment and their relationships to it. In this day of advancing technology, expanding populations, energy developments, and other events that modify the environment, people who a few years ago were only vaguely concerned about their physical environment have now become greatly concerned.

This concern has been expressed in numerous local, state, and federal laws designed to protect the environment. It has also led to a growing awareness of the complexity of the relationships between people and many aspects of the environment and has generated an interest in these relationships in numerous areas. Architecture, urban and regional planning, civil and sanitary engineering, forest and park management, geography, biology, sociology, and psychology are only a few of them. As Wohlwill (1970) points out: "there are few, if any, fields that do not at some point touch on the relationship between man and his environment" (p. 303). In this book we will be particularly concerned with the kinds of relationships that have been studied primarily by psychologists and other behavioral scientists and that make up the new discipline of environmental psychology.

SOME PROBLEMS OF DEFINITION

In 1970 in their textbook *Environmental Psychology: Man and His Physical Setting*, Proshansky, Ittelson, and Rivlin questioned whether it is possible to arrive at an adequate definition of environmental psychology. They concluded:

> We think not. There are, in general, two ways in which the definition of a field of study may be stated. One—and in the long run, the only really satisfactory way— is in terms of theory. And the simple fact is that as yet there is no adequate theory, or even the beginnings of a theory, of environmental psychology on which such a definition might be based [p. 5].

Nearly a decade later this statement is still basically true. We still have no adequate theory on which a definition of environmental psychology can be based, although we do have the beginnings of several theories that may prove useful. The newness of the field accounts for this lack of a solid theoretical base. As Proshansky, Ittelson, and Rivlin state in the 1976 revision of their book, "Perhaps the most important indicator of the maturity of a scientific field is the level of its theoretical formulation. In this regard it must be said that environmental psychology is still very much in its infancy, although the infant has indeed grown considerably in the past few years" (p. 7).

If the best way of defining a field is in terms of its theory and if the field does not have an adequate theoretical base, how can we define it? In their discussion of the problems of defining environmental psychology, Proshansky and his associates (1970) suggest that we must use an operational definition; that is, environmental psychology is what environmental psychologists do. From this perspective, we will have defined environmental psychology when we have surveyed the activities of researchers who consider themselves environmental psychologists. Although we will find these activities to be quite diverse, the researchers will have in common a concern about the relationships between people and the physical environment. Thus, we can arrive now at a working definition of the field. *Environmental psychology is the discipline that is concerned with the relationships between human behavior and the physical environment.* To clarify this definition, however, it is necessary to discuss several aspects of it in more detail. In this section we will be concerned with a more precise explanation of what is meant by the *physical environment*, by *human behavior,* and by the *relationships* that exist between the two.

The Physical Environment

Psychologists and other behavioral scientists have always talked about the role of the environment in shaping behavior. Usually, however, they have thought of the environment as social or interpersonal and have considered other people to be the major determinants of human behavior. When behavioral scientists have referred to other environmental influences, they have generally done so in nonspecific terms, with the concept of environment "used to refer to the most diverse set of conditions of experience, ranging from attendance in nursery school to socialization practices of parents; from the provision for practice or training on a task to the role of culture or society in a global sense" (Wohlwill, 1970, p. 304). Although environmental psychologists recognize that social or interpersonal factors are important determinants of behavior, they also recognize that the physical environment influences behavior and are interested in determining the relationships between the two.

In its broadest sense, the term *physical environment* connotes everything that surrounds a person. As typically used in environmental psychology, the term has a more limited meaning—although, as will become apparent, it is still quite broad. Environmental psychologists divide the physical environment into two types, the *built* or *modified* and the *natural.*

Much of the interest in the built physical environment has centered on the relationship between behavior and such features of the built environment as the rooms of buildings in which the behavior occurs, various types of housing, the design of institutions, and the conditions of life in cities. Built features of the environment have also resulted in pollution, overcrowding, and other undesirable consequences. The effects of these conditions on behavior have been of considerable interest to environmental psychologists. It is these aspects of the built environment with which we will be primarily concerned in this text.

The distinction between the built or modified environment and the natural environment is mostly one of convenience, since very little of the "natural" environment has not been modified to some extent. However, there are still many national parks and wilderness areas where human modifications are at least minimal and where millions of visitors every year perceive themselves as interacting with the natural environment. Some research has been conducted on the relationship between behavior and these kinds of environments as well as on other types perceived as natural environments by various users. Researchers have also been interested in another kind of natural environment, the *geographic,* which includes climate, terrain, and such natural hazards as floods, earthquakes, and hurricanes, all of which influence behavior.

It should be pointed out that other psychologists often use the term *natural environment* somewhat differently. They may use the term simply to refer to a situation or setting that has not been modified by the experimenter. Thus, a psychologist studying the behavior of schoolchildren in a classroom would report that their behavior was observed in a natural environment.

It is important to realize that the environmental psychologist, in attempting to study the relationship between a physical setting and human behavior, seldom deals with a situation in which the individual being studied is not influenced in some fashion by other people. There are virtually always social factors that will influence the response to the physical environment and that may have far more profound effects on behavior than the physical setting itself. These social factors have been studied under the headings of privacy, personal space, territory, and crowding. When we discuss the work of Irwin Altman (1975) and others in Chapter 6, we shall see that this is an area of environmental psychology with a more solid theoretical foundation than most of the other areas we will deal with.

Studying the relationships between human behavior and the many features of the physical environment is a challenging task. It is difficult, if not impossible, to isolate one feature of the environment and study its effects on behavior without having the behavior modified, at least to some extent, by other features. For example, suppose a researcher is interested in the relationship between the shape of a room and the behavior of its occupants. The researcher could design a study in any one of several ways, and various types of behavior could be involved. In addition, however, the room would be only one unit of a building having a number of characteristics that also influence behavior. The building, in turn, might be one of several in a complex forming part of a neighborhood. The neighborhood would be part of a city having hot or cold weather and subject to possible natural hazards, such as floods or earthquakes. The physical environment can be thought of as a system composed of a number of subsystems—climatic conditions, cities, buildings, and so forth—all interacting and influencing behavior. This concept of the physical environment as a system will be discussed later in more detail. For now, keep in mind that it is difficult to isolate one of the subsystems and determine the relationship between it and human behavior. As we shall see in the following chapters, this is a problem in much environmental-psychology research.

Human Behavior

When we speak of human behavior, we are referring to an almost limitless range of activities. As Skinner (1953) states:

> Behavior is a difficult subject matter, not because it is inaccessible, but because it is extremely complex. Since it is a process, rather than a thing, it cannot be easily held for observation. It is changing, fluid, and evanescent, and for this reason it makes great technical demands upon the ingenuity and energy of the scientist [p. 15].

As we shall see, because of the nature of the relationships between behavior and the physical environment, the demands upon the ingenuity and energy of environmental psychologists are often great indeed. In the next chapter, some of the methods used by these researchers in attempting to study these relationships will be considered in some detail.

Broadly defined, behavior is any form of activity that is observable either directly or with the aid of instruments. Elaborate equipment is required to observe some kinds of behavior—electrical changes within the brain, for example. Various types of tests can be used to detect mental and psychological processes. Still other kinds of behavior are overt, so the researcher need only jot down what is seen or heard. The point to keep in mind is that behavior ranges from very subtle forms of activity to overt activities that are easily observable.

Although the types of behavior that might be influenced by the physical environment seem almost limitless, a review of the environmental-psychology literature suggests that researchers have tended to focus on relatively limited kinds of behavior. For example, much of the research has dealt with perception of or attitudes about the physical environment. Although we shall see in the next chapter that these can be useful types of measures, we shall also see that there are major difficulties involved in identifying and measuring attitudes and perceptions and that there is some question about their meaningfulness.

There has also been considerable research dealing with the impact of the physical environment on various affective states, such as mood, and with the effects of physical or social stimuli in the environment on emotional states. For instance, in one of the recent attempts to establish a theoretical framework for environmental psychology, Mehrabian and Russell (1974) suggest that environmental stimuli have emotion-eliciting qualities and that the emotional responses (pleasure, arousal, and dominance) serve to determine a variety of what they term "approach–avoidance behaviors such as physical approach, work performance, exploration, and social interaction" (p. 8). In their book *An Approach to Environmental Psychology,* these authors summarize a great deal of the available literature in an attempt to substantiate their theory.

There are, of course, a number of other types of behavior that have been studied by environmental psychologists frequently enough to merit discussion. These will be considered in the next chapter.

In discussing the behavior that is of interest to the researcher, it is easy to forget an important point. To discuss relationships between physical settings and behavior meaningfully, it is necessary to define carefully not only the behavior that is to be measured and evaluated but also the physical setting. This requirement has led to interest in the development of methods for adequately describing the physical stimuli influencing behavior. However, a statement by Craik (1970) should be kept in mind: "While the everyday physical environment is its unifying theme, the subject matter of environmental psychology is human behavior *as it relates to,* for example, rock formations, downtown streets, and corners of rooms, not the rock formations, downtown streets, and corners of rooms themselves" (p. 13). Thus, although environmental psychologists may spend a good deal of time and effort describing characteristics of the physical environment, their ultimate objective is relating these characteristics to human behavior.

Relationships between Behavior and the Environment

When environmental psychologists refer to the relationships between human behavior and the physical environment, they are usually referring to relationships in which the environment has an effect on behavior. In this section, for the most part, we will be discussing these types of relationships, but it is important to keep in mind that much human behavior also has an effect on the environment. Thus, instead of studying the effects of air pollution on behavior, a researcher might have wished to study the kind of behavior that results in air pollution.

There are several views of human behavior as a function of attributes of the physical environment. Wohlwill (1970) believes that the relationship between behavior and the physical environment takes three forms. First, he points out that behavior occurs in a particular environmental context. This context imposes major restrictions on the kinds of behavior that can occur in it and "frequently serves to determine in a more positive sense particular aspects or patterns of an individual's behavior" (p. 304). For example, the behavior that a person living on a farm or in a small town can engage in differs considerably from the behavior that a city dweller can engage in. One kind of relationship, then, is that the environment determines the range of behavior that can occur in it.

In the second type of relationship, certain qualities associated with a particular environment may have a broad effect on the behavior and personality of the individual. Wohlwill cites as examples the "wonted brusqueness of the typical New York City bus driver on the job [and] the proverbial 'mad cabbie' of Manhattan." Wohlwill suggests that, at least to the extent that these stereotypes hold true, "it seems plausible to relate them to the conditions of stress and tension to which these individuals are subjected in their daily battle with urban traffic and congestion" (p. 304). This type of relationship may also explain reported differences between urban and rural incidences of mental disease and various physical disorders, as well as bystander apathy in the face of violence.

The third kind of relationship is one in which the environment serves as a motivating force:

> Individuals give evidence of more or less strongly defined attitudes, values, beliefs, and affective responses relating to their environment. . . . They develop diverse forms of adjustment and adaptation to environmental conditions. They exhibit temporary and permanent responses of approach to and avoidance of or escape from given environmental situations, ranging all the way from recreation and tourism to migration to the suburbs, or to a different part of the country [p. 304].

This last type of relationship thus has three important facets: (1) affective and attitudinal responses to environmental features, (2) approach and avoidance responses to various attributes of the environment, and (3) adaptation to environmental qualities. As Wohlwill (p. 305) points out, not only are these kinds of relationships directly connected with many current environmental problems, but they can also be analyzed in terms of existing principles or hypotheses in psychology.

Much of the research conducted by environmental psychologists has dealt with the first of these relationships, the environment as a source of affect and attitudes. As we shall see in the following chapters, the physical environment can elicit strong feelings and attitudes, both positive and negative.

In the second relationship the physical environment results in approach or avoidance behavior. Thus, individuals may move from an area they dislike for some reason—a cold climate or overcrowding, for example—to a region they find more attractive. This kind of behavior is also involved when a person selects one vacation spot over another, one building site over another, and so forth. This aspect of the behavior/environment relationship is now beginning to receive more attention from researchers and, as already pointed out, is a key feature of the conceptual framework presented by Mehrabian and Russell (1974).

Finally, the question of how people adapt to their physical environment is also of considerable interest to environmental psychologists. We know that people are capable of adapting both behaviorally and physiologically to a wide range of environments. Although much of the research in this area has been conducted in the laboratory and has dealt with adaptation to temperature, light, and so forth, people also adapt to life in the ghetto, to noise from jet aircraft and freeway traffic, to pollution, and to other features of the physical environment. We will discuss this adaptive process at several places in the text, since it raises a number of intriguing questions.

Irwin Altman (1973) takes a somewhat different approach to behavior and the environment. He discusses several models that have guided many researchers in the environmental–psychology field and have partly determined the nature of the behavior/environment relationships studied.

The first model, called the *mechanistic* model, originated in the human-engineering field of psychology. This field is primarily concerned with designing equipment to fit the capabilities of the human operator—that is, to modify the physical environment to fit people. Consequently, investigating performance-related behavior has been emphasized. As Altman (1973) points out, although this approach was popular 15 or 20 years ago and is still relevant, it is not often used in current behavior/environment research.

Altman suggests that the present-day approach in environmental research uses a model that can be labeled the *perceptual/cognitive/motivational* model. In this model, people are seen in terms of various internal processes, including perceptual, motivational, emotional, and cognitive reactions to the environment. Researchers using this model have tried to determine how individuals perceive their environment and how they react to it. These researchers emphasize subjective perceptions or impressions of the environment, regardless of its physical or "objective" aspects.

A third model is called the *behavioral* model. Researchers basing their work on this model are not interested in subjective states developed in relation to the environment but in overt behavior that can be observed, recorded, and analyzed. This approach is becoming increasingly popular.

The last model Altman calls a social-systems, ecological model. According to Altman, this one holds considerable promise for better understanding of behavior/environment relationships. One of the most important elements of this model is that it treats both people and environments as equally important; each influences and shapes the other. In other words, people help create their own environment. Altman states that this model "may be useful in establishing connections between the other models. Furthermore, it seems to fit more appropriately the complex nature of man-environment relationships" (p. 123).

From our discussion of the kinds of relationships that can exist between people and the physical environment (and there are others that have not been mentioned), it should be apparent that we are dealing with situations involving complex causes and complex behaviors. For example, when we study behavior, we must be aware that the behavior observed is the result of existing motivational factors, of past experience, and of a host of other variables, some of which may not have any relationship to the physical environment. It would be appropriate at this point to discuss some of these factors—such as the role of previous experience or learning in determining the way a person behaves in a given situation—but space limitations do not permit doing so. We are assuming that most readers will have had at least an introductory course in psychology, in which these topics would have been covered.

WHY AN ENVIRONMENTAL PSYCHOLOGY?

As we have indicated, there are many possible relationships between human behavior and the physical environment. But why study these relationships? Of what use is the information that the shape or color of a room will have an effect on the behavior of the occupants or that certain features of a natural environment may result in strong approach responses while other features result in avoidance responses?

Research is conducted for many reasons. In some fields of psychology, as well as in many other scientific disciplines, much research is undertaken only to increase our general fund of knowledge. The researchers are not concerned about whether the data collected will be, or can be, used to solve any of the practical, real-world problems that confront us. This type of research is called *basic* or *pure* research. However, many other investigators—and their number appears to be increasing—are concerned with solving practical problems. Studies dealing with these kinds of problems are called *applied* research. Most research by environmental psychologists is of the applied variety.

Environmental-psychology research has many potential uses. For example, people in a number of professions concerned with various aspects of "environmental design" routinely make decisions that modify the physical environment in such a fashion that the behavior of many individuals may be affected. Thus, an architect should know about the relationships between various physical characteristics of buildings and human behavior, a city planner should be aware of the findings of studies dealing with life in cities, and managers of wilderness areas should have some understanding of people's interactions with the natural environment.

Although the people in such professions generally recognize that data from research in environmental psychology may be useful, a number of problems must be overcome before environmental designers will routinely use the data in making their decisions. First, research in the field has concentrated on some areas and neglected others, so that in many areas the behavioral data necessary for intelligent planning do not exist. Moreover, as Ward and Grant (1970) suggest:

> Another and greater problem has been that the designer has not known what sort of data he needed in the first place, let alone whether or not it existed. A third problem, the greatest of all, is that if the designer has known what sort of data would be useful and if, as has increasingly been the case in recent years, the data has been found to be available, the designer has not known how to incorporate it into his decision-making processes [p. 2].

There are no easy solutions to these problems. Perhaps the most important step would be to improve communication between the researchers and the designers, so that each understands the other better. As Altman (1973) points out, further progress in the behavior/environment field will depend on their joining forces, but that will be difficult because the differences in style between the groups give rise to misunderstanding.

A better understanding is now developing. At professional meetings dealing with environmental psychology or with environmental design, researchers and designers are both heavily represented, and a common topic of conversation is the necessity of bridging the gap between the two groups. However, there is still a long way to go.

RESEARCH AREAS IN ENVIRONMENTAL PSYCHOLOGY

We have stated that environmental psychology is the discipline that is concerned with the relationships between human behavior and the physical environment. In this chapter we have attempted to elaborate on this definition and define further the key terms in this definition. Our discussion of the relationships between the physical environment and behavior has been in general terms. In this section we will outline some specific research areas that have been of interest to environmental psychologists. Since these research topics will be covered in detail in the following chapters, this section will also serve as an overview of the organization of the book.

We pointed out earlier that studying the relationships between human behavior and features of the physical environment is a challenging task. However, a number of research methodologies are available to the investigator attempting to design studies dealing with these relationships. These research methods are discussed in some detail in Chapter 2. For the reader who has had some exposure to research methodology in the behavioral sciences, it will quickly become apparent that, while the areas investigated by environmental psychologists may be quite different from those studied by other psychologists, the research approaches are very similar.

The physical environment, as mentioned earlier, can be thought of in systems terms. Thus, in viewing the built environment, we can think of a room as one of the smaller subsystems in the total system, the room as part of the building, the building as located in a neighborhood in a city, and so on. In discussing the relationships between the physical environment and behavior, we will attempt to follow this systems approach. Thus, in Chapter 3, we will first consider some of the research dealing with rooms and the various factors associated with rooms that may have an effect on the behavior of the occupants. This will include research on such variables as room shape, furnishings, color, and ambient environments and the relationships between these variables and the perceptions and behavior of people occupying the rooms. Studies dealing with single-family dwellings and multiple-family dwellings and the behavior of occupants will also be discussed.

Environmental psychologists have been interested for some time in the design of buildings that best serve the needs of the occupants—whether they are office workers or patients in a hospital or a mental ward. For example, what type of office design is most effective from the users' point of view? What kind of ward design in a mental institution will encourage social activity among the patients? Research areas such as these will be discussed in Chapter 4.

Rooms, houses, buildings, neighborhoods, and so forth are often part of what we consider the largest component of the built environment—the city. There has been a considerable amount of research conducted by environmental psychologists and others dealing with life in the city. The research has been aimed at determining sources of satisfaction and dissatisfaction with city living, with the image of the city, including cognitive or psychological mapping, and with other types of perceptions of city living. Much of the research has been concerned with city living as a pathogenic experience. Is city living stressful? Does life in the city contribute to physical and mental pathology? How do people living in the city respond to the stress associated with it if it is in fact stressful? Other researchers have concentrated on studying the behavior of urbanites. Studies in all of these areas will be discussed in Chapter 5.

The behavior of people in the built environment seldom occurs in isolation. Consequently, social behavior in relation to the physical environment has been of considerable interest to environmental psychologists, especially crowding, territoriality, personal space, and privacy. In Chapter 6 we will look at several of these areas and some of the theoretical frameworks developed around them.

Finally, in Chapter 7 we will deal with the natural environment and behavior. Although environmental psychologists have tended to concentrate on the built environment, there is a substantial amount of research dealing with the relationships between the natural physical environment and behavior. Much of this research has been concerned with determining the characteristics of the users of various outdoor recreation facilities and the frequency with which they are used. Other studies have dealt with perceived requirements of these facilities and motivations of users. Some research has been aimed at developing a better understanding of the relationships between people and the geographic environment, such as a region's geology, climate, and natural hazards. Chapter 7 also deals with such topics as pollution and its behavioral effects.

CHAPTER 2

RESEARCH METHODS IN ENVIRONMENTAL PSYCHOLOGY

Research is a process designed to find answers to questions by means of scientific techniques. In this chapter we will be concerned with the techniques employed by environmental psychologists in studying the relationships between human behavior and the physical environment.

The research process by which these relationships are studied can be thought of as consisting of a number of steps or stages. Although the specific stages may differ from one study to the next, certain procedures are common to nearly all investigations. We will briefly discuss these common stages of the research process before considering specific methodologies.

The initial stage in any investigation is the formulation of the research problem. In this stage the researcher gets an idea about some area of interest and then states the idea in the form of a question that can be answered by some research approach. This procedure may sound relatively simple, but it is often difficult, and numerous articles have been written on the criteria for good research-problem statements. As pointed out by Ellingstad and Heimstra (1974), "This transformation of an often vague initial idea into a precise statement of a research problem, or question, that is amenable to scientific research is critical if the research is to produce meaningful information" (p. 6).[1]

Normally, the second step in the research process is a detailed review of the available literature in order to become familiar with previous studies that may be similar to the one the researcher has in mind. A review of this type not only prevents investigators from duplicating previous work but helps clarify their research idea and shape it into a researchable form. The review should

---

[1]This and all other quotations from this source are from *Methods in the Study of Human Behavior*, by V. S. Ellingstad and N. W. Heimstra. Copyright © 1974 by Wadsworth Publishing Company, Inc. Reprinted by permission of the publisher, Brooks/Cole Publishing Company, Monterey, California.

also give investigators some ideas about experimental designs and methods employed by other researchers that may be useful in designing their own studies. A variety of sources can be used in a literature review, depending on the particular research idea being considered.

After the literature review the investigator designs the study. The proper design of an investigation requires a high level of sophistication obtained only through considerable training and experience. It is not appropriate here to discuss experimental design other than to say that it is critical. If the investigation is designed properly, the researcher can have confidence in the results and know that the study will answer the research question that was formulated. If the study is not properly designed, the results will be of little, if any, value.

The next stage of the research process is the actual running of the study. Following the design established in the previous stage, the investigator will use one or more of a variety of methods, which may include testing subjects in experimental settings, observing individuals or groups in natural settings and recording the observed behavior, conducting field experiments, and so forth. Some of these methods will be discussed in some detail later in the chapter.

After a data analysis, the final step of the research process is writing up the results of the study for publication or, in some other fashion, making certain that the findings will be available to the scientific community. This is a critical step, since research findings that do not get reported are not much use to anyone except the investigator who conducted the study.

An additional step in the research process is essential for many investigators. This step, obtaining the money to conduct the investigation, usually takes place between the design stage of the research process and the phase when the study is actually conducted.

An investigator can obtain funds to conduct a research project in several different ways. Sometimes the research is supported by the investigator's own institution or organization. Sometimes the investigator may simply pay for the research. Typically, however, the researcher seeks funds from an organization whose function is to support research in various areas. This procedure, in nearly all cases, requires a *research proposal.*

Most research proposals are of one of two types—a *solicited* proposal or an *unsolicited* proposal. The former is prepared by an investigator in response to a "request for proposal" (RFP) from some granting agency. For example, suppose a government agency wished to know what the attitude of park users would be toward some proposed changes in the way national parks could be used. The agency would prepare an RFP, which would be made available to a relatively large number of potential investigators. From the RFP, which would describe (generally in relatively sketchy fashion) what the agency wished to have done, some investigators would prepare and submit a proposal. An unsolicited proposal, as the name implies, originates with an investigator. It is based on a question the investigator wishes to see answered by means of a research project. The investigator submits this unsolicited proposal to a granting agency in the hope that the agency will fund the project.

Regardless of whether the proposals are solicited or unsolicited, they have many similarities. Nearly all have an introductory section reviewing the current status of the field, a methods section outlining the approach the investigator hopes to use to answer the research question, and a budget section presenting the costs of the project, as well as other material that might be useful in helping a review group decide on the merits of the proposal.

Typically, the proposal is reviewed by a group of experts in the area that the proposal deals with. Though different types of review procedures are followed, most investigators hope that, if the procedures in their proposal have merit, the project will be approved. Unfortunately, in this era of tight funding for research, many proposed research projects are approved by review panels but cannot be funded. Some areas of research are "hot" in that there is a considerable amount of money available; other areas are less appealing. Although funds for environmental-psychology research seem to have increased somewhat during the past few years, it certainly cannot be considered one of the hot areas.

SOME RESEARCH METHODS

As we have pointed out, research is a process designed to find answers to questions by scientific techniques. The question the investigator seeks to answer depends on many factors. Sometimes the question is generated by a practical problem encountered in our technological society. At other times the question is abstract. But regardless of the type of question, the same methods may be used by researchers to arrive at an answer.

Although any classification of these research methods is somewhat arbitrary, one scheme is based on the control that the investigator exerts over the situation in which the behavior occurs and over the conditions that influence the behavior. In this classification scheme, researchers use what is called the *experimental method* when they have direct control over the behavior and can manipulate the appropriate variables or conditions. At the other end of the spectrum is the *naturalistic-observation method*, in which researchers make no attempt to manipulate or control variables. (See Figure 2-1.) Between these two extremes are a number of other methods, several of which will be discussed later in this section.

These methods are not unique to environmental psychology. As Proshansky, Ittelson, and Rivlin (1976) state in discussing research methods in environmental psychology:

Figure 2-1. Research methods in the behavioral sciences range from strictly observational techniques to carefully controlled experiments that make use of minicomputers such as the one shown in the lower photograph.

What we find, then, is a variety of measurement techniques and research methods being employed which have been borrowed from the other behavioral sciences or research problem areas. Apart from the nature [of the] problem to be studied, there is little to distinguish the use of these research techniques and methods in environmental psychology from their use in other fields of research [pp. 323–324].

Because of the nature of the relationships between people and the physical environment, some environmental psychologists question whether the research strategies that we will be discussing are the most appropriate ones for studying these relationships. However, environmental psychology has not yet reached a stage—nor is it likely to in the near future—where new and unique methods for studying them will be developed. Thus, books dealing with research methods in the area, such as *Behavioral Research Methods in Environmental Design* (Michelson, 1975), describe the use of standard methods rather than new ones.

The Experimental Method

Basically, the experimental method of studying behavior involves manipulating certain aspects (*independent variables*) of a behavioral situation and observing the effect of the manipulation on behavior (*dependent variable*). For example, suppose a researcher is investigating the effects of noise level on the ability to concentrate. In this study, noise is the independent variable, while ability to concentrate, a form of behavior, is the dependent variable.

In an experiment the investigator generally uses several levels of the independent variable to determine whether changes in its level will result in changes in the measure of the dependent variable. Thus, in the noise study the investigator might use four levels of the independent variable, noise. A group of subjects might be tested under a no-noise condition (the control group), another group under 70 decibels (db), another under 80 db, and the fourth group under 90 db. Under each of these conditions, the subjects would be required to proofread an article containing a number of typographical errors. A composite score on length of material completed and number of errors missed would serve as the measure of concentration, the dependent variable. If the subjects' performance on the proofreading task differed under the various noise conditions, the investigator would use a statistical test to determine whether the differences were due to chance alone or were statistically significant.

The experimental method is generally used in laboratory studies because they can be conducted under carefully controlled conditions. As will be apparent, relatively little research in environmental psychology has been conducted in laboratories. The experimental method can, however, be used in field experiments in many natural settings, such as a school, a city, and a forest or wilderness area.

Although the experimental situation in a field study often cannot be as tightly controlled as in the laboratory, the field study has several virtues that make it a useful method for researchers interested in the effects of the built or natural environment on behavior. One important advantage of the field study is that the setting is much more realistic than the laboratory. This realism usually makes generalizations from the research findings more valid.

For example, let us contrast our laboratory noise study with one that might be conducted in a field setting. Suppose that in this case we were interested in the effects of aircraft noise on the performance of school-children. We could select several schools with children generally similar in socioeconomic background, race, and so on but with unequal exposures to aircraft noise. Our dependent variable would be some measure of academic performance. The study would tell us whether the aircraft noise had any effect on academic performance. Although we would try to control as many variables as possible, we would be unable to exert the same type of control that we could in the laboratory. However, our findings might be more meaningful.

Many kinds of behavior, ranging from relatively simple reactions to complex social processes, that are difficult to study in the laboratory can be studied in field experiments. Although researchers may not have *full* control over the variables, they can still exert a considerable amount. Field experiments, particularly in environmental psychology, are an extremely useful method of studying relationships between the physical environment and behavior.

The Naturalistic-Observation Method

Regardless of the method used to study behavior, observation of the behavior is fundamental. In the experimental method just described, the behavior of interest (the dependent variable) is observed either directly or with instruments, and the investigator determines the effect on the behavior of manipulating the independent variables.

With the naturalistic-observation method, unlike the experimental approach, behavior is observed and studied as it occurs in an uncontrolled, natural setting. The researcher does not have to depend on the willingness of the subjects to respond verbally or otherwise to the experimental variables but observes and records the behavior of interest as it takes place in a particular environment. Although the researcher may be interested in the effects of certain variables on the behavior being observed, no attempt is made to manipulate these variables or to influence the behavior that takes place.

Although it may seem that simply observing and recording behavior should present no difficulties for an investigator, some methodological decisions confront the investigator wishing to use this approach. Careful thought must be given to the setting for the study, the behavior that is to be observed, and the way in which the observations will be recorded.

Generally, the setting to be used is determined by the objectives of the study. For example, if a researcher wishes to observe the behavior of patients in a ward of a mental hospital, the setting is determined by the purpose of the study. However, other decisions concerning the setting might have to be made. Possibly the ward is designed in such a fashion that clear observations cannot be made. Should the ward be modified, or will a modification destroy the meaningfulness of the data? What about the observer in the setting? Will the presence of an observer disrupt the behavior? Should the observer be concealed? Should the observer become an active member of the group to be observed? These and other questions must be asked by the researcher about the setting for the observational study.

The researcher must also give careful thought to the question of what kind of behavior to observe. Again, the behavior of interest is generally determined by the objectives of the study. Possibly the greatest difficulty in deciding what behavior to observe is overcoming the impulse to attempt to observe, record, and analyze all the behavior that takes place. Obviously, many kinds of behavior—both verbal and nonverbal—can occur in a given setting, but the observer usually concentrates on only one or two categories.

A last decision concerns the method to be employed in recording the observations. The observer may use equipment ranging from a note pad and pencil to very elaborate photographic or videotaping systems. However, regardless of the system used, the important consideration is that the data recorded can later be summarized, analyzed, and interpreted.

The observational method has been popular with investigators in many different areas. For example, much of what we know about animal behavior, particularly that occurring outside laboratory settings, has been obtained by researchers observing animals in their natural habitats. For years, behavioral scientists have also been using the observational method to study humans in such "natural habitats" as small towns, urban areas, and schools and other institutions. The area of psychology concerned with studying naturally occurring human behavior in these and other types of settings is often called *ecological psychology*. Ecological psychology, like environmental psychology, is concerned with examining the relationship between the environment and human behavior. Possibly the best-known research in this field was conducted by Roger Barker (1968), who made detailed observations of people's activities in various environments.

Ecological psychology, with its emphasis on observing behavior in natural settings, has made a considerable contribution to environmental psychology. According to Mercer (1975), ecological psychology "is having a very powerful effect, not only on environmental psychology but also on psychology as a whole, an effect which will do much to expand the narrow horizons of a great deal of modern psychology" (p. 18). Similarly, Irwin Altman (1973) states in discussing the increasingly important role of behavioral observations in environmental psychology: ". . . Barker-type work occupies more and more time at conferences, sessions are increasingly crowded, students and practitioners now talk about committing themselves to behavioral observations. It is likely that the coming years will show a surge of energy in this direction" (p. 117).

The Testing Method

The testing method includes several approaches used by environmental psychologists. Typically, the researcher using one of these approaches is investigating a particular characteristic of a group of individuals. A standard stimulus situation (called a test) is designed to measure the characteristic. Tests have been designed to measure intelligence, personality, aptitude, and affective states. Interviews, questionnaires, opinion polls, and attitude surveys also are tests. Although the actual instruments used in testing may differ, they all involve a controlled stimulus situation designed to elicit responses that reveal something about the individual in which the researcher is interested.

The testing method is frequently employed by environmental psychologists interested in attitudes of groups of people about an environmental problem, such as air or water pollution. To obtain this kind of information, the researcher typically uses a special testing method called *survey research.*

We are frequently exposed to information gathered by surveys; indeed, before an election the public is bombarded with the results of one kind of survey research—public-opinion polling. In survey research the investigator attempts in some systematic fashion to obtain data from a population (more typically, samples of a population) in order to assess some characteristic of it.

Conducting a survey so that the results are meaningful is a complex procedure that we cannot discuss in any detail. Several aspects of the procedure are, however, of particular importance. One is that only on rare occasions can an entire population be studied by a surveyor. Consequently, in most studies the researcher draws samples from the population and, from these samples, attempts to infer its characteristics. How the sample is selected is critical. There are a number of methods for selecting the sample to be used in a survey, and an investigator must use a correct procedure if a generalization of the findings from the sample to the population is to be valid.

Another critical feature of survey research is the construction of the interview questions. It is relatively easy to get almost any kind of response from a person if the question is worded in a particular fashion. For example, virtually everyone asked the question "Does smog bother you?" would be likely to reply in the affirmative, so the researcher might conclude that smog is really a matter of great concern to the people interviewed. The researcher might get quite a different response if the question were "What do you consider to be the most serious environmental problem in this area?" The interview instrument must be constructed so as to get at what the investigator is interested in but also to avoid distortion or feigning of responses. That is often difficult.

Evaluative or Impact Research

Classifying methods of studying behavior as falling within the experimental, the testing, or the observational method is somewhat arbitrary. Many research designs do not neatly fit any one of the strategies but combine features of two or even all three of the methods. There are many examples of these *mixed models* of research, which will be discussed at various times in the text. A researcher may combine methods for a number of reasons, such as finances, availability of subjects, availability of facilities, and so on. Or the researcher may feel that a mixed design will give more reliable results. Often, however, a research project is so large that it is necessary to use all the methods to answer the research questions. This is frequently the case in a type of research that is becoming increasingly common in environmental psychology and in many other areas. This type is called evaluative or impact research.

At any given time there are usually numerous large-scale "action" programs funded by the government that are designed to modify behavior in one way or another. These programs may be designed to reduce drug and alcohol problems, reduce mental-health problems, reduce smoking, conserve energy, and on and on. Though at one time the granting agencies assumed that these programs were effective if they "looked good," the agencies now insist that the programs do what they actually set out to do. This demand has resulted in evaluative research that often does not fit neatly any of the models we have discussed.

Action programs are designed to bring about changes in behavior. For example, suppose the government wished to start an action program that would significantly reduce the use of various forms of energy. The change in the behavior of interest would be reduction in the use of energy. Evaluative research, in this instance, would assess the effectiveness of the program in bringing about a reduction. As pointed out by Ellingstad and Heimstra (1974):

The evaluation research project is designed with the objectives of the action program in mind. The investigator takes into consideration the nature of the objectives (*what* kinds of behavior the action program is aimed at changing); whether the objectives are *unitary* or *multiple* (in that a single change or a series of changes may be the goal); the desired *magnitude* of the change; *when* the desired change is to take place; *who* the target of the program is (the groups or populations the program is aimed at); and *how* the objectives are to be gained. These questions are crucial to the design of the project, and the answers determine the methodological procedures—sampling, controls, measuring instruments, and analysis of the data [p. 95].

Much more could be said about the methods of studying behavior that are commonly used by researchers in many different fields. However, in the remainder of this chapter, we will be concerned with how these methods are used by environmental psychologists and with some of the problems encountered.

VARIABLES IN ENVIRONMENTAL RESEARCH

We have emphasized that the experimental method of studying behavior involves manipulating certain aspects (the independent variables) of the environmental situation and observing the effect of the manipulation on behavior (the dependent variable). In the testing method and the naturalistic-observation method of studying behavior, the independent variables are not manipulated.

The experimental method has not been employed as frequently in environmental-psychology studies as in other areas of behavioral research because of the nature of the independent variables involved. Many of the variables do not lend themselves to manipulation, and it is difficult, if not impossible, to use different levels of the independent variable, as is required in the experimental method. For example, suppose an investigator is interested in the effects of air pollution on some form of behavior. It would be difficult to exert any control over the level of pollution that the subjects would be exposed to at any given time. Similarly, it would be difficult to manipulate the level of pollution in a stream, the population density in an urban area, noise pollution near an airport or a lake, and so forth.

It is important to keep in mind, however, that there are several kinds of independent variables and that some types are more easily dealt with in environmental research than others. In general, the independent variable in behavioral research can be one of two basic types. One type of independent variable is some particular aspect of the research situation in which the dependent variable is measured. These environmental independent variables are the type that we have been referring to—noise, air pollution, features of the physical environment, and so on. It is these independent variables that the environmental psychologist may have difficulty manipulating in order to study the effect on a dependent variable. However, the second type of independent variable may, in some instances, be easier to use. This type is referred to as a classificatory variable and represents some characteristic of the research subject. Thus, age, sex, intelligence, educational background, and socioeconomic status are examples of classificatory independent variables. Research with independent variables of this type is often referred to as *ex-post-facto research*. Kerlinger (1964) defines this as "research in which the independent variable or variables have already occurred and in which the researcher starts with the observations of a dependent variable or variables. He then studies the independent variables in retrospect for their possible relations to, and effects on, the dependent variable or variables" (p. 360).

Research using classificatory independent variables is common in environmental psychology. In the next section we will consider the use of independent variables in environmental-psychology research.

Independent Variables

Virtually any aspect of the built or natural environment with which people interact can influence their behavior and, consequently, could be selected as an independent variable. Because there are so many potential independent variables, we will make no effort to discuss them in any exhaustive fashion here. Rather, we will briefly mention some of the types of variables that have been studied and take up many of them in much more detail in later chapters.

For many years, researchers have been interested in how various aspects of the built environment influence certain types of behavior. For example, psychologists and engineers have systematically studied the effect on work efficiency and comfort of such variables as lighting, noise levels, heating, ventilation, and machine design and position. Although studies such as these can certainly be considered environmental research, they are more appropriately dealt with in books on industrial or engineering psychology and will not be discussed in any detail in this text.

Architects, engineers, urban planners, behavioral scientists, and others have recently become interested in variables of the built environment that influence behavior and so are now trying to take the "human factor" into consideration. Among the variables that can influence behavior are such features as size and arrangement of rooms and passageways, number and size of windows and doors, and arrangement of furniture; interior illumination, temperature, and noise; community layout, recreational facilities, and shopping convenience; and transportation facilities, including location and speed of public transport, parking space, and street layout (McCormick, 1976, p. 407).

Similarly, numerous features of the natural environment may affect behavior. Among these are the physical characteristics of a natural environment, such as the presence or absence of trees, mountains, streams, or lakes. Features such as accessibility, perceived "wildness," cost, and many others are also variables that must be considered. Climate and such natural hazards as floods, droughts, and earthquakes are additional features of the natural environment that may influence behavior.

As the level of technology in our society has increased, so has the deterioration of the environment. Thus, air pollution, water pollution, noise pollution, and desecration of the landscape have become major issues to large numbers of people. These features of the environment, then, are another important class of independent variables having an effect on behavior.

The independent variables we have listed can be thought of as physical, nonliving influences on behavior. It is important to keep in mind, however, that when individuals are exposed to these variables they generally are not in isolation but in the company of other people. Consequently, each individual not only reacts to these variables but also interacts with other individuals, and this interaction may modify the effects of environmental variables. In many cases the existing social condition may be an important environmental variable in its own right. For example, one variable of particular interest to researchers is the effects of varying levels of population density on behavior. We will consider this variable in some detail in a later chapter.

It should be apparent, then, that a wide variety of environmental features can serve as independent variables. It should also be kept in mind that they are not the neat, easily quantifiable, readily controlled and manipulated variables that make for a tidy experimental design of research projects.

Presenting the Independent Variable

Because environmental researchers study the effect of some feature of the environment on a particular type of behavior, that feature must, of course, be exposed in some fashion to the persons in whose behavior the researchers are interested. In much of the environmental research that has been conducted, the persons whose behavior is being studied have already been exposed to the environmental feature of interest. For example, most of the research dealing with attitudes toward air, water, and noise pollution is of this type. Researchers also frequently compare attitudes or other forms of behavior of persons exposed to different types of environmental features. Thus, the attitudes toward pollution of persons living in polluted areas may be compared with the attitudes of those living in "clean" areas, the behavior of people living in high-population-density areas compared with that of people living in low-density areas, the attitudes toward earthquakes or other natural disasters of people living in regions where these events occur compared with the attitudes of people living in areas where they do not occur, and so on. In studies such as these, the exposure (or lack of exposure) to the environmental feature has occurred, so that the investigators do not have to be concerned with how the independent variable is presented to their subjects.

In many other types of environmental-psychology studies, however, presenting the environmental feature to the subjects is an important consideration for the researcher. Moreover, the manner in which it is presented is critical to the success of the investigation. The exact methods used will, of course, depend on the particular variable or variables that the investigator is concerned with, and we cannot attempt to describe all the possible approaches. But as Craik (1970) has pointed out, several methods of presenting environmental features encompass, with some modifications, many of the approaches used by environmental psychologists, and we will discuss these general techniques.

When referring to the environmental feature that is to be presented to a subject, Craik uses the term *environmental display* (pp. 65–66). An environmental display may include virtually all the independent variables that we have discussed in this section. Thus, a room, a building, a forest glade, a crowded street, and a smoggy atmosphere are all examples of environmental displays. Craik discusses three general methods by which environmental displays can be presented to subjects: *direct presentation, representation,* and *imaginal presentation.*

Direct presentation. In this type of presentation, subjects are exposed to the actual environmental feature, or display, and can view it, possibly touch it, perhaps walk or drive around or fly over it. For example, suppose an investigator is interested in the effect of a badly polluted stream on the mood or feelings of people who view it. The investigator might take a group of subjects to an area near the stream, measure their mood (techniques for doing this will be discussed later), then have them walk along the stream, look at it, perhaps even taste it, and finally again measure their mood to see whether it was changed by exposure to the stream. Although there are a number of environmental displays to which subjects can be exposed by the direct-presentation method, obviously in many studies it would be difficult actually to get subjects to the display. For these studies, then, the representation method is a much more feasible approach than the direct-presentation approach.

Representation. As Craik points out, "The various representational media offer attractive alternatives to direct presentation, being less expensive, more convenient, and more standard methods" (p. 68). An experimenter might choose to employ any of a number of devices in lieu of direct presentation. Drawings, maps, models, and replicas of the environmental feature can be presented to subjects and their responses to these representations studied. Photographs, movies, and television can also be used.

With this approach the investigator interested in the effect of a polluted stream on the mood of observers could conduct the study in a laboratory and not have to worry about transporting the subjects to the actual stream. In this case the investigator might measure the mood of the subjects, show them a movie or some other representation of the stream, and then measure the subjects' mood again to see whether the environmental display had any effect. Obviously, the pollution would not be as "real" to the subjects as a direct presentation would, and one drawback of this method is that we do not know whether people respond to a representation of an environmental display in the same manner as they would respond to a direct presentation of it.

Imaginal presentation. The researcher using this technique asks the subjects to visualize a display. This method is a convenient one because the researcher does not have to take the subjects to the display or prepare representations for the study. The researcher using imaginal presentation to gauge reaction to a polluted stream might measure the mood of the subjects, ask them to imagine a polluted stream (perhaps describing such a stream in some detail to the subjects), and then again measure their mood. Imaginal presentation has been used in a number of environmental studies, some of which will be described later. Obviously, the same drawbacks listed for the representation method would also hold true for the imaginal presentation; that is, we do not know if people respond to an imagined display in the same fashion as they do to a real display.

Dependent Variables

Exposing subjects to some feature of the environment is only one aspect of investigation. Researchers must also be concerned with the selection and measurement of the behavioral response they wish to study.

Behavior involves many activities, some easily observed by the experimenter, some observed only by sensitive electronic equipment, and some "observed" by tests and interviews. The exact behavioral response selected by a researcher will be determined by the research question. In the following chapters we shall see that even though environmental psychology is a new field, researchers have already studied a number of behaviors.

In some studies these variables involve overt behavioral responses. Movement through a room served as the dependent variable in one study about the effects of room color. In other studies the dependent variable has been the number of people visiting a particular national park. Other variables have been reaction time, detection of infrequently appearing signals in a vigilance or monitoring task, eye irritation as a function of smog level, and performance on a task under crowded conditions. Typically, measurement of these variables is relatively straightforward and poses no great problem for the investigator.

Most work in environmental psychology involves variables that are more difficult to deal with. Frequently the researcher is concerned with how people feel about a particular environmental feature rather than with how the feature affects their overt behavior. Since feelings, judgments, and other similar reactions are more difficult to measure in a reliable fashion than are reaction time, locomotion, and other dependent variables of this type and since the former are so common in environmental research, we will consider them in some detail.

There are several ways of eliciting and recording these types of responses to the environment. Craik (1970) categorizes these responses as *descriptive responses, global responses, inferential responses, attitudinal responses,* and *preferential responses.* Though all of these have been used in environmental research, some are more common than others; these will be emphasized in the following discussion.

Descriptive Responses

In some instances, subjects are asked to describe, either verbally or in writing, their reaction to an environmental display. Researchers using this technique, called *free description,* make no effort to structure the subjects' responses; they only analyze what is said or written. A disadvantage of this technique is that it is difficult to quantify and compare the responses obtained with it. Consequently, most researchers who wish to elicit descriptive responses use a *standardized description* technique instead. The numerous standard descriptive formats include rating scales and adjective check lists.

Rating scales. Although rating scales exist in a variety of forms, all have certain features in common. Typically, subjects are presented with several categories from which they select the one that they feel best characterizes the environmental display or feature of the display. The categories are usually assigned numbers, which can be directly used in statistical analysis. If a researcher wished to measure, for example, reactions to air pollution, the researcher might ask the subjects to select on the scale shown below the category best describing their feelings about air pollution. The subjects' answers to a number of such rating scales, each with different descriptive categories, would give the researcher a relatively broad picture of the subjects' feelings about air pollution.

Very Harmful	Harmful	Not Very Harmful	Not at All Harmful

One rating-scale method that has been used a great deal in behavioral research is the semantic differential. With this technique, which was developed by Osgood, Suci, and Tannenbaum (1957), the subjects are asked to make a judgment about an environmental display on a scale with opposing adjectives—such as pleasant/unpleasant, comfortable/uncomfortable, or friendly/unfriendly—at opposite ends. For example, assume that an investigator wishes to determine how people view two rooms in a building that are identical except for wall and carpet color. The researcher shows each room to the subjects and asks them to complete semantic differentials like the ones shown below. If the positions on the scales from left to right are numbered from 1 to 7, then the individual who completed the scales shown felt that this room should be rated as a 3 on the pleasant/unpleasant scale, a 5 on the comfortable/uncomfortable scale, and a 4 on the friendly/unfriendly scale. Normally, many more scales than are shown in our example would be administered. The numbers assigned to the judgments would then be averaged to determine whether the subjects viewed the two rooms differently.

Room A		
Pleasant	__ __ **x** __ __ __ __	Unpleasant
Comfortable	__ __ __ __ **x** __ __	Uncomfortable
Friendly	__ __ __ **x** __ __ __	Unfriendly

Rating scales have some definite advantages in behavioral research. Usually they require less time than other methods, have a wide range of applications, are interesting and easy for the subjects to use, and are more economical than other measures.

Adjective check lists. An adjective check list consists of a long list of adjectives (sometimes several hundred) that the subject checks as being applicable or not applicable to an environmental feature. Thus, the researcher who is interested in how people view the two rooms with different-colored walls and rugs could use the list of adjectives shown below (together with many others) instead of the semantic differential. The researcher would then ask the subjects to view the rooms and check whether each adjective is or is not applicable to them. Check lists of this type are easy to administer and can be used effectively with many kinds of environmental displays.

Room A		
	Yes	*No*
Pleasant	✗	—
Comfortable	✗	—
Friendly	—	✗
Cold	✗	—
Large	✗	—
Coherent	✗	—

A common response to certain kinds of environmental features is a change in affective state. For example, viewing a mountain stream may make people feel happy; if the stream has been polluted, they may feel sad. One form of adjective check list that has been developed to enable persons to describe their mood in a quantifiable fashion is the Nowlis (1965) Mood Adjective Check List (MACL). The MACL consists of a group of adjectives that describe eight mood factors, such as anxiety, fatigue, aggression, and concentration. For each of the adjectives, the subjects rate how they feel at the moment on a four-point scale like the one below. They circle *VV* if they definitely feel relaxed, *V* if they feel slightly relaxed, *?* if they cannot decide, and *no* if they definitely do not feel relaxed. Analysis of the responses (which can be assigned numbers) gives the experimenter a comprehensive picture of the subjects' mood.

Relaxed	VV	V	?	No

The MACL can be used in a number of ways in environmental research. By administering the check list both before and after the presentation of an environmental display, the researcher can determine the effect of the display on the subjects' mood. Sometimes, different environmental displays are presented to different groups of subjects, with members of each group completing a MACL. In this way the researcher can compare the effects of various environmental displays on the mood of viewers.

Other techniques for eliciting descriptive responses that can be used in environmental research have been developed. However, rating scales and adjective check lists such as those described are the most common techniques used.

Global Responses

Although the simple descriptions of reactions to the environment provided by rating scales and adjective check lists are useful, recording subtle responses to environmental displays may require different techniques. For example, as Craik (1970) points out, "One seemingly implicit reaction to displays such as buildings, rooms, rural valleys, and urban alleys is an automatic scanning response answering the question 'What might go on here?' " (p. 73). To elicit this reaction, subjects could be asked to write a brief story about the display they were shown. Readers familiar with some of the personality tests commonly used by psychologists will recognize the similarity between this procedure and the use of the Thematic Apperception Test (TAT). Global responses, then, typically involve little structuring by the researcher. Subjects respond to an environmental display by telling a story about it, by describing how a display makes them feel, by interpreting what effects a display might have on other persons, and so forth.

Another technique for obtaining global responses requires that subjects draw environmental displays. In studies of urban areas, subjects have often been requested to sketch maps to convey their concepts of cities. In a later chapter the results of this "cognitive mapping" technique will be discussed in some detail.

Inferential Responses

We continually make inferences about features of the environment and gradually build up notions about them. These beliefs may or may not correspond to reality. There are several ways to elicit and record these inferential responses. Suppose, for example, that we are interested in finding out how people in a small town in South Dakota view people living in New York City and vice versa. Persons in each locale could be given adjective check lists on which to describe what they think the kinds of people living in the other locale are, what they do for a living, how they entertain themselves, and so forth. Inferences about an environmental feature can also be elicited by having people list as many consequences as they can imagine that might be associated with the presence of some environmental display (such as a new lake formed by a dam) or the removal of some display (a wooded area's being destroyed for a new housing development).

Although these and similar approaches entail some difficulties in quantification and analysis, they can show the investigator a dimension of behavior that is important in better understanding people/environment interactions.

Attitudinal Responses

Much of the research in environmental psychology has been concerned with measuring people's attitudes toward such features of the environment as air and water pollution, aviation and other transportation noise, and outdoor recreation areas. Sometimes the surveys have been aimed at the public in general and sometimes at more restricted populations, such as wilderness campers or persons living near an airport. Attitudes can be measured in several ways, but most researchers use detailed questionnaires.

The term *attitude* means different things to different psychologists, and we cannot go into detail concerning attitude theory and the nature of attitudes. Many psychologists feel that attitudes have at least three components, with the central component being a relatively permanent *feeling* about something. The feeling can be positive or negative and is learned. An attitude also typically has a *cognitive* component in that the individual holds some belief or view about the thing at which the attitude is directed. The feeling, or emotional, component and the cognitive component interact in that if a person has, for example, an unfavorable belief (cognitive component) about air pollution—that is, thinks that air pollution is bad—then a negative feeling is probably also present.

The third component of an attitude can be labeled the *action* component. This is the component that environmental psychologists are usually most interested in. An attitude is often defined as a mental readiness to respond that is organized through experience and will influence behavior. In other words, based on the feeling and cognitive components, there is a tendency to act. At least, this has been assumed to be the case. Attitudes, however, do not always modify behavior; as we shall see later, people have very strong negative feelings and beliefs about air, water, and noise pollution but apparently do very little about it. Although many psychologists argue that we must change attitudes if we wish to change behavior, others suggest that this approach is actually backwards. If we wish to change attitudes, we must first change the behavior.

The concept underlying most educational programs aimed at changing people's behavior toward their environment is that acquiring new knowledge about and concern for the environment will change behavior. As pointed out by Goldsmith and Hochbaum (1975), this is a simplistic view. They suggest that knowledge and concern—that is, the feeling and cognitive components of attitudes—are only two of several conditions that must exist in order for behavioral change to take place. They state that the following are conditions that influence behavioral change:

1. Awareness that the environmental issue in question is actually or potentially detrimental to the person's own health and welfare.

2. Enough concern with the hazardous condition to be motivated to do something about it.
3. Knowledge of what one can do about the issue.
4. Knowledge of how to carry out this action.
5. Ability to carry out the action.
6. Belief that one's action will have a substantive impact on the environmental condition.
7. Assurance that the gains from taking the action will outweigh any sacrifices required (that is, the perceived cost-effectiveness of changing one's behavior) [p. 232].

Simply attempting to change attitudes through educational processes may not result in significant behavioral change. Unfortunately, this is too often forgotten, and costly campaigns aimed at changing various attitudes toward the environment are undertaken with little success.

As pointed out earlier, measuring attitudes toward an environmental feature requires considerable care on the part of the investigator. It is particularly important that questions be constructed in such a way that they do not put words in a respondent's mouth. For example, people who live near an airport may not be bothered by the noise enough to complain about it or even be particularly concerned. However, if they were asked, "Do you think aircraft noise is the most serious neighborhood problem?" they would probably answer in the affirmative.

Although attitude measurement is an important area of research in environmental psychology, too much emphasis may have been placed on it. Consequently, other kinds of research, which might result in more useful information, may have been neglected.

Preferential Responses

Eliciting and recording preferential responses are relatively simple procedures. Subjects can, for example, give their preferences after simply looking at photographs of environmental displays, whether landscapes, neighborhoods, wilderness areas, or camping facilities. The researcher with a number of photographs of, say, different camping facilities can ask the subjects to choose between paired alternatives, to rank the photographs in order of preference, or to rate them. After the subjects have expressed their preferences, the researcher can analyze the displays in detail to determine what features may be associated with high or low preference ratings.

Our discussion of various kinds of responses has not by any means exhausted the possible responses that have been and could be used as dependent variables in environmental research. The natural and built environments influence behavior in so many ways that virtually any aspect of behavior can be considered an appropriate variable for study.

SELECTION AND USE OF SUBJECTS IN ENVIRONMENTAL RESEARCH

We have emphasized that two critical decisions the investigator must make have to do with the selection and manipulation of independent variables and the selection and measurement of dependent variables. A third decision deals with the selection and assignment of the subjects to be used in a study.

In some instances the investigator must decide whether to use human subjects or some species of lower animal. As we shall see in Chapter 6, much of the research on the physiological and behavioral effects of population density has been conducted with rats and mice as subjects. Generally, though, researchers in environmental psychology are interested in the effects of environmental features on human behavior and recognize that generalizations of findings from studies with animal subjects can be made to humans only with a great deal of caution. Thus, although the researcher who plans to use animal subjects is confronted with some problems of selection, we will be concerned here with selection and assignment of human subjects.

Samples and Populations

In nearly all studies in the behavioral sciences, the number of subjects that an investigator actually uses is relatively small. Nonetheless, researchers can often generalize the findings of their studies to a larger number of people if they select a sample of subjects from a population with the characteristics in which they are interested. For example, suppose an investigator wants to determine the attitudes toward aircraft noise of the inhabitants of a small city where, each day, overflights by military jets produce sonic booms. In this case the population is all the inhabitants of the city—perhaps 40,000 people. Because interviewing all of them would not be feasible, the researcher would select a sample. If the sampling strategy was adequate, the views held by the persons making up the sample would very closely reflect the views of the entire population. This procedure, of course, is the one followed by the various professional survey groups, who, on the basis of information obtained from a sample of only a couple of thousand people, can quite accurately determine what the nation thinks about a particular topic.

The researcher studying behavior in a laboratory setting must also be concerned with the manner in which subjects are selected and assigned to experimental conditions. Though all too often the subjects in laboratory research are college students in introductory-psychology courses who may or may not be willing participants, investigators can take steps to make the generalizability of their data more valid. Normally, their strategy involves some type of random selection of subjects as well as random assignment of the subjects to the different levels of the independent variable.

The selection of samples is often a complex procedure and is beyond the scope of this text. Detailed discussions of sampling strategies can be found in Ellingstad and Heimstra (1974) and in Babbie (1973). The point to keep in mind is that the subjects for a study, whether it is a large-scale survey or a small laboratory experiment, must be selected carefully if the researcher hopes to generalize the findings.

Characteristics of the Subjects

The characteristics of the subjects selected obviously depend on the research question. If a researcher were interested in the effects of aircraft noise on children's classroom performance, the sample would consist of children drawn from a noisy area. Similarly, if a researcher were interested in the attitudes of wilderness campers toward a new highway being built through a wilderness area, the sample would consist of persons who camp in the area. In some instances, subjects are selected on the basis of a personality characteristic, such as extroversion or introversion, and their responses to various types of environmental displays are compared. Because many questions about the effects of the environment on behavior remain to be answered, virtually any person could be a member of a group with some characteristic of interest to environmental psychologists.

Often, however, subjects are drawn from what Craik (1970) refers to as *special-competence groups* and *special user/client groups.* In the former groups are engineers, architects, city planners, landscape architects, and others with competence in a particular area. In special user/client groups are elderly persons, hospital patients, inmates of prisons or other types of institutions, wilderness-area campers, and so forth. The type of special-competence group or special user/client group selected depends, of course, on the objectives of the study.

A last category from which subjects are drawn is the large number of people who happen to live in areas where some aspect of the environment is deteriorating. In many areas, air pollution has reached an extremely high level, or the residents are bombarded with aircraft or other transportation noise, or the population density is very high. A single area often has all these environmental features. Much of the research in environmental psychology has been an attempt to determine how the environmental deterioration affects these people's behavior.

Use and Misuse of Human Subjects

It should be apparent that environmental psychologists conduct investigations that involve a number of different types of behavior and techniques. Although some investigations relevant to environmental psychology use animals as subjects, the majority of studies use humans. The way in which human subjects are obtained for a study and the way in which they are used during the study have become major issues in behavioral research.

We have pointed out that there are methodological considerations that must be kept in mind when selecting subjects for a study. There are also ethical considerations. According to Ellingstad and Heimstra (1974):

> One of the most important ethical questions a researcher must consider in obtaining human subjects for his experiment has to do with the subjects' freedom of choice to participate in the experiment. Coercive measures are often used to obtain the cooperation of subjects in research projects. For example, students in introductory psychology classes (one of the most common sources of subjects) must frequently participate in various experiments to meet the course requirement. Similarly, employees in business and industry are often required to take part in studies, as are military personnel [p. 15].

"Informed consent" should be obtained from subjects. Basically, this means that a subject decides to participate (or not to participate) in a study on the basis of accurate information about what the subjects will be called upon to do. Often, however, the experimenter runs into difficulty with the informed-consent factor because many studies cannot be conducted if the subjects are informed about all the details of the investigation. Potential subjects often have to be deceived in one way or another if the results of the study are to be meaningful. Though considerable care is taken by most researchers to protect their subjects from any physical harm (and there are many safeguards built into the system to prevent this), what about the possible psychological harm that may arise from deception?

Deception can take many forms. A subject may be brought into a laboratory and told that the researcher is interested in studying the effects of noise on reaction time when the researcher is actually observing the effects of the noise on social interaction. This is probably a relatively harmless form of deception. Sometimes, however, the deception may lead to severe mental stress. Suppose that, on the basis of a test, some subjects in a group were told that they had homicidal tendencies when the test revealed nothing of the sort. Perhaps the investigator wished to determine what effects this type of information would have on various forms of behavior. Even if the subjects were "debriefed" at a later date, some psychological damage may have been done. The long-term effects of some kinds of deception can only be guessed at. As Kelman (1967) says:

> Serious ethical issues are raised by deception per se and the kind of use of human beings that it implies. In our other interhuman relationships, most of us would never think of doing the kinds of things that we do to our subjects— exposing others to lies and tricks, deliberately misleading them about the purposes of the interaction or withholding pertinent information, making promises or giving assurances that we intend to disregard. We would view such behavior as a violation of the respect to which all fellow humans are entitled and of the whole basis of our relationship with them. Yet we seem to forget that the experimenter–subject relationship—whatever else it is—is a *real* interhuman relationship, in which we have responsibility toward the subject as another human being whose dignity we must preserve [p. 5].

The problem of deception of subjects, then, is a serious one that must be considered by researchers in designing their investigations. There are many kinds of studies that could not be conducted without deception of subjects. Essentially, researchers must ask, "Is the research important enough to warrant the use of the kind of deception that would be involved?" If the answer is "yes," they should be as careful as possible to reduce the mental stress involved and to make sure that the subjects understand the reason for the deception after the study is completed.

CHAPTER 3

THE BUILT ENVIRONMENT: ROOMS AND HOUSING

The two principal types of physical environments are the built environment and the natural environment. They should not, however, be thought of as mutually exclusive but as part of a continuum on a number of dimensions. For our purposes, the most important of these dimensions is the relative contribution (in number or in space occupied) of designed and built structures in a particular physical setting. Consider, for example, the difference in the composition of the overall physical setting between a suburb or a classroom and a campground or a trail through a national park. Both types of settings contain designed structures or features, but designed and constructed features are dominant in the composition of the suburb or classroom. A built environment, then, is one that has been designed and formed, to a large degree, by people.

According to this general concept of what is meant by the term *built environment,* much of our behavior occurs in built environments of one type or another. As stated by Raskin (1974):

> Most of mankind spends the major part of its time indoors, in environments of its own creation, emerging only once in a while to plant a radish, chop down a tree, or complain about the weather. We are born indoors, live, love, bring up our families, worship, work, grow old, sicken, and die indoors. . . . This man-created environment, consisting of hospitals, schools, residences, office buildings, and churches, is what we call Architecture [p. 3].

Obviously, then, the built environment has great potential for influencing our activities.

The built environment can be considered to be a system made up of many subsystems. Although these subsystems vary tremendously in physical size, function, and amount of social interaction taking place within them, each can be broken down into elements that may affect human behavior in the system. By the same token, the human element in different built environments also varies, providing unique behavior/environment relationships in each built environment. Thus, behavior in a room in a house may differ substantially from the types of behavior that occur in a large airport terminal. We will therefore first consider interactions between people and the built environment at the relatively simple level of rooms and their furnishings and then consider more complex behavior/environment systems, such as houses, large buildings and facilities, and social institutions.

In this chapter and the next, we will focus on the manner in which different built environmental settings influence behavior. We will discuss these settings as though they were independent of other physical or social variables, although obviously this is not the case. From a systems point of view, each of the physical and behavioral settings will be influenced by the system of which it is a part. As shown in Figure 3-1, although we may be interested in the physical features of a room that influence the behavior of the person in that room, it is but one room in a specific building in a neighborhood of a city in a geographical region. Each of these systems (the building, the neighborhood, the city, and the geographical region) possesses unique physical features that may influence the behavior of the individual in the room. Moreover, these same physical features affect other persons in each level of the system and thus may promote social behavior that involves the single person under consideration.

It should also be kept in mind that the physical features of all built environments are subject to additional social, cultural, technological, economic, and political considerations.

As an example, consider the process of designing, constructing, and maintaining an office building in a city. The initial motive for construction is most likely economic—the developers have determined that they can profit from building and leasing office space in a particular location. To realize a profit, they must construct the building within some cost range. Further, their decisions on building location and type of structure are tempered by zoning laws, structural codes, and the possible whims of the political bodies governing that city. The legal and political constraints, as well as the economic criteria, are then turned over to the design team, which must use the current state of technology in construction and maintenance while adhering to sometimes ambiguously defined social and cultural expectations in producing a building. Obviously, creating a built environment is not a very freewheeling enterprise. This fact is an important one to keep in mind as we discuss all environmental influences on behavior.

ROOMS

The most significant influence of a room on behavior is the purpose of the room. In many cases a room's function is partially defined by the purpose of a larger system—a single classroom in a school building, for example. That

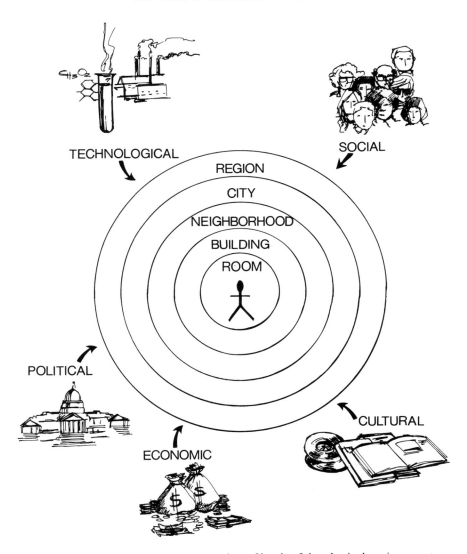

Figure 3-1. Although there are a number of levels of the physical environment that may affect behavior, there are also social, cultural, technological, economic, and political factors.

this room is part of a school typically places constraints on the behavior occurring there. The type of influence on behavior depends on whether the room is a lecture hall, a chemistry laboratory, or a small seminar room.

Moreover, for each type of room, we expect a certain shape, certain furnishings, and certain ambient conditions, all of which affect behavior.

In other cases the purpose of a room is not so explicit. An example of such a room is a family room in a private home. Because many different kinds of behavior may occur in this room, the specifications for its physical structure and contents are not nearly so clear as for a particular type of classroom.

When, however, a room is to encourage specific kinds of behavior, certain design considerations must be kept in mind. For a classroom the most obvious consideration is provision for student learning. Thus, if a classroom is to serve as a lecture hall, the seating should be arranged so that each student has as clear a view as possible of the instructor and the teaching aids to be used. This consideration means that all the students will typically be facing the instructor in some type of desk or table arrangement. Associated with this type of classroom are implied social-behavior regulations; for example, student interaction must be minimized in order not to interfere with the lecturer. This behavioral prerequisite means additional specifications for the seating arrangement.

From these examples it should be apparent that there exist two potential modes of physical design that affect behavior. The first is those aspects of the built environment that must be incorporated into the design of a room if it is to fulfill its function; for example, room for laboratory tables must be provided in a chemistry lab. The second mode is the physical attributes of a room that are not directly required by its function. Both categories of physical design contain independent variables that exert considerable influence on behavior. One such variable in the latter category is color.

Color

Color is probably the one physical dimension of a room that suffers least from the restrictions imposed by the planned function of a room, even though wall and ceiling color are frequently chosen to complement window and lighting-fixture placement in reducing glare and increasing reflected light. Accordingly, the color scheme of a room is generally left to the architect or interior decorator. The decision on color should not, however, be purely an aesthetic one; as shown in the research discussed in this section, colors elicit affective states and influence overt behavior.

Characteristics of Color

Colored light has three dimensions, *brightness, hue,* and *saturation.* Brightness is the intensity of the color, and hue is simply the color of an object, or the wavelength in the color spectrum that predominates in the composition of the color. Saturation is the amount of white present in any color; the more saturated a particular color, the less white it contains. For example, red is more saturated than pink.

In specifying colors composed of pigments rather than light, the term *hue* is retained, but the term *chroma* is often substituted for *saturation,* and the dimension of *value* is added. Value is "the degree of lightness or darkness of the color relative to a white-to-black scale" (Woodson & Conover, 1966, pp. 2–211). Because one or more of these dimensions can be varied in planning color layouts for rooms, designers have considerable latitude in attempting to produce desired subjective reactions in the people who use the rooms.

Basic Studies of Color and Behavior

Research dealing with relationships between color and behavior is complex. In many instances, studies of these relationships have not yielded clear-cut results. The effects of color on behavior can vary depending on the nature of the three different color dimensions, the context in which they are perceived, and the quality of the light illuminating the colors. Color effects can also vary depending on the type of behavior being measured and the way in which the behavior is measured. Finally, the effects of color may differ for persons of different ages, sex, cultural backgrounds, or mental states. A point to keep in mind is that if the "simple" variable of color and its effects on behavior is this complex, how much more complex the situation becomes when all other variables present in the built environment are included in the behavioral equation rather than being ignored or held constant. Nonetheless, each variable must be investigated to determine its effects on the prediction of behavior in the built environment.

The effects of color on behavior can be dealt with on several different levels. At the most basic level is the effect of sensing and perceiving different colors on physiological responses. Mehrabian and Russell (1974), in their review of studies dealing with color and arousal, offer general but tentative conclusions on the physiological effects of color. They cite studies indicating that red is generally more likely to bring about arousal than is green. In two studies employing the galvanic skin response (GSR) and patterns of brain activity as measures of basic physiologic arousal, red was more arousing than green when slides of the two colors were viewed (Erwin, Lerner, Wilson, & Wilson, 1961; Wilson, 1966). Nakshian (1964) arrived at a similar conclusion when he measured hand tremor and speed of movement in a perceptual/ motor tracking task as the subjects were exposed to panels of red, gray, and green. The subjects were found to show more hand tremor and speed of movement when exposed to red as opposed to gray. In turn, the gray panels were found to elicit faster movement than the green panels. Birren (1969) also concluded that red "excites" more than blue in studies using muscle tension, brain waves, heart rate, and respiration. However, a general caution stated by Mehrabian and Russell is appropriate when considering these results. They point out that the studies used to generate these conclusions can offer only qualitative impressions because color-elicited arousal responses have not been systematically investigated.

The next level of color/behavior relationships deals with how colors elicit judgments of preference and pleasantness. The studies on preference and perceived color pleasantness have direct implications for the design professions. For example, if the population that a designer is dealing with has some specific color preferences or dislikes some color combinations, the designer can emphasize or delete these in developing the color schemes. For these reasons the work on color preference and pleasantness deserves attention.

Some investigators have been concerned with personal or group differences in color preferences as defined by cultural background, age, or sex. Child, Hansen, and Hornbeck (1968) investigated the effects of hue, chroma, and value in determining the color preferences of children in elementary and secondary school. Children were shown pairs of color patches that differed on one or two of the three color dimensions. Hues from what is commonly referred to as the cooler end of the spectrum (green, blue, violet) were preferred by all ages, but the preferences decreased with age. Highly saturated colors were also preferable and also declined as a function of age. Brighter colors were generally preferred to darker ones. In comparing the girls' color-preference patterns to those of the boys, the researchers noted that the girls generally preferred colors higher in saturation and brightness.

In a study of cross-cultural color preferences, Child and Iwao (1969) presented Japanese and American college students with pairs of Munsell[1] color patches and asked them for their preferences on each color pair. The colors of each pair varied in either brightness or saturation or were complementary or very close to each other on the color spectrum. All the subjects preferred colors from the cooler end of the spectrum. The females showed no consistent preference for lightness. The American males showed more preference for lightness than the Japanese males, while the Japanese males preferred lighter colors than the Japanese females. The reverse of this finding was true for the Americans. Although all the subjects preferred more highly saturated colors, the degree of preference was influenced by culture and sex. Finally, the American students showed more individual consistency in their choices than did the Japanese participants.

These studies show that different groups of people may have different color preferences, at least in one or more dimensions. Although these data are

---

[1]The Munsell color system is the most widely used standard system of color identification.

useful for members of the design professions, it would be more useful for us to know how individuals and groups feel about the pleasantness of different colors. The rationale is that, although people may prefer one color or group of colors to another, they may judge both colors or color groups as pleasant and therefore be quite satisfied with either if they were included in an environmental display. Further, if the color ranges in any of these investigations were somewhat limited, the participants might have been choosing between colors that they did not find at all pleasant. Studies using color pleasantness as the measurement dimension would add the quality of an absolute rather than a relative judgment to the color-preference process. The following study by Helson and Lansford (1970) provides us with such judgments of color pleasantness.

Helson and Lansford compared the effects of illumination sources and background colors on pleasantness judgments of different colors. Their study is different from the typical study, which asks for pleasantness judgments of object colors under one source of illumination against neutral background colors (white, gray, or black). The size of this investigation is of particular significance. The investigators used 125 different colors on 25 different backgrounds under five different illumination sources. The object colors were also varied on the three dimensions of hue, value or lightness, and chroma or saturation. The color chips used were taken from the Munsell color system. Preference ratings were obtained from the subjects by placing 25 different color chips on a solid-color background under each of the different illumination sources. Each chip was rated from 1 (very, very unpleasant) to 9 (very, very pleasant). Five men and five women were used as judges in the study. This gave the investigators 156,250 different observation ratings, which makes it a remarkably comprehensive study.

The ratings revealed that both the type of light source used to illuminate the colors and the background were highly significant in predicting the pleasantness of the colors. There were also color-preference differences between the sexes. Finally, differences in hue, lightness, and chroma in the development of pleasing color contrasts were discovered. For light sources, the average rating of object colors over all backgrounds showed that the two best light sources were a fluorescent cool white and an incandescent filament (2854k). (There were many situations, however, in which the rankings of the light sources were different from this final result.) Background color was found to be more important in determining pleasantness ratings than source of illumination. This general finding has significance for designers; if an optimum light source is not available, it may be possible to use object-color and background-color contrasts to rectify the situation.

Generally, the best background colors for providing high pleasantness ratings were found to have either very dark or very light values in combination with very low saturation. (Recall that value or lightness is the amount of white in a color and that chroma goes from a very saturated color to a neutral gray. A low-chroma color is less saturated and closer to gray.) Across all sources of illumination, the best background colors were white, light yellow, light red, light green, dark green, light purple-blue, and black. In terms of hue, or actual color, the highest-rated object colors were blue, purple-blue, green, and blue-green. Red ranked slightly better than average. Yellow and purple turned out to be ranked quite low. The dislike for yellow also showed up in colors with strong yellow components, such as green-yellow and yellow-red. Women rated the warm colors—red, yellow-red, and yellow—higher in almost all sources of light, while males tended to find the cooler colors—blue, purple-blue, purple, and red-purple—more pleasant. High-chroma or highly saturated colors were generally rated higher than low-chroma colors. Lightness contrasts were judged to be the single most important source in yielding pleasant color combinations between object and background colors. Chroma contrasts also had an effect on object/background pleasantness ratings, but not to the same degree as lightness contrasts. Hue differences were not found to be as important as either lightness or chroma contrasts in providing pleasant color combinations.

From the wealth of results in this study, the authors offer one general formulation:

> . . . a certain amount of variety, change, differentiation or contrast is pleasant; sameness, monotony, repetition tend to be unpleasant. The organism adapts to same conditions of stimulation, rendering them neutral or unpleasant. Hence, in the field of color, static configurations of color should contain some variations in hue, lightness and chroma, and over a period of time different configurations of colors should be employed to prevent satiation of overfamiliar patterns of stimulation [p. 1539].

Due to the comprehensiveness of this investigation, we can offer only the general findings here. The interested reader should go to the original work for more specific information. In any event, this study can provide important information to designers who are concerned with the manipulation of color.

Studies of Room Color and Behavior

In our previous discussion of color, we referred to persons having preferences for "warm" or "cool" colors. Colors toward the red end of the spectrum (yellows, oranges, and reds) are commonly considered warm, while colors at the other end (blues and greens) are considered cool. This idea probably arose from commonsense associations. Blue water and green forest glades suggest cool temperatures; yellows, reds, and oranges evoke thoughts of the sun or fire. These kinds of associations have led to the seemingly intuitive hue/heat hypothesis "that an environment which has dominant light frequencies toward the red end of the visible spectrum feels warm and one with dominant blue frequencies feels cool" (Bennett & Rey, 1972, p. 149).

These authors tested a logical extension of the hue/heat hypothesis: the perceived warmth obtained from the color of a room and the actual temperature in the room may interact to affect differentially the thermal comfort of the room's occupants. The room used for the investigation was an environmental chamber, a room with strict controls over humidity and temperature. The temperature in the chamber was changed by circulating hot or cold fluid through coils attached to the walls, which were aluminum. Color, the other independent variable, was controlled by requiring each subject to wear successively red, blue, and clear goggles. Under each color condition the wall temperature was increased to 101 degrees and then decreased to 58 degrees. The subjects, who were seated close to the walls, were required to rate periodically their feelings of thermal comfort. Temperature readings were obtained at the points at which the subjects shifted from one thermal-comfort condition to another—for example, from "slightly warm" to "warm"—in each of the color conditions. The investigators' analysis revealed that red did not affect the subjects' feelings of thermal comfort any differently than did the blue or the clear condition. Bennett and Rey suggest that the hue/heat hypothesis is only intellectual, a pervasive belief that some colors make rooms seem warmer than do others.

Evidence of this intellectual effect was also obtained by Berry (1961) in a similar investigation. The subjects in his study were placed in a room under different colors of illumination and, as the experimenter raised the air temperature in the room, asked to report when they felt too warm. Although no differences between colors and the point at which the subjects stated a feeling of discomfort were discovered, the participants indicated that the warmer colors (usually amber and yellow) conducted more heat than did the cooler colors (green and blue).

These two studies illustrate an important point. Although no behavioral effect of room color on thermal comfort could be established, the subjects in the studies still maintained that cognitive perception of warmth varied as the colors were changed. Thus, this perceptual effect of color may be as important as actual behavioral indications of comfort in color choice for a room.

Color affects perception of not only a room's warmth but also such qualities as its spaciousness, complexity, and social status. Acking and Küller (1967, 1972) asked subjects to rate colored slides of rooms on an extensive list of adjectives that could describe an environment. The ratings were used by a team of architects and psychologists to select a set of adjectives that would best describe the pleasantness, social status, complexity, unity, and enclosedness of a room. Using this derived rating list, the participants in the second investigation evaluated slides of room sketches in which the colors of walls and some of the room details varied. The social evaluation of the rooms was found to vary as a function of lightness; as the darkness of the color and the detail increased, the subjects thought the rooms more rich or expensive. The dimension of value also accounted for the perceived spaciousness of a room. As the room colors became lighter, the rooms were generally judged to be more open. The effect of openness was also achieved by increasing the chromatic intensity of a room's details while leaving the color of the walls relatively weak in saturation. A room's judged complexity was also found to depend on the chromatic strength of the hues, with the more saturated room colors receiving higher complexity ratings. The rooms' pleasantness ratings varied from individual to individual, with no firm color preferences being established.

Up to this point our discussion of color as an independent variable has dealt with the effects of different dimensions of color on perceptions of a room. Although a person's perceptions of warmth or spaciousness can be considered behavior of a sort, they are difficult to measure. Another approach to studying the effects of color attempts to link a person's perception of a room to behavior that is more observable, or at least more subject to objective assessment. However, such behavioral measures become increasingly difficult to obtain as people/environment relationships become more natural.

An ingenious device that measures "locational" behavior and how it is affected by environmental features has been developed at the Environment Research Foundation in Kansas. This apparatus records the locational behavior of unknowing subjects in a museum room at the University of Kansas. The device, referred to as a *hodometer (hodos* is a Greek term for pathway), consists of a network of square switchmats similar to those used for automatic doors. The mats are laid on the floor, covered by a carpet, and wired to counters placed in a side room unnoticeable to people in the museum viewing room. The number of places where visitors go in the room, the time they spend at a particular location, and other kinds of behavior can thus be measured. Betchel (1967) has used this hodometer to establish correlations between locational behavior and picture preference in art displays.

Of more immediate interest, however, is a study by Srivastava and Peel (1968) using the hodometer to measure the exploratory behavior of museum-room visitors. In each of the two conditions in the study, the color of the carpet concealing the switchmats and the color of the walls were changed. When the walls and carpet were light beige, the subjects explored less (used less of the available floor space) than did the subjects in the room when the carpet and walls were chocolate color. The subjects under the latter condition took more steps, covered nearly twice as much area, and spent less time in the room.

This section has provided at least a preliminary statement of the effects of color perception on other forms of behavior. In addition to providing important information on behavior/environment interactions, such thought-provoking studies suggest future research directions. The study by Srivastava and Peel, for instance, suggests that color in rooms should not be disregarded or relegated to fulfilling purely aesthetic functions in future design considerations.

Ambient Environment

The experience of color in a room is visual. Other aspects of a room impinge on different sensory modalities. These aspects, collectively known as the *ambient environment*, are noise, temperature, illumination, and odor. Traditionally, these have been given more consideration in discussions of work environments, such as offices and factories, or of special environments, such as hospitals. The concept of noise as an environmental stressor will be covered in detail in a later chapter, as will the ambient environmental aspects of offices and special-purpose building systems. However, a few general statements about the effects of the ambient environment on perceptions of rooms can serve to provide an awareness of their existence in the scheme of any room environment.

An acceptable ambient environment is a prerequisite for aesthetic satisfaction. According to Fitch (1965), "the aesthetic process only begins to operate maximally, i.e., as a uniquely human faculty, when the impact upon the body of all environmental forces is held within tolerable limits. . . . A temperature of 120 degrees F or a sound level of 120 decibels can render the most beautiful room uninhabitable" (pp. 707–708). Thus, not only must all ambient conditions be acceptable, but no one stimulus should be allowed to dominate the others even though that stimulus may be tolerable. If the stimulus is extreme, sensory overload can result, which constitutes a stressful situation for the individual. The concept of the environment as a creator of stress will be examined in depth in a later chapter. Although the examples presented in that chapter deal with pollution, overcrowding, and other stress-creating attributes of the physical environment, it should be kept in mind that stressful aspects of the ambient environment in a room can elicit much the same type of behavior. Even if not stressful, an excessive amount of one or more aspects of the ambient environment in a room may cause an individual to perceive the room as unpleasant, which may lead to a more active behavior—avoiding the room in the future, for example.

The ambient conditions required for satisfaction and appreciation vary from room to room because they are a function of the purpose for which a room was designed. Thus, depending on the purpose of a particular room, different aspects of the ambient environment can be manipulated to produce an atmosphere that, in turn, will elicit the desired behavioral state in the occupants of the room. The following examples of common rooms, together with an examination of their ambient environments and the desired behavior, are illustrations.

In a discotheque two ambient conditions, lighting and sound, are highly manipulated. Music and other sources of sound often reach a sustained overall level of more than 100 decibels. Although the overall lighting level is often quite low, the lights may be in unusual places—for instance, under a Plexiglas floor—and may be programmed in flashing or blinking sequences in an attempt to produce an exciting visual experience. Moreover, the temperature in establishments of this sort is likely to be higher than the occupants would consider pleasant in other situations.

In a dentist's office, light and sound are usually manipulated to help give the impression of a pleasant atmosphere. Sound levels are much lower than in a discotheque, although soft music is likely to be played. Lighting, on the other hand, is at a higher level, not only because the dentist needs it but also because it seems cheerful. Such ambient conditions help to create an environment that is advantageous for both the patients and the dentist. From the point of view of the dentist, the more pleasant the atmosphere of the office, the greater the chance of a favorable impression on the patients. The impression that the patients receive may influence their returning or referring their friends. Patients appreciate a soothing, cheerful office while they are waiting for and undergoing treatment.

Obviously, other conditions are also operating in these two situations, and among the most prevalent may be social conditions. Social interactions and how they are affected by various aspects of a room will be discussed later in this chapter.

In these examples of a discotheque and a dentist's office, the two ambient environmental conditions that are subject to manipulation are lighting and sound, or acoustics. These are the variables that receive the most design attention. A third factor is temperature. These ambient environmental factors can influence a person's perception of an environmental space—in this instance, a room. In certain cases they can also have an impact on the person's observable behavior.

Since one objective of environmental psychology is to provide designers with relevant data about human behavior in environmental settings, it is useful to discuss these factors from a design standpoint. Raskin (1974) has discussed the architectural features of sound and light, and we will use a summary of his concepts as a framework for our discussion of these factors.

Sound has several dimensions that can be of design importance. The first is volume, more commonly known as intensity or loudness. The primary design consideration is to keep loudness below the level that would be perceived by the inhabitants of a room to be unpleasant. Thus, in many cases the designer's objective is to control volume by suppressing it.

Reverberation is a second dimension of importance to designers, especially when the room is designed for a special purpose, such as for a theater or a concert hall. Reverberation is simply the physical sound bouncing off the various surfaces of the room until it fades below the threshold of hearing. The time from the emittance of a sound until it falls below the hearing threshold is the critical value in reverberation and is referred to as t. Raskin states that t should be shorter in rooms used for speaking than in such rooms as a concert hall. Reverberation time is rather easily calculated and manipulated by the use of either sound-absorptive or sound-reflective materials. The acoustical quality of reverberation takes on a psychological meaning when the t criterion is not met. We have all experienced situations in which a multipurpose room, such as a gymnasium, is also used as a public-speaking facility. We may have had trouble understanding the speaker, which leads to unpleasantness or at least annoyance. Another possible result of the t criterion's being violated is the perception of an echo. Echoes can be interesting in a cave, but they tend to be disrupting if we are trying to understand what someone is saying.

Another acoustical dimension is the phenomenon of focusing. Here the shape of a room can set up sound-reflecting characteristics that can result in loud spots and soft spots by "funneling," or dispersing, sound throughout the room. In many cases, people attempt to eliminate sound focusing by the use of amplification systems. Sometimes these systems only serve to make the problem worse rather than alleviate it.

Raskin's last acoustical dimension is ambience. Ambience appears to be an aesthetic dimension in which the quality of the room environment elicits a certain behavior from the room occupants because of an unwritten social expectation. Examples are persons whispering in cathedrals or talking softly in luxurious restaurants. This dimension, then, is certainly present in our example of discotheque sound levels.

Four architecturally relevant dimensions of lighting are reported by Raskin. Illumination is the amount of light that falls on a surface, measured in foot-candles. A second dimension is the distribution of light within the room. As one might expect, the distribution of light is governed by the activity that the room was designed for. We have provided an example of light distribution in the discotheque and the dentist's office. Distribution can be further broken down into the categories of general and local lighting. Activities in different parts of the room (typing at a clerk's desk, for example) may require more local lighting than the average illumination level provided by the general lighting system. The third lighting dimension is glare, which is essentially light reflected from room and furnishings surfaces or direct glare from the light source. Glare is usually something to be avoided from both an architectural and a performance standpoint. Raskin also lists ambience as a dimension of lighting because certain environmental spaces seem to demand certain lighting characteristics.

Temperature also has four dimensions of importance from both the architectural and the psychological standpoint. The first is the ambient temperature of the air in a room. Second is humidity. The third is the circulation of the air, or the speed with which the air is moving past an individual. Fourth is the temperature of objects in the room, such as the walls and ceiling. These object and surface temperatures are translated into an index of mean radiant temperature (MRT).

In each of the ambient environmental factors we have mentioned, the dimensions are interrelated, just as they are in color, in which hue, chroma, and brightness interact to produce something we react to as color. These interrelationships serve to complicate attempts to relate specific behavioral responses to specific ambient environmental dimensions as they would occur in natural settings in the built environment.

Having considered the physical dimensions of the ambient features of sound, lighting, and temperature, we will now turn our attention to their behavioral effects. As we shall see, different dimensions of each of the environmental factors can prompt different levels and kinds of behavioral responses.

Sound

Sound has definite physiological effects, especially if loudness as measured in decibels is beyond the bounds of human tolerance. This is true in any environmental setting, whether in a room or an airport flight line. Too much sound will cause tissue damage, resulting in deafness. Sound also has effects that can be considered perceptual. For the purposes of this book, the most important perceptual effect is the effect labeled noise. It is discussed extensively in Chapter 5.

Lighting

As is the case with sound, light can have physiological effects. Too much light can cause tissue damage, although in the built environment this would be extremely rare. We will concentrate on light as it affects different perceptual processes, ratings of comfort and discomfort, and possible behavioral responses that are related to those perceptual processes.

In the area of perceived effects of light, a study by Cuttle (1973) has dealt with purely aesthetic considerations. Cuttle points out that the focusing of light on different objects in a room can either enhance, neutralize, or detract from the perceived aesthetic value of the lighted object. He provides pictorial examples of how, under different lighting conditions, objects can assume attractive, neutral, or aggressive characteristics. From these examples Cuttle infers that directionality of lighting is important for aesthetic experience. For example, side windows and overhead skylights provide different light patterns and effects in a room.

Other investigators have taken a more functional approach to the perceived qualities of different lighting conditions. Martyniuk, Flynn, Spencer, and Hendrick (1973) provide information that different lighting conditions in a room will yield different perceptual evaluations. These investigators conducted a study of lighting conditions in a conference room. Six different lighting conditions were used. Four of the conditions held the illumination level constant but varied the type and the location of the light sources. Overhead/focused, peripheral wall/indirect, overhead/diffuse, and a combination of the overhead/focused and peripheral wall/indirect lighting were used in the constant-illumination conditions. Two additional conditions used increased amounts of light. One used high-intensity overhead/diffuse light. The other used the additive combination of overhead/focused, peripheral wall/indirect, and overhead/diffuse light. In this portion of the experiment, the subjects were brought into the room and exposed to the six different lighting conditions. They were asked to rate the configurations with semantic-differential scales on five factors. The first factor was evaluative and used friendly/hostile, harmony/discord, and sociable/unsociable pairings on the semantic differential. The second factor was perceptual clarity, with clear/hazy and focused/unfocused pairs. The third factor, spatial complexity, used a simple/complex pair. A spaciousness factor used large/small, long/short, and spacious/cramped pairings. The formality factor used rounded/angular and informal/formal pairs.

Three general findings developed from the ratings of the lighting configurations on the factors of evaluation, perceptual clarity, and spaciousness. The higher-intensity overhead lighting yielded higher ratings of perceptual clarity than the lower-intensity overhead conditions. Second, the overhead/diffuse lighting conditions received lower scores on the evaluative factor than the other conditions. Finally, when overhead and limited wall lighting were compared to overhead/focused lighting used in isolation, they were rated higher on the evaluative and spaciousness factors.

The second portion of this study determined the means by which subjects rate the similarity or dissimilarity of different pairs of lighting conditions. The results indicated that the subjects judged similarity or differences in the lighting conditions using three dimensions—peripheral/overhead, uniform/nonuniform, and brightness. The dimensions derived from the pair-comparison procedure were compared to the five original factors used by the subjects in rating the six lighting configurations. Perceptual clarity contributed much to the bright/dim dimension. The evaluative factor was highly associated with the overhead/peripheral dimension. The spaciousness factor was associated with all three of the derived dimensions.

In summary, it should be noted that the study's objective was not to delineate specific items of information that could be immediately applied by designers. Rather, the purpose of this study was to show that lighting conditions can be differentiated from one another by the way they are perceived and to determine what dimensions are used in judging different lighting configurations. Although it has no immediate application to design, it is this type of methodology that must be developed if we are to evaluate lighting conditions.

Temperature

Temperature is the last ambient environmental variable to be considered in this basic review. Like sound and light, it has its own physiological-response components. As air temperature increases or decreases, involuntary control systems in our bodies act to maintain a stable internal temperature. At extremes this is observable by our profuse sweating or shivering. Since these responses are involuntary, they are of no real intrinsic interest to the environmental psychologist. The behavioral responses that are of interest center around comfort ratings or their derivations. Representative of state-of-the-art research in perception of the thermal environment are several studies by McIntyre and Griffiths (1974). The emphasis of their research is the development of a methodology and reliable measures of individual reactions to the thermal environment. Their experiments were conducted in a climatic chamber similar to the one used in the Bennett and Rey (1972) study.

One dimension McIntyre and Griffiths discuss is mean radiant temperature (MRT). MRT is contrasted to air temperature in that it is defined by the average temperature of all the surfaces of the environmental unit under consideration—in this case, a room. These researchers consider MRT to be more important than air temperature in determining perceived and reported warmth. They also imply that for a given room environment a higher MRT could be used with a lower mean air temperature, thereby manipulating the room environment to induce feelings of freshness.

The subjects were placed in the environmental chamber in one of a number of conditions in which the air temperature ranged from 15 to 35 degrees C and the MRT varied from 17 to 29 degrees C. In some cases there was as much as a 10-degree difference between the MRT and the air temperature. The subjects stayed in the chamber for 45 minutes and then were asked to rate their warmth on a standard scale. Their judgments of subjective warmth were more predictable from mean air temperature than from mean radiant temperature. Also, reports of freshness could not be related to warmth, nor were the higher MRT conditions preferred. The authors feel that these results are particularly relevant for designing cooling and heating systems. For example, if mean air temperature is deemed to be more important, it appears that there can be a difference of up to 10 degrees C between the two measures with no judgmental differences in comfort. Second, the results suggest that radiant-heating systems are not superior in perceived comfort, as was once believed.

A second study reported by McIntyre and Griffiths (1974) deals with asymmetric radiation fields. A room may have relative hot and cold spots, especially when the room has windows and a radiant-heating system. The authors wished to determine whether asymmetric radiation fields about the head have any effect on the perceived or reported warmth of room occupants. For the purposes of this investigation, the authors attempted to set limits for a particular case of asymmetric radiation, that around the head, coming from the heated ceiling of the climatic chamber. Their predictions were that ceiling temperatures above 33 degrees C in a domestic situation or 27 degrees C in a large building would prove unacceptable because of the temperature differentials felt by an individual on different parts of the body. They felt that this effect would be increased at higher subjective temperatures. During the experiment, as ceiling temperatures were increased, wall temperatures were decreased in order to maintain constant subjective temperatures. In this manner the researchers controlled for subjective perceptions of temperature going beyond the bounds of tolerability through an increased absolute temperature in the room rather than an increased ceiling temperature.

The experiment was conducted at low-MRT and high-MRT conditions, with ceiling temperatures ranging from 26.5 degrees to 46 degrees C. The subjects rated their perceptions on three different scales—discomfort, warmth, and nonuniformity of the room temperature—from both sitting and standing positions. Only the highest ceiling temperature in the standing position was felt uncomfortable for the high-MRT condition. Subjective warmth was reported as decreasing as the ceiling temperature increased. (Recall that wall temperature was always adjusted so that the MRT remained constant.) The subjects reported that the temperature became less uniform as ceiling temperature increased at both MRT conditions and both rating positions. These findings do not support the authors' hypothesis, since the subjective rating of discomfort was reported only at the highest ceiling temperature and did not proportionately increase in the high-MRT condition.

The practical implication of this study is that people appear to be able to tolerate a significant amount of asymmetry in their radiation fields. Also, the research does not support the common concept that high temperature differentials on different surfaces of a room affect people's comfort. The authors suggest that the results of this research can be applied in an interactive fashion with room lighting. Designers have been cautious about increasing the power of the lighting source for fear of increasing ceiling temperatures beyond the bounds of comfort. McIntyre and Griffiths' research suggests that this need not be a concern until ceiling temperatures approach 45 degrees C.

What implications do the results of studies such as these have for those engaged in designing buildings? Although we have dealt with sound, light, and temperature as though they were independent of one another, it is obvious that each factor is present in every room we enter. Therefore, these features are in dynamic interaction and will elicit some response from individuals in a room.

We have mentioned the physiological bounds of tolerance for these ambient environmental features. The tolerance ranges for the factors can be combined to construct a three-dimensional "tolerance envelope." Any point in this tolerance envelope depends on the interaction of the values for each factor. Similarly, the three factors can be combined to produce a perceived "comfort envelope," in which each of the factors interacts with the others in producing a composite comfort space. Any time individuals enter a room they may make unconscious or conscious judgments about their position in that perceived comfort space. What becomes important to behavioral scientists and designers alike is to develop the ability to predict the relative contribution of each ambient environmental factor to that perceived composite comfort rating. Second, we must be aware that different values on the comfort/discomfort continuum for any one or two of the ambient features will place constraints on the values that the remaining ambient feature can approach without venturing outside the boundaries of the comfort envelope.

Obviously, as we discussed in the two examples of the discotheque and the dentist's office, there are factors that can override people's perceptions of their position in the comfort envelope. These factors may also override any expected behavioral consequences that exceeding the boundaries of the envelope could have. In a discotheque, for example, the boundaries of the perceived envelope may be exceeded in all three dimensions discussed, but the excesses probably would not have any direct impact on a person's approach/avoidance behavior since the social variables involved and the perceived function of the room would be more important in predicting behavioral response to the room environment.

Size and Shape

If we think of the various features making up a room as either fixed or flexible, size and shape are undoubtedly the most rigid. Although, as we shall see later, the nature of rooms can be altered by rearranging the furnishings, the physical dimensions of a room do not lend themselves to change without considerable effort and expense. Thus, the size and shape of any particular room have been largely accepted as fixed, and researchers have concentrated on manipulating other aspects of the room environment, such as color, ambient conditions, and arrangement of furnishings.

The primary reason for the lack of research on the effect of room shape on behavior is our almost total lack of variety in shapes. For the most part, the North American room is rectangular; it is difficult to remember seeing a room that does not consist of 90-degree angles. Only in futuristic architecture and in other cultures—the igloo in Eskimo culture and the tepee in Indian culture, for example—do rooms have different shapes. Indeed, the rectangular room is so common that we tend to believe a particular room is rectangular even though cues from objects within the room tell us it is not. Ittelson and Kilpatrick (1951) provide an excellent example of this phenomenon's occurrence in a distorted room:

> . . . the floor slopes up to the right of the observer, the rear wall recedes from right to left and the windows are of different sizes and trapezoidal in shape. When an observer looks at this room with one eye from a certain point, the room appears as if the floor were level, the rear wall at right angles to the line of sight and the windows rectangular and of the same size. Presumably the observer chooses this particular appearance instead of some other because of the assumptions he brings to the occasion [p. 55].

The relevance of this study for environmental psychology is that viewers' perceptions of the distorted room are influenced by their previous experiences with rooms. Unfortunately, little other research has been reported on different behavioral effects of various room shapes. We will report the results of a single study that bear some relationship to the influences that the size and shape of a room have on the perception and description of room spaces.

Hall, Purcell, Thorne, and Metcalfe (1976) conducted a study designed primarily to develop a procedure for determining the dimensions people use to describe a room. They were also concerned with validating the statistical technique of multidimensional analysis as a tool in helping to find the descriptive dimensions. In the subjects' perceptions and descriptions of a room, one of the dimensions that surfaced was related to the size and shape of the room.

Every possible paired combination of 11 entrance halls in commercial buildings was rated on similarity or dissimilarity. These data were then subjected to a multidimensional scaling analysis, and the number of dimensions needed for perception or description was determined. The resultant dimensions were warm/cool, shiny/matte, patterned/plain, large/small, and deep/shallow. The investigators considered the dimensions of large/small and deep/shallow to be descriptive of the size of the foyer. It appeared that the shape of the room in terms of the deep/shallow rating was also related to the large/small rating. In a subsequent analysis the size dimension was retained as an important contributor to the description of the foyer spaces. The small/large dimension was also shown to have associations with the patterned/plain and shiny/matte descriptive scales. From this it can be inferred that texture and the quality of visual reflectance are important in judgments about room size. It also appears that individuals do take size into account when describing the distinctions between rooms.

Furnishings and Their Arrangement

Thus far we have emphasized the effects of some aspect of a room—size and shape, color, or ambient conditions—on the perceptions, appreciation, and locational behavior of the individual. In this section we will expand our discussion to include the furnishings and arrangements of furnishings in rooms and how these variables may influence perceptions of the room and the behavior that takes place. We will see that the effects of room furnishings on an individual are generally confined to perceptions of efficiency, beauty, comfort, or purpose. However, when two or more persons are interacting in an educational, work-related, recreational, or some other setting, other behavioral effects of furnishings and their arrangement can be more readily observed.

Furnishings and Perceptions of Rooms

Furniture can influence people's perception and evaluation of room size. Imamoglu (1973) asked subjects to evaluate the spaciousness of an experimental room and give estimates of its size compared to a regularly furnished office room. The experimental room was presented in three different conditions: empty, normally furnished, and overfurnished. The amount of furniture in the room therefore served as the independent variable. The results followed commonsense prediction and supported his hypothesis that when more furniture is placed in a room the room will appear smaller. The subjects tended to rate the experimental room as less spacious when it was empty than when it was appropriately furnished. However, they judged it much less spacious when the room was in the overfurnished condition.

A study by Samuelson and Lindauer (1976) also dealt with furniture arrangement. They asked their subjects to evaluate a room under "neat" and "messy" conditions. In this case the same room, an office with the expected furnishings, was used for both conditions, with the items in the room differing only in their arrangement. The neat room had a small desk and a chair, a wastebasket, and a second chair. On the desk were newspapers, books, and other office paraphernalia arranged in an orderly fashion. The messy room had an overflowing wastebasket, crumpled papers, pens and pencils strewn about, and newspapers scattered on the desk. The subjects were asked to rate the two room conditions on an evaluative measure, using adjective pairs such as cheerful/gloomy and pleasant/unpleasant, to obtain affective reactions to the room. The descriptive items of small/large and empty/full were used to indicate the subjects' perceptions of the size and spatial aspects of the room. Generally, the subjects saw the messy room as fuller than the neat room. The neat room was also perceived as larger than the messy room. These results provide an interesting addendum to the Imamoglu study. It appears that the objects in a room do not have to be changed or increased to create a significant change in the perceiver's judgment about room size or fullness.

Furnishings and Social Interaction

As stated at the beginning of this chapter, many components of the built environment are designed to meet both functional and behavioral objectives. The function of a chair, for instance, is obviously to provide something to sit on. At the same time, however, a chair may be designed to affect behavior. Sommer (1969) reports that a Danish furniture designer was contracted to design a chair that would become so uncomfortable after a short time that an occupant would be forced to get up. This design was requested by restaurant owners who did not want their customers lingering over coffee. Sommer also describes similar design considerations in the seating arrangements at a typical airport and points out that in most airports it is difficult for people to converse comfortably. He states:

> The chairs are either bolted together and arranged in rows theatre-style facing the ticket counter, or arranged back-to-back, and even if they face one another they are at such distances that comfortable conversation is impossible. The motive for the sociofugal arrangement appears the same as that in hotels and other commercial places—to drive people out of the waiting areas into cafes, bars, and shops where they will spend money [pp. 121-122].

If the objective of the seating arrangements in airports is actually to discourage social interaction and promote financial gain, the arrangement is highly appropriate. In a series of experiments, Sommer (1959, 1962) investigated the seating preferences of persons engaged in conversation. In the first study, pairs of subjects were asked to sit on two couches in a lounge and discuss a prepared topic. The couches were placed across from each other at distances depending on the experimental conditions. Sommer found that up to a distance of about 3 feet between the couches, his subject pairs preferred to sit across from each other. When the distance was greater, they preferred to sit on the same couch.

Using the findings from this experiment, Sommer conducted a second study in which the couches were replaced by four chairs to allow greater variety in side-by-side distance. The experimental situations were constructed so that the distance between side-by-side and facing chairs could vary from 1 foot to 5 feet. Again pairs of subjects were assigned to an arrangement of chairs and given a topic to discuss. As in the previous study, the subjects generally preferred to sit across from each other if the distance was equal to or less than the maximum side-by-side distance (see Figure 3-2). In interpreting these findings, however, Sommer cautions that they were obtained in one room and in one structured interaction. He emphasizes that manipulation of other environmental variables, such as room size and function, as well as the social situation may elicit different responses.

The classroom and what happens in it have always been of much interest and concern to administrators, teachers, and parents. New educational techniques, such as modular scheduling and the open classroom, with broadly defined goals of increasing the quality of the educational experience,

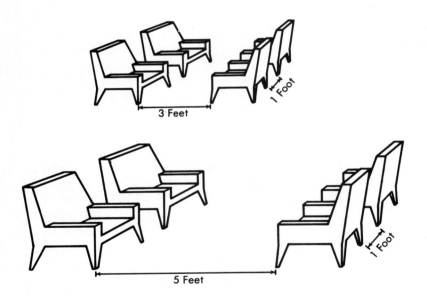

Figure 3-2. Research indicates that chair arrangement influences the seating choice of two persons who wish to converse. People prefer to sit across from each other while talking if the chairs are close enough, as they are at the top of the illustration. If the distance separating the chairs is too great for comfortable conversation, as it is at the bottom of this illustration, people will sit beside each other.

have accelerated this interest substantially. However, not nearly so much attention has been directed toward the contribution of the physical classroom environment to the educational process. More often than not, if the classroom environment is altered in any way, it is altered to promote some behavioral objective—for instance, to increase class discussion. Researchers then are confronted with a host of independent variables. If class discussion is shown to have increased, was it because of the new teaching technique, or was it possibly because of arranging the furnishings in a manner more conducive to student/teacher interaction? Research designed to answer this type of question is rare. However, Sommer (1969) and Richardson (1967) provide some insight into the question of physical classroom conditions and student behavior.

Richardson maintains that the traditional physical arrangement of the classroom—students' desks in straight rows facing the instructor—may not be the best way to encourage student involvement and satisfaction. She cites a number of reasons: (1) Students may not be able to see the instructor or what the instructor is doing because other students may inadvertently block their view. (2) Many students may be so far from the instructor that they feel isolated from the class and its subject matter. (3) Students may have difficulty seeing and hearing other students. If a person in the front row answers a question, students in the rear may not be able to hear. Moreover, it is difficult for the front-row student to gauge the class's reaction to the answer. Students in the rear answering a question also cannot see and hear their classmates' reactions. (4) The dominant role of the instructor is accentuated by the use of furniture different from that of the students and by the distance between class and instructor. (5) The row-by-row arrangement inhibits "action" types of lessons.

Richardson offers several alternatives to the traditional furnishings arrangement that would encourage class participation. One suggestion is to arrange the desks in one or more circles or semicircles. She also notes that substituting large tables for desks would enhance class unity and cooperation. Although Richardson's opinions were derived from observation and represent no more than anecdotal evidence, her basic ideas are supported by Sommer (1969), who investigated seating arrangements, room properties, and class participation.

Sommer used six rooms in his study. Four of the rooms had the traditional arrangement of straight rows. Two of these rooms were student laboratories containing the usual equipment in addition to the fixed tables. The other two traditional rooms differed in another dimension: one was windowless, and a wall of the other consisted of windows. The remainder were seminar rooms, with tables in a square in one of the rooms and on three sides in the other. Observation of students during regular classes showed that a higher average number of students per session in the straight-row arrangements participated in class discussions. However, the absolute number of statements per session was higher for the classes held in the seminar rooms. Sommer also notes that students said they did not like to have their classes in the laboratories and the windowless room. The results of this investigation suggest that the physical characteristics of a classroom are important determinants of the behavior occurring there.

HOUSING

The logical next level in our discussion of the built environment is housing. Here rooms become components of a larger system and are bound by the system's objectives: providing physical shelter for the family, places for family activities, and psychological shelter from the pressures of the outside world. Each individual dwelling is in turn a component of a larger housing system, whether in a suburban neighborhood or an apartment house.

Houses and housing units are considered to be important factors in the investigation of environment/behavior relationships for reasons ranging from the commercial to the social. One obvious reason is the amount of time that is spent in or around a family dwelling. From this standpoint there is no other feature of the built environment that has the potential for such intimate contact for such extended periods. Interest in the effects of housing on behavior has also grown with the recognition of the tremendous need for new housing to allay current and projected shortages. A conservative estimate is that the nation's current total number of housing units should double by the end of the century. New dwellings of all types will be required: suburban developments to satisfy the demands of the growing middle class, additional public-housing projects for the economically deprived, and increased numbers of structures aimed at enticing people to remain in the cities. People in the construction industries indicate that it is impossible to meet new housing needs by using conventional methods. Thus, factory-fabricated housing is rapidly expanding to fill the gap left by on-site construction methods. Advocates of both types of construction, however, lack knowledge about the behavioral correlates of present design and construction methods, not to mention the possible influences of new housing concepts on behavior.

Single-Family Dwellings

Our discussion of the single-family dwelling and its importance in the spectrum of people/environment interaction will center around four basic questions. First, why has North American society placed such an emphasis on the single-family dwelling? What sociological, psychological, and economic needs are met by living in a single-family dwelling? Second, what are the salient factors involved in choosing a residential area and a particular dwelling in that area? Third, what effect do physical characteristics and areas within our homes have on our everyday behavior? Finally, what are the physical relationships between dwelling units, and what impact do these physical features have on our interactions and social activities?

At times during our discussion of these topics, the answers to these questions may seem quite elusive. There are several possible reasons for the lack of definitive research findings in the area of single-family dwellings. First, the population to be studied is obviously heterogeneous, transient, and quite independent. Much of the time the researcher is confronted with a generally satisfied sample because people can often either modify their environment or move away from it if it proves unsatisfactory. Even if the residents are not wholly satisfied with their physical home environment, the human organism has proved to be remarkably adaptable. Thus, any small dissonance between people and their dwellings may not be operating at a level the respondents can verbalize. Second, single-family-dwelling residents may not be convenient to study as a group. Unfortunately, from the point of view of many behavioral scientists, there is no payoff for studying such a difficult population when relatively captive audiences living in prisons, hospitals, and public-housing projects are available. Finally, research on single-family dwellings may not have any impact on future design activities. Even if design considerations could be identified, they would have to prove economically feasible for the developers and builders to incorporate them. Given the high demand for single-family dwellings, such behavioral dictates for design are highly unlikely to be readily adopted.

Attributes of Single-Family Dwellings

One primary attribute of the single-family dwelling and its environment is the treatment of space. Typically, the family is assured a space where they can engage in activities without interference from neighbors. Although we have little data showing that space other than that within the house itself contributes to resident satisfaction, denial of this type of space has proved to be detrimental to family relations and activities in multiple-family dwellings.

Michelson (1970) provides evidence from a survey that desired lifestyle to some extent determines the quest for family space. He notes that a substantial number of families who moved from cities to suburbs indicated that the primary reason for their move was to break away from intense relationships with relatives outside the immediate family. Apparently, these people perceived the suburban single-family-dwelling environment as a means of changing their emphasis from extended-family to nuclear-family activities. Thus, the space provided by the single-family dwelling, as well as the increased distance from their relatives, served as a source of satisfaction with their new lifestyle.

Another factor that may be partly responsible for the choice of single-family dwellings is the traditional role of the man in the household as keeper of the physical plant and all-around "pioneer" handyman. Evidence for the importance of space to play this role is again provided indirectly by pointing out the negative aspects of multiple-family dwellings:

> When a man lives in a multiple dwelling, particularly when he is surrounded on all sides by other tenants, he can't perform any activity which is violent inside his own dwelling without provoking his neighbors—not unless there is adequate soundproofing, an expensive proposition. He can by no means alter the interior of his dwelling to any major extent without typically invoking the wrath of his landlord and probably a lawsuit.
>
> But where else can he perform this role? Private outdoor space provides a suitable outlet. The man who has just completed an active job and stands talking with his neighbor, foot on split-rail fence, is out of the American dream. Yet most multiple dwellings, particularly high rise apartments, have no provision for private open space for such purposes [Michelson, 1970, p. 81].

Michelson also cites Kumove (1966), who conducted a study comparing high-rise apartment buildings and town houses. An informal visitor in a high rise generally sees no men about, whereas in town-house complexes, in which each unit has direct access to ground level, the males are observed to be engaged in a variety of activities, mostly recreational. Kumove feels that these activities help fulfill the man's expected social role.

Although such sociological variables influence choice of a home, more personal variables are also involved. The desire for single-family dwellings and the space they provide can be considered to be an extension of the need for territory. The possession of a house and lot can satisfy the need to exert territorial influence. An additional advantage of territorial possession in the form of home ownership may be a reduction in the social tension that can exist when possession of a space is ambiguous, as in the case of public areas used for family activities in multifamily dwellings.

Michelson's study also investigated relationships between individuals' values and their judgments of different types of housing. From the results of a standard inventory designed to determine a person's value structure, Michelson obtained measures of his subjects' instrumentalism, expression, group-indebtedness, individualism, and activity-mindedness. Each of his subjects was then asked to rank photographs of four different types of housing, ranging from a single-family house to a high-rise apartment, on the same types of value dimensions as were used in the inventory. The subjects were also asked to sketch a map of their ideal environment, including the position of their ideal home in relationship to neighbors' houses and commercial establishments. From these sketches and the responses to the photographs, Michelson attempted to distinguish relationships between the individuals' value structures and their housing preferences. For instance, if a man valued group activities, which type of housing environment seemed group-minded to him? Although Michelson's overall results were inconclusive, a number of suggested relationships did emerge. In general, the subjects who expressed a desire for large lots in their sketches were high in individualism. Also, the single-family dwelling was thought by the subjects to be highly related to the pursuit of family activities, much more so than any of the other housing types presented. Further, regardless of whether the subjects expressed a desire for a large or a small lot in their sketches, they consistently stressed that the purpose of the lot was to provide for family and individual activities they felt could not be undertaken in a public area. The findings of this investigation provide some indication of the importance of single-family housing and the kinds of behavior that its space fosters.

Factors in Home Choice

There are many reasons for choosing a particular residential location. For example, there are a number of personal or family variables related to home choice. Among these are education, income, age, occupation, and race. Feldman and Tilly (1960) demonstrated the importance of these variables in location choice by using census data and correlating the location of an individual's residence in an area with a number of the factors listed. Education was a relatively high determinant of where someone lived in a particular city area. Income was also related to location within an area. When the occupational and income data were considered together, it appeared that higher-paid blue-collar workers (craftsmen and foremen) used their higher disposable income to disassociate themselves from other members of the blue-collar class. They tended to move to residential areas that their higher salaries allowed them to afford.

Hallowitz (1969) sought to find the relationship between selected goals of prospective home buyers and the extent to which these goals were met by their choice to move from one house to another. The principal reasons, as identified by Hallowitz, for the purchase of a house were the desires to have more space, to secure benefits for the children, to develop equity, and to enjoy greater freedom. These factors were significant enough to override the general increase in the husband's commuting time and the wife's expectation that she would be separated from her old friends and would have to make new ones. Another motive for choosing the new housing was to provide the children with the quantity and quality of space they needed to play constructively and safely. In a follow-up study the mothers confirmed that this objective was met.

One outcome hypothesized by Hallowitz—that adult activities and involvement in local community dealings and organizations would increase in the new home environment—did not materialize. These more formal activities were infrequent in the locations that the families had lived in before and continued to be infrequent after the move. However, the families appeared to engage in more informal social activities with their new neighbors as long as they belonged to the same social class.

There are two sets of possible reasons for a family's wanting to relocate. These reasons, classed as social and economic, are in accord with the two theories of location choice discussed by Moriarty (1974). Moriarty reviews the concepts underlying what is considered the economic-competition hypothesis and the social-choice hypothesis in predicting where different families will choose to make their home.

The economic-competition hypothesis is based on the ability to pay. Those whose incomes enable them to live on the periphery of an urban core with more spacious and private sites are the ones who will live in those areas, assuming they can pay the basic site costs and the higher operating costs due to increased travel. According to the social-choice hypothesis, people choose a place to live based more on whom they want to associate with than on what they can or cannot afford. In this manner the social distance between groups would explain segregation of different housing areas or different residential-location choices rather than primarily economic considerations. Moriarty's analysis of different residential areas within a medium-sized city reveals that both employment accessibility, as predicted by the economic-competition hypothesis, and social accessibility, as predicted by the social-choice hypothesis, are important in predicting where a family will live. In other words, socioeconomic status and the status of the people in the neighborhood help determine where the family will live. However, in determining these relationships, it was found that a social-accessibility index as derived from the social-choice hypothesis was better able to predict the composition of different housing areas than was the index derived from the economic-competition hypothesis.

We have discussed the variables that influence a person's choice of residential location in terms of social factors of communities or neighborhoods. We might then ask whether there are any data to indicate that physical characteristics of either the neighborhood or specific dwellings influence people's choice of a house. Recall from Michelson's (1970) study that values and judgments about different housing types are related to the activities, such as children's play, foreseen in the different housing types. Pyron (1972) found that physical composition and structure in site groupings at the neighborhood level affect the fulfillment of perceived requirements. In a rather detailed study the subjects were shown films of models of housing areas with different housing forms and arrangements of the forms. Generally, Pyron's subjects indicated that the more complexly grouped forms arranged around courts would provide more and better opportunities for children's play. At the same time there was some uncertainty about preservation of privacy in the court type of groupings. This concern over privacy in clustered or court arrangements is a well-founded one, as we shall see in our discussion of neighborhood orientations and their effects on development of social relations and on perceived privacy.

Once a neighborhood has been chosen, a person may not be able to exercise much choice in the physical attributes of a house. The decision on which type of house or which house of a number of similar houses may be based primarily on the square footage available. Once the neighborhood and space requirements are met, the degree of freedom in choosing a particular house is again reduced, so the actual choice of a house based on particular physical amenities may be quite constrained. However, there may be some room left for decisions based on topics described in Cooper's "The House as a Symbol of Self" (1974). A person may be able to make a house a symbol of self by choosing among houses with the same basic floor plan but with different types of ornamentation or by changing the interior from Colonial to Spanish or from Mediterranean to the contemporary natural look. Cooper implies that the most common way of making houses symbols of self is decorating the interior spaces, not making choices in the basic design of the exterior or the interior.

Up to this point we have been concerned with behavior in the built housing environment in terms of choices based on social, economic, and, to a small extent, physical factors. For whatever reasons choices of neighborhood and of a particular dwelling in that neighborhood are made, certain activities revolving around the family will take place in that dwelling environment. The extent to which that environment influences the activities and the attitudes of the family living in it is our next area of consideration.

Dwelling Design and Family Activities

The activities that can be expected to take place in a home are almost limitless. They include production-related tasks, such as homemaking and food preparation; maintenance tasks; management of the activities of spouses, children, and possibly live-in relatives; leisure activities, which can range from reading to gardening to constructing boats or planes; sleeping, which is the single activity that accounts for the largest proportion of time spent in the home; and other family social and interactive events. We will make the implicit assumption that the home environment is designed around the support and/or containment of these activities.

In this section our discussion will center around a sampling of the activities that can be expected in a home and the extent to which the expected location of the activities is supportive of them. Specifically, we will be discussing the kitchen, bedroom, and bathroom. At the outset we should point out that we will be talking about activities and the rooms associated with them from a Western cultural standpoint. This is an important consideration, because Tagg (1973) has established that, as far as Westerners are concerned, certain rooms have certain activities associated with them. In Eastern cultures, activities are associated with their functions and are not delineated by location (Canter & Lee, 1974).

Kitchens. The kitchen is felt by many to be the most important room in any single-family dwelling. Historically, the kitchen has been used as a family-gathering place for many activities besides food preparation and consumption. At one time the kitchen table, with its surrounding chairs, served as the major functional piece of furniture for the family living as well as dining area. For many families the kitchen has retained its influence as the hub of family activity, partly because other rooms do not provide a proper environment for many activities (Mehrabian, 1976). The end result is that the spaces originally planned for those activities are not used.

The kitchen is also the central point for many of the more demanding household tasks. Steidl (1972) reports that the kitchen is the site for both some of the most cognitively demanding tasks (such as meal preparation) and some of the most disliked and monotonous tasks (such as after-meal cleanup). She maintains that the same design considerations that go into any work station can and should be applied to the kitchen. When the subjects in her study were asked what made their household tasks more or less difficult, they cited inadequate or poorly located work surfaces and inconvenient storage areas as factors that made homemaking tasks more difficult than they needed to be. On the other hand, homemakers who were fortunate enough to have well-planned kitchens said that the design forethought made their tasks less difficult. Steidl implies that, although performance may not be affected to the point where the tasks are not completed satisfactorily, any design factors that contribute to the difficulty of homemaking functions can be considered sources of annoyance and that these cumulative annoyances in addition to problems of day-to-day living can create stressful situations. Steidl's study has direct implications for designers of houses and certainly deserves further consideration, since homemaking constitutes the largest single occupation that we have today.

Bedrooms. As Parsons (1972) points out, by the age of 65 most people have spent nearly 40% of their lives in their bedrooms, yet the bedroom "has received little systematic investigation from psychologists, engineers, physicians, or architects" (p. 421). In a systematic review of the literature on bedrooms and their furnishings, Parsons discusses the activities of bedroom users and the characteristics, requirements, and standards of bedrooms. Space limitations do not permit a detailed discussion of his article, but we will consider his approach to the topic and a few of the points he raises.

Parsons employs what can be called a systematic human-factors approach in his discussion of the bedroom. This approach involves a detailed analysis of bedroom activities, with design considerations based on these activities. Although sleeping may be the most obvious bedroom activity, this behavior can be analyzed in detail, for it includes lying, falling asleep, dreaming, snoring, talking, waking up, and various physiological processes. Bedrooms are also used for sexual behavior, housekeeping, sitting, and observing as well as dressing and social, recreational, and occupational activities.

After considering the activities of bedroom users, Parsons discusses the design of the bedroom. He points out that the bedroom has tended to become larger. This may be due to a variety of reasons, including the desire to put more furniture in the bedroom, the need to express personal territoriality, the trend toward using the bedroom for many activities besides sleeping, and the need to get away from the bustle of family life and enjoy some degree of privacy and solitude. Parsons also deals with the available information on the ambient environment of bedrooms, including sound, illumination, temperature, and ventilation, as well as decor and interroom relationships.

In his discussion of the design of the bed, Parsons states that "The components of the bed of greatest human engineering interest are the mattress and bedstead . . ." (p. 434), but he also considers sheets, blankets, and pillows. There are some guidelines on mattress design, but they are not based on substantial research. Similarly, the appropriate length and width of a mattress are still not firmly established, though it has been suggested that it should be 8 inches longer than one's height.

We have not attempted to present any data in our brief review of Parsons's article because when data are available they are often conflicting. Parsons concludes by saying that the need for much research in this area is apparent. He adds, "The bed is the device with which human beings have the most intimate contact, and in the bedroom they spend more time than anywhere else. Need more be said to excite the interest of those who study man–machine–environment relations?" (p. 488).

Bathrooms. If any room in the house has been neglected more than the bedroom or the kitchen, Kira (1975) would nominate the bathroom for that dubious distinction. Kira has spent nearly 20 years studying the design of bathrooms and has concluded that the bathroom, as found in North American homes, is nearly beyond hope. Although he has been concerned with the subjects of modesty, privacy, and sexuality and their relationship to room and fixture design, Kira's research has dealt primarily with an-thropometric considerations in the design of bathroom fixtures. For example, he points out that the present height of the toilet is not appropriate for bodily functions but is based simply on industry standards that have developed over the years.

Kira's assertion that bathrooms and their fixtures are poorly designed is given substantial credence in a report by Willis (1975) on bathtub and shower accidents. He states that 200,000 people are injured each year in bathroom accidents, many of which involve a slip or a fall. This finding has direct implications for the design of tub and shower enclosures as well as the areas around these fixtures. The number of accidents is a prime example of a direct relationship between features of the built environment and serious behav-ioral consequences.

Environments of Single-Family Dwellings and Social Behavior

In this section we will expand our discussion to residential areas made up of varying numbers of single-family dwellings. These areas are much smaller than what could be considered a suburb or an urban neighborhood, which are discussed in a later chapter. The present discussion focuses on the role of the physical properties of a residential environment in determining social interaction among the people who live there.

One aspect of the residential environment that affects behavior is socioeconomic. The planners and builders of a particular development often purposely minimize cost variation from dwelling to dwelling. The result of this practice is that the families who live there are fairly homogeneous in income, social and educational background, and occupational status and generally have compatible, if not similar, interests. Although the overall behavioral ramifications of this fact are sociological and beyond the scope of this text, that socioeconomic factors exist in any housing area should be kept in mind while examining the physical aspects of these environments that also influence behavior.

Two primary features of residential environments shown to affect behavior are spatial: *distance between houses* and *relative locations of houses.* A number of investigators have studied the relationship between residence proximity and the social relations of the occupants. An early study by Festinger, Schachter, and Back (1950) surveyed friendship patterns of stu-dents in a university housing project consisting of single-family detached homes grouped around public yards. The study revealed a direct relationship between interhouse distance and friendship. In general, families were more likely to establish social contact with others living in the same residential grouping. Moreover, the probability of friendship tended to increase as the distance between houses located in the same courtyard decreased. The authors point out, however, that the relationships revealed in their investigation may be due to social homogeneity.

Taking this factor into consideration, Yoshioka and Athanasiou (1971) interviewed 300 residents of single-family dwellings on a variety of differently planned sites. The subjects varied considerably in income and occupation, so that any relationships discovered between the residential environment and social behavior could be interpreted with more confidence than was the case in the study by Festinger and his co-workers. The subjects were asked about their family's lifestyles, attitudes, and social, educational, and occupational backgrounds. All the subjects were also asked to draw a map of their residential area, including the location of friends whom they saw on a regular or an occasional basis.

Among the number of relationships discovered was that the distances to friends' homes were a function of the particular site plan. Generally, the families living on culs-de-sac, or dead-end streets, lived closer to their friends than did the subjects living on through streets. The authors suggest that two features of residential arrangement may contribute to this pattern of social interaction. The first is that the lower population density of the through street may require its residents to travel farther to satisfy their needs for social interaction. The second suggestion is that a main street may act as a barrier to social contact whereas a cul-de-sac does not.

Other investigators provide evidence of yet another feature of the residential environment that influences social behavior: door placement. Caplow and Forman (1950), in a study of university housing, observed that friendships were likely to develop among residents whose doors opened onto a common sidewalk. This finding held even for doors that were closer together but opened onto different sidewalks. Thus, the orientation of the doors, in addition to the shared public space, was shown to affect friendship patterns.

One of the most significant studies of residential environment and behavior is presented by Whyte (1956), who conducted a survey of part of a new, fast-growing suburb south of Chicago. The residents of this suburb were generally homogeneous; most were young, in managerial or professional positions, and quite mobile in both social status and location of residence. Accordingly, there was a substantial annual turnover in residents. Whyte was interested in whether certain social activities were related to the locations of houses or to characteristics of the residents. He found, as might be expected from the research previously discussed, that people living close to one another engaged in the same social activities. For example, people who lived next door or across the street from one another met regularly to play bridge.

Three years later Whyte returned to the area and again surveyed the residents. He found that, although many of the families had moved and the nature of some activities had changed, by and large the residents in the same houses or locations were still involved socially, regardless of the identity of the people there at the time. Whyte concluded that house-to-house distance and orientation of houses significantly influenced the retention of social-interaction patterns even when the individuals involved had changed.

From the research thus far discussed, we have obtained an idea of the important environmental features of the single-family dwelling, particularly the space it provides for private family activities and its fulfillment of the territorial need. The results of these studies have also shown the importance of interhouse distance, relative locations of houses, and orientation of doors in determining friendship formation and social interaction. Much of the research also reveals that the residents are highly satisfied with their housing.

Although the same concepts of privacy, space, residence arrangement, and dwelling-component orientation have been considered in research on multiple-family dwellings, the results often reveal resident dissatisfaction or antisocial behavior. Before discussing the possible reasons for the differences reported in resident satisfaction and behavior between single-family and multiple-family dwellings, however, one important point should be noted. The socioeconomic status of residents of single-family dwellings is often vastly different from that of residents of multifamily housing. The typical subjects of studies on the multifamily dwelling live in public-housing projects. These people are usually economically deprived, are often exposed to racial or ethnic prejudice, and generally live in such places out of necessity, not choice. Undoubtedly, these factors, as well as the physical aspects of the environment, significantly influence behavior.

Multiple-Family Dwellings

Multiple-family dwellings allot, of course, less land area for each family than do single-family dwellings. Whether the family has access to a private land area for family activities depends on the type of multiple dwelling. In any event, such families are almost certain to be closer to their neighbors than are people living in single-family dwellings. Another feature of multiple-family dwellings is the sharing of walls, ceilings, and floors. The number of shared partitions increases from single walls in garden apartments and town houses to walls, floors, and ceilings in walk-up and high-rise apartment buildings. Clearly, as the number of common partitions increases, privacy decreases.

Lack of privacy is heavily emphasized in a report by Kuper (1953), who conducted an extensive survey of Braydon Road, a housing complex in Coventry, England. Built in the late 1940s of prefabricated steel, the semidetached units were based on a standard plan employing both through streets and culs-de-sac. Figures 3-3, 3-4, and 3-5 show the interior arrange-

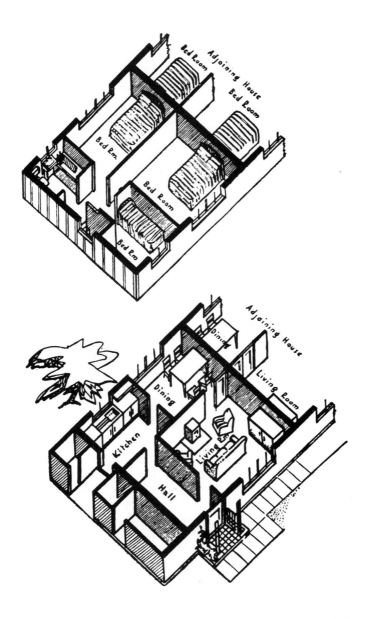

Figure 3-3. The first and second floors of a unit in Braydon Road. Common partitions can be a source of annoyance between neighbors. From *Living in Towns,* Leo Kuper (Ed.). Copyright 1953 by The Cresset Press. Reprinted with permission of the publisher, Barrie & Jenkins, Ltd., London.

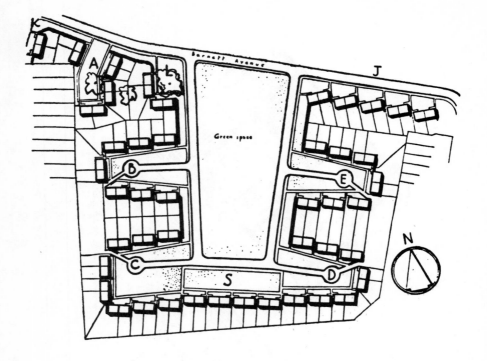

Figure 3-4. The first floor of two adjacent units in Braydon Road. The short distance between the lobbies provides for intense social relationships, either positive or negative. From *Living in Towns,* Leo Kuper (Ed.). Copyright 1953 by The Cresset Press. Reprinted with permission of the publisher, Barrie & Jenkins, Ltd., London.

ment, the orientation of units, and the entire complex. As can be seen from these illustrations, the physical relationships within, between, and among the housing units, in addition to the unusual structural material, provided Kuper with a host of environmental features potentially affecting behavior.

One of the major sources of dissatisfaction on the part of the residents was a pronounced lack of privacy. The common walls between units resulted in nearly constant annoyance of each family by the other. Because both living areas shared the partition, much of the activity of one family in their living room was heard by the other family and vice versa, whether the noise was a result of daily routines or of boisterous celebrations. This infringement of privacy also existed at a more personal level, because the units shared bedroom walls as well. Many residents expressed embarrassment at being able to overhear clearly what they considered private conversations and

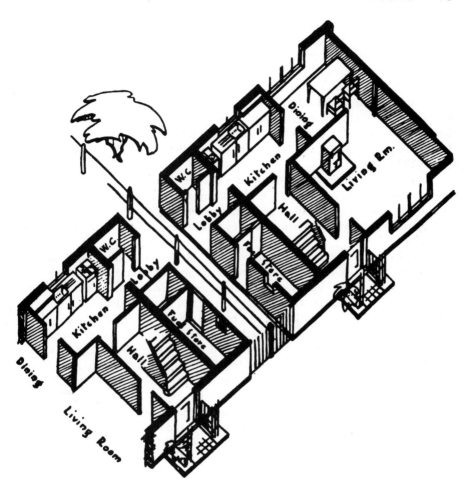

Figure 3-5. Diagram of the Braydon Road complex. The cul-de-sac arrangements of B, C, D, and E provide an opportunity for increased social interaction but also allow for visual invasion of privacy. From *Living in Towns,* Leo Kuper (Ed.). Copyright 1953 by The Cresset Press. Reprinted with permission of the publisher, Barrie & Jenkins, Ltd., London.

activities. Since the residents were aware of the problem, most attempted to keep noise at a minimum. However, doing so often meant curtailing the normal play of children, keeping radios, televisions, and musical instruments very low, and hurrying through daily cleaning chores if the neighbor was asleep. Kuper expresses concern about the possible long-term effects of such enforced behavior on the development of healthy intrafamily relations.

Invasion of privacy was not restricted to the auditory dimension in Braydon Road. The arrangement of the doors between the buildings provoked considerable annoyance in a number of residents. Although the arrangement of the side doors encouraged social relations between residents of the units, a resident of one unit could easily see into the next if both doors were open. Even more detrimental to privacy was the arrangement of the buildings in the culs-de-sac. Anyone entering or leaving any dwelling could be seen by others. Residents also stated that it was difficult to look out their living room or bedroom windows without inadvertently looking into the units across the court.

Another fault cited was the fences between the backyards and gardens of each dwelling. Solid fences would have ensured each family considerable privacy in their yards, but these fences were little more than symbolic, consisting only of wires. In brief, privacy in Braydon Road was highly desired but scarce.

If we were to rely on the previously cited research findings on single-family dwellings, we would assume that a number of environmental features of the Braydon Road complex were conducive to friendship formation and healthy social interaction. The placement of doors, the culs-de-sac, and the informal lines of demarcation in the backyards all increased visual contact between residents, which is assumed by some to increase social interaction (Michelson, 1970). However, Kuper notes that, although the neighbors with a common wall were physically closest, he observed very little social interaction between sets of these neighbors. One reason for this situation may be the considerable involuntary contact between the sets of neighbors, which can result in mutual avoidance. Another possible reason is the orientation of the doors of each unit. As can be seen in Figure 3-4, the main entrances to the two units in each building are at opposite ends of the structure. In terms of social interaction, this distance (referred to by some investigators as the *functional distance)* is actually much greater than the physical distance separating the two apartments. Even if the mutual violation of privacy is ignored, this feature of the environment would tend to discourage social interaction within the buildings. On the other hand, the arrangement of the side doors provides for maximum neighbor contact *between* the structures. However, depending upon the nature of the relationship between the neighbors, this door placement could encourage either friendly conversation or hostile confrontation. Kuper observed both kinds of behavior at Braydon Road.

It should be noted that the violation of auditory privacy is a concern not only for people who live in public-housing projects, such as Braydon Road, but also for those in other multifamily dwellings, such as apartment houses. Prestemon (1968) cites the results of surveys of residents of apartment buildings also constructed after World War II. He asked the residents about whether they were bothered by noise, the extent of their annoyance, and what type of behavior they would be willing to engage in (specifically, how much more they would be willing to pay) for greater acoustical privacy. Of the individuals surveyed, 12% indicated that quietness was a feature they liked about their current apartment, and 35% objected to the existing noise levels. When asked directly, 40% of the occupants said that the noise level in their apartment was annoying. The sources of annoyance were radios, televisions, stereos, other activities in adjacent apartments, and plumbing noise. Some 8% of the tenants indicated that they would be willing to pay about 20 dollars more for a quieter apartment. The feature of common walls was shown to have an impact on the proportion of tenants complaining about noise. Of those who shared common walls with two apartments, 53% indicated that noise was an annoying factor, compared to 37% of those who had only one adjoining apartment. A smaller percentage of tenants who lived alone objected to the noise level than did the tenants who were couples or had families.

Behavior in Public Housing

As mentioned previously, the occupants of public-housing complexes typically are more handicapped socially and economically than are residents of other types of dwellings. A substantial number of the people living in public-housing projects are welfare recipients. Absent fathers are common, so that many mothers must give up full-time care of their children in order to earn a living. Many projects are managed by Whites, though the tenants are non-Whites, a situation that contributes to racial tensions.

Another factor that may have an undesirable effect on behavior is that public housing is generally constructed with one objective: providing low-cost accommodations for the maximum number of families. Consequently, to the builder space is usually at a premium, both within the buildings and around them. This strictly budgeted, high-density housing environment combines with the characteristics of the project's residents to produce a setting unparalleled for adverse reactions.

As will be discussed in a later chapter, residents of slums often staunchly defend them as suitable places to live, yet urban-renewal programs have often resulted in razing slums and erecting housing projects in their place. A critical question is whether the public-housing projects provide more satisfaction to the residents than did the slum neighborhoods. Generally, the reverse has been found to be true.

Lewis (1970) provides an account of an interview with a woman who had moved from a slum neighborhood to public housing at the suggestion of her social worker. Although she indicated overall satisfaction with her apartment, she expressed distaste for other people living in the project, fear for her children's safety, desire for the informal interaction of the old slum, and general regret at having moved.

More objective accounts of resident surveys are presented by Yancey (1972) and Hollingshead and Rogler (1963). Yancey reports the results of a survey querying residents of Pruitt-Igoe, a large public-housing project in St. Louis, and residents of a nearby slum about their satisfaction with various aspects of their environments. Of the Pruitt-Igoe residents, 78% indicated general satisfaction with their apartments, while 55% of the slum dwellers felt the same about their housing. However, when asked whether they were satisfied with the neighborhood, 74% of the slum residents answered affirmatively, in contrast to 53% of the Pruitt-Igoe residents. The reasons most often cited for dissatisfaction in the public-housing complex were inability to survey children's activities, mistrust of others in the building, and fear of being assaulted or robbed outside the apartment.

Hollingshead and Rogler's findings support those of Yancey. Comparing slums and public housing in Puerto Rico, they found that 7% of the men in public housing felt that it was a suitable location for raising a family, while 38% of the slum dwellers stated that their area was adequate for this purpose. The proportion of public-housing residents expressing overall satisfaction with their situation was approximately 25%, in contrast to more than 60% of the slum residents. These are typical findings of research on resident satisfaction with public housing.

The survey data reported by Hollingshead and Rogler and by Yancey and the anecdotal account by Lewis tend to point to dissatisfaction of public-housing residents in some specific areas. For example, some persons feel that public housing is not a suitable place to raise a family. As we shall see later, there are specific physical attributes of public housing, and high-rise dwellings in particular, that cause anxiety on the part of the mothers living there. Generally, however, the inadequacy of locations for children's play is a prime reason that respondents label public housing as an unsuitable place to raise children. This factor has been investigated by Becker (1976), who determined the level of satisfaction of residents of high-rise and low-rise multifamily-housing facilities in terms of their being a desirable place to raise children. Residents of low-rise facilities, which had better playground areas, were much more positive than residents of high-rise facilities.

It appears that, in general, people are often not satisfied with public-housing environments, especially when it comes to perceiving them as places to raise their families. Also, there is a definite difference in satisfaction between high-rise and low-rise public-housing projects. However, before we assert that public housing is the sole cause of this dissatisfaction, we should consider an alternative explanation offered by Onibokun (1976).

Onibokun states that studies dealing with resident satisfaction have usually focused on the physical or architectural qualities of the site, the maintenance of the site, management-related activities associated with the site, or the quality of the social services offered in the housing-project package. He suggests that social variables, in addition to the variables associated with the physical features and the services of the projects, have an impact on resident satisfaction.

To investigate this hypothesis, Onibokun administered questionnaires to tenants of a number of different housing projects located in Canada. In addition to asking the usual questions about satisfaction with their housing situation, he collected data on the tenants' social characteristics: age, marital status, education, occupation, employment status, income, urban/rural background, time in their residence, data about previous homes, perceived image of the social status of their housing area, and their own perceived social status. The population was predominantly White, and 75% of the households had a male head; 49% of the households were considered to be at the poverty level (less than $5000 per year in income), and 70% were self-supporting. However, the majority of the residents lived in the projects not from choice but because they could not afford commercial housing. These characteristics should be kept in mind as we discuss the results of Onibokun's study.

The respondents' answers to the questions about residential satisfaction were consolidated into an index, which was used as the dependent variable in comparing various groups and subgroups derived from the tenants' social characteristics. The results of this phase indicated less satisfaction in larger households and in one-parent families. Respondents with a higher so-cioeconomic status were also less satisfied. Persons who perceived the neighborhood project to be of a middle-class nature appeared more satisfied than those tenants who perceived the project to have a lower-class or an upper-class status. Also, those tenants who perceived themselves to be in the middle or working class evidenced more satisfaction than those who per-ceived themselves to be of a higher or lower social status.

Onibokun's interpretation of these survey results supports the results of studies discussed previously. For example, respondents with large families were concerned about the space available to them and the adequacy of outside recreation facilities for their children. This was also true of families with no male head. However, Onibokun adds some interesting new dimen-sions to the explanations for residential satisfaction or dissatisfaction that have been presented. First, he notes that families with no male head of household had a disproportionate amount of expressed dissatisfaction with the physical facilities of the project, maintenance of the project, lack of privacy, and presence of fear. He hypothesizes that this finding may be due to the relatively large amount of "life stress" that the female heads of house-holds experienced. For example, they most likely were on welfare, typically had large families, and could be considered to have a low socioeconomic status. Such a combination did not yield much hope in their situation. Second, living in public housing has a definite stigma attached to it, no matter what class the respondents are in. Public housing is often looked upon as a hovel for the poor, at least in the North American societies, and the stigma attached to being labeled a public-housing tenant can be quite overwhelming. It tends to contribute to the reduction of self-esteem in an already disadvantaged group of persons. Finally, public housing in both the Canadian and the U.S. point of view is designed to be temporary housing. However, it often becomes permanent because the simple provision of housing does not typically pay off in terms of tenants' eventually achieving the socioeconomic stability that would allow them to move out of the project. Once in public housing, people tend to remain there indefinitely. Also, the longer they live in the housing the more dissatisfied they typically become.

In summary, there are many reasons that people who live in public housing are there. These social, economic, cultural, and psychological factors bring to public-housing projects a group of individuals who have lowered self-esteem and not too much hope for the future and who can take a dim view of the "Great Society" and what it has done for them. Onibokun sums this up quite appropriately by stating:

> . . . finally the evidence . . . shows that when tenants or the public complain about public housing we should not assume that the fault lies with the public housing per se . . . at times the fault stems from the social, cultural, pathological, and psychological state of the tenants, and public housing is being used as the scapegoat, or public housing may be only serving as a reminder to the tenants of their discontentment and dissatisfaction with things that had nothing to do with public housing per se [p. 341].

Onibokun's position is thought provoking and deserves serious consideration. However, the physical design of public housing is still cited by the residents as a source of dissatisfaction. Although changing the design of public housing will not affect the situations that bring or keep the tenants there, it could make their lives much easier. In fact, since the typical population of public housing is at a disadvantage with the rest of society for various reasons, we could consider design objectives centered around the concept of a prosthetic environment. For example, the physical features of the housing environment could be manipulated to support the female head of household in her task of raising a family with some peace of mind. For these reasons, the design features of public-housing projects still deserve consideration.

Design and Behavior in Public Housing

As we have stated, the physical design of public housing is a major contributor to resident dissatisfaction. This conclusion is based on two factors. The first is that the physical characteristics of the buildings do not foster either social relations among the residents or normal family activities—

children's play, for example. The second factor is a result of the first: because of the inadvertent discouragement of informal group relationships by the design, certain types of public housing promote a disproportionate amount of undesirable behavior. The remainder of the chapter will center on the research support for this conclusion.

A typical structure in public housing is the high-rise apartment building. This type of structure appears to have the largest number of design features that produce resident dissatisfaction and fear. One of these features is the height of the building itself. Mothers of children in high rises are quick to express concern about their lack of control over their children's where-abouts and activities. (See Figure 3-6.) Yancey (1972) relates one mother's answer to questions about her satisfaction with living in a high rise:

> "Well, I don't like being upstairs like this. The problem is that I can't see the kids. They're just too far away. If one of them gets hurt, needs to go to the bathroom, or anything, it's just too far away. And you can't see outside. We don't have any porches" [p. 131].

Hall (1959) supplies a similar comment from another high-rise resident: " 'It's no place to raise a family. A mother can't look out for kids if they are fifteen floors down in the playground' " (p. 159). The results of a survey by Kumove (1966) suggest that the problem in high rises of control over a child's activities increases with the child's age. He observed that, after the age of 7, children living in high rises tend to spend much more time outdoors than do their counterparts living in single-family dwellings.

An indirect result of rearing families in high rises is the mother's reduced opportunities for social interaction. If, for example, the family has a young child, the child's play will be restricted to the apartment rather than to the enclosed yard of a single-family dwelling, where the mother has more opportunity for informal contact with neighbors. Similarly, if the mother is occupied in the apartment, she will not go down to ground level to supervise her older children's play. Thus, the mothers in two adjacent apartments are denied the opportunity for social interaction by the greater functional distance involved.

We have already pointed out that designers of public-housing units are forced to use the space as economically as possible. This emphasis often results in the double-loaded corridor, a straight hallway with apartments on both sides. This corridor is considered by residents and administrators alike to be public space, since many persons must use it to reach their apartments. Thus, because of the traffic in the rather limited space and the implied function of the hallway (if a resident is in it, he or she should be going somewhere), informal social interaction is unlikely to occur there. Another disadvantage of this type of corridor is the lack of symbolic or physical

Figure 3-6. According to mothers living in multistory apartment buildings, the situation in the top photograph is much preferred for the supervision of children's play. Photos by Sam Sprague and John Tesnow.

boundaries to act as territorial markers for individual or small groups of apartments.

Two other features of high rises and their surroundings are also thought to weaken the residents' social cohesion. One is that the typical high-rise building has stairways to satisfy fire regulations as well as a central elevator. Thus, residents can enter or leave at a number of different points, and this lack of a common entrance reduces social interaction. The second feature is that the buildings often have large open spaces between them. The frequent lack of fences or walls serves to discourage the residents from engaging in activities within the boundaries of their building's territory.

A more serious behavioral result of these physical features is crime. In discussing this problem, Newman (1973a, 1973c) presents the concept of *defensible space*, defined as:

> . . . the range of mechanisms—real and symbolic barriers, strongly defined areas of influence, and improved opportunities for surveillance—that combine to bring an environment under the control of its residents. A defensible space is a living residential environment that can enhance the inhabitants' lives while providing security for their families, neighbors, and friends [1973a, p. 57].[2]

Newman implies that the provision of defensible space fulfills two objectives that may in turn discourage criminal behavior. First, defensible space encourages social interaction, which hopefully promotes feelings of group cohesion, resulting in mutual aid by group members. Second, it provides for increased visual contact or surveillance, both informally by residents and formally by members of policing units.

Another physical feature of public housing that has been shown to have a significant relation to the incidence of crime is building height. From data on crime in New York City's public housing, Newman (1973a) reports substantial differences in crime rates between buildings of six or fewer stories and those of seven or more stories. In projects involving structures with six or fewer stories, the crime rate was approximately 46 per 1000 dwelling units, whereas the rate was approximately 59 per 1000 dwelling units in projects with higher buildings. An analysis of the felonies committed in or near the buildings of the projects revealed an equally dramatic difference. Figure 3-7 shows the felony rate for four different categories of building height. The rate for buildings in the shortest category (two or three stories) was about half that for buildings in the tallest category (16 or more stories).

Newman points out a number of factors that can account for the increased crime in high-rise buildings. One is the number of persons living in each of the building types. By its nature the larger building contains more

2From *Architectural Design for Crime Prevention*, by O. Newman for the National Institute of Law Enforcement and Criminal Justice, United States Department of Justice, 1973.

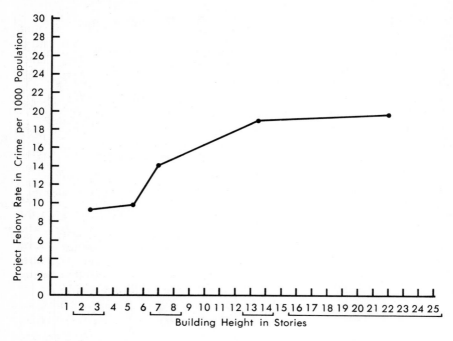

Figure 3-7. Felony rate in public-housing projects and height of the buildings in the projects. From O. Newman, *Architectural Design for Crime Prevention.* Washington, D.C.: National Institute of Law Enforcement and Criminal Justice, U.S. Department of Justice, 1973.

people, thereby resulting in more anonymity. It is difficult for residents of a high rise to identify another person as a resident of the building.

Another factor is stairwells and elevators. Larger buildings have more of each than do shorter structures. As might be expected, Newman found a direct relationship between building height and crime rate when crimes committed in elevators were given separate consideration. Newman's defensible-space hypothesis may explain why these differences exist. In most public housing the stairs are closed off from the hallways, thus eliminating not only any claims of territory by the residents of the nearby apartments but also the opportunity for informal surveillance. Consequently, stairways are notorious for frequency of criminal acts. This situation is also noted by Yancey (1972), who relates that the residents of high rises in his study expressed great fear of using the stairways. Even more obvious, however, is the privacy afforded an offender in a closed elevator.

Another physical feature of public housing discussed by Newman is hall size. Recall that a common occurrence in public-housing units is the double-loaded corridor, which may serve as many as 20 families. Newman hypothesized that halls serving small numbers of apartments would tend to inhibit criminal behavior because of possible increased informal surveillance and the establishment of territorial behavior. Conversely, the absence of these kinds of behavior in larger halls would increase crime. This hypothesis is supported when crime rates are computed for different types of hallways; less crime is reported to occur in halls leading to five or fewer apartments.

Newman suggests that large projects (those containing 1000 or more dwelling units) composed of high rises were found to have the worst overall crime rate not only because of the problems of the structures themselves but also because of project layout. High rises require, of course, much less land than do lower buildings to provide the same number of dwelling units. Consequently, high-rise projects often have large open areas between the buildings. These areas are not easily observed by the buildings' residents, who normally feel no particular attachment to the grounds. Lower buildings, on the other hand, are thought better to define areas of informal resident control and promote feelings in the residents of responsibility for particular territories around their buildings.

Unfortunately, more complete treatment of the research reported by Newman is beyond the scope of this book. Although his research has been criticized on methodological grounds, it is exciting, thought provoking, and suggestive of the role that aspects of the physical environment can play in fostering or inhibiting certain kinds of behavior.

CHAPTER 4

THE BUILT ENVIRONMENT: BUILDINGS AND SOCIAL INSTITUTIONS

In our earlier discussions of built environmental systems, we stressed the importance of a system's function in determining the major physical features of structures. In this chapter, function again determines the charac-teristics of built structures as well as the behavior that occurs in them. However, we will deal here with built environments designed for occupa-tional and service-related activities or for the modification of behavior. These different functions result in a number of differences between the characteris-tics of these systems and those of the systems discussed previously.

One major difference is the number of persons involved. In Chapter 3 we were concerned primarily with the environmentally influenced behavior of individuals and families. Structures such as offices and hospitals typically contain more persons interacting to accomplish a general objective, whether the management of business affairs or the provision of health care to a large number of patients. Such common objectives do not exist in public-housing projects even though they may contain more people; the residents have no binding common interest aside from involvement in their own families. Large numbers of individuals are also brought together to achieve a common purpose in the environmental systems constructed to produce behavioral change in certain segments of the population—those in penal institutions and mental hospitals, for example. Obviously, the functions of these institutions are important determinants of the physical features incorporated in any given structure.

A second difference between the built environments discussed in this chapter and those considered earlier is the types of behavior of interest to researchers and their reasons for studying them. For example, wall color in an office is likely to be an important independent variable to consider. Although researchers may be interested in the overall aesthetic appeal of a particular color layout to employees, they are more likely to be concerned with its effect on job performance. Moreover, the kinds of behavior that would give them information on aesthetic satisfaction and job efficiency would differ markedly. In a hospital, however, color is likely to be considered aesthetically for its contribution to a pleasant atmosphere and the alleviation of unnecessary patient discomfort and dissatisfaction. In penal institutions, color may be used to provide the inmates with a source of environmental variety.

The last difference has to do with the variety of persons involved in these larger systems and their varying needs in a particular structure. The two major factions in the systems discussed in this chapter are clients, patients or inmates, and staff or employees. The needs of these two factions are often nearly opposite. Moreover, different segments of the same faction may have different needs.

A particular system is designed to support persons engaged in fulfilling the system's objectives. The extent to which these efforts have been successful and the physical features that have proved important in determining success or failure are the topics of this chapter.

OFFICES

Typically, behavior in offices is geared toward one purpose—maximum output within reasonable cost limitations. To make achieving this goal possible, the designer of an office building must provide for, among other considerations, optimal communication between departments, work flow within and between various groups, supervisor/subordinate relationships, and allocations of jobs between people and machines. An integral part of these considerations is the continuous provision for individual-worker efficiency, whether a worker is a clerk or an executive.

Factors important for maximum individual efficiency are job design, adequate training, and effective employee/task matching. These factors have received considerable research attention and management interest for many years. Until recently, however, the relationships between the physical features of office environments and job performance have received comparatively little attention from researchers. The reason may be that, if the other factors mentioned have been provided for, the physical environment may have so little effect on job performance that its consideration is not economically feasible. Nonetheless, the small but growing body of research on office equipment and accommodations, ambient conditions, office layout, and general employee satisfaction suggests that these factors deserve further research and design emphasis.

Furnishings and Arrangements

The immediate office environment of an employee is often dependent upon the employee's function and stature in the organization. It may consist of a desk, chair, typing table, and typewriter or possibly a more specialized piece of furniture or equipment, such as a drafting table or a card-punch machine for a computer.

For those persons who must spend the majority of their time seated at their equipment cluster, comfort and efficiency of their furnishings and arrangements are of great importance. For a number of years, investigators in the field of ergonomics, the study of human performance in work situations, have collected data and formulated standards on the acceptable dimensions for desks, chairs, and other office equipment. These standards are based on measurements taken from several thousand men and women to determine, for instance, how far from the floor a chair's seat can be and still permit the average person's feet to touch the floor. These standards are useful only in preventing unnecessary gross bodily movements and positioning resulting in fatigue, inconvenience, or injury. Other investigators have dealt with furnishing and seating design by measuring behavior at a physiological level, such as monitoring subjects' muscle tension in various seating positions in the hope of eventually developing standards based on the amount of muscular tension caused by the interaction of different seats and seating positions (Floyd & Ward, 1969).

Some investigations have included an additional furnishing-design consideration, that of comfort. Grandjean, Hunting, Wotzka, and Scharer (1973) had 50 judges evaluate, for various aspects of comfort, 12 different chairs of the types used for general seating in offices. The rating method was paired comparisons in which each chair was compared for comfort with every other chair. The judges rated each chair on how comfortable it felt to the neck, shoulders, back, legs, and arms while leaning forward and while sitting back in the chair. The investigators also took detailed measurements of each chair's seating angle, width, height, and curvature and noted the type of chair and its upholstery. From the judges' ratings the researchers determined what features contributed to maximum comfort and incorporated these features into one design recommendation, shown in Figure 4-1. If the designers and suppliers of office equipment use these types of standards for furniture dimensions and comfort, they may improve worker efficiency.

Another factor in the individual's immediate work environment is the arrangement of furnishings. Although furnishing arrangement has remained much the same, it has been proposed that different arrangements can facilitate different work activities and consequently enhance overall effi-

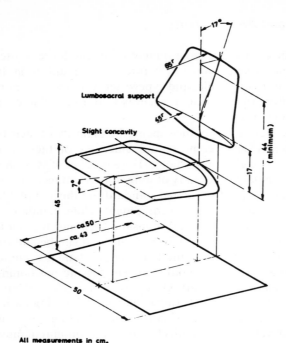

All measurements in cm.

Figure 4-1. The use of design recommendations for office furnishings as illustrated in the figure can contribute to increased employee comfort and efficiency. From E. Grandjean, W. Hunting, G. Wotzka, & R. Scharer. An ergonomic investigation of multipurpose chairs. *Human Factors,* 1973, *15*(3), 247–255. Reprinted by permission of the Human Factors Society.

ciency. Propst (1966) designed an office that he labeled the "Action Office," whose furnishings and arrangement he considered conducive to better efficiency, alertness, and creativity. Figures 4-2, 4-3, and 4-4 present examples of offices he thought appropriate for a plant manager, a research specialist, and a physician.

Fucigna (1967) attempted to evaluate the effectiveness of the Action Office. As he points out, among the features of the Action Office thought to induce maximum performance are these:

1. Both a sit-down and a stand-up work surface to give relief from the seated position.
2. File wells at the rear of desks as well as flip-up display panels to facilitate storage and retrieval of information.
3. Roll-top desks and flip-down panels to provide privacy of information. These also keep work surfaces neat.

Figure 4-2. An Action Office for a plant manager. From Robert L. Propst. The Action Office. *Human Factors,* 1966, *8*(4), 299–306. Reprinted by permission of the Human Factors Society.

Figure 4-3. An Action Office for a research specialist. From Robert L. Propst. The Action Office. *Human Factors,* 1966, *8*(4), 299–306. Reprinted by permission of the Human Factors Society.

Figure 4-4. An Action Office for a physician. From Robert L. Propst. The Action Office. *Human Factors,* 1966, *8*(4), 299–306. Reprinted by permission of the Human Factors Society.

4. A communications center, with a phone, dictation equipment, and so forth.
5. A variety of information racks for coded data folders to be reviewed. Portable box drawers, shelves, and bins limit blind accumulation [p. 593].

Fucigna's criterion for evaluation of the Action Office was the degree to which it facilitated activities assumed to be important in planning and decision making. He suggests that a process like the one described below is involved in planning and decision making.

From information *received,* individuals *determine* that a decision must be made. They then *identify* the information necessary for an effective decision. The next step is *retrieval* of the information from various sources and by various means and temporary *storage* of some of it until all the pertinent facts have been collected.

The information is then *processed,* which may include discussions with other personnel, reading, writing, modifying the information, comparing it, and so forth. This step may, of course, take a long time, so again *storage* and *retrieval* may be involved. Finally, the information is put into suitable form for making a *decision* and taking appropriate *action.*

To evaluate the Action Office, Fucigna asked office workers to keep logs of the time spent on each of the above activities, the work station used, the data used, the location of the data, and the involvement of other individuals.

The workers were observed for one month in their conventional offices, given time to adjust to the Action Office, and then studied in the Action Office condition.

No differences between the two office layouts were found in the percentages of time spent on each activity (reading, writing, visiting, storing and retrieving information, and so on). Analysis of conferences and phone calls revealed that in the Action Office they were fewer but lasted longer. The presumed reason is that more information was readily available in the Action Office, so that the worker accomplished in one conference or phone call what might have taken more in a conventional office. Although efficiency did not improve, many subjects said that they liked the Action Office organization, information availability, neatness, and physical convenience. Fucigna concludes that, although the structure of the office did not affect activities, the workers' perception of the Action Office as more efficient and convenient should not be ignored.

To this point we have limited our discussion to the operational or efficiency dimensions of furnishing arrangements. There is another dimension of furnishing arrangement that is especially relevant in offices. This dimension is social interaction. Recall that in the previous chapter we briefly discussed various aspects of furnishing arrangement and their effects on social interaction. Research in this area typically uses subjects who are naïve about the experimental situation and have no vested interest in the outcome of the investigation. Situations involving the conduct of business are different. For the most part, the participants in a business-related interaction have distinct organizational roles and associated statuses. Each interaction typically has a formal agenda and may also have what is referred to as a hidden agenda as well as the formally stated objective for the transaction. In addition, the past, present, and future interactions between all parties concerned may be a consideration in any business interaction. These factors have implications for furnishing arrangement in business settings. Given a rudimentary knowledge of how furnishing placement can affect interaction and territorial behavior, various arrangements can be made to produce desired outcomes, at least from the point of view of the person who can arrange the furniture (Howells & Becker, 1962; Joiner, 1976; Korda, 1975).

Korda discusses these ideas in his popular-press book. He proposes that status is afforded individuals in an organization by the type of furniture and the accessories, plants, and pieces of art they have and by the placement of their offices within the organization. Further, the arrangement of the furniture in the offices can imply power and authority by manipulation of the relative territory given to visitors. Korda suggests that, to establish the maximum amount of territory, an office occupant should face the desk toward the door and put most of the space in the office behind the desk, leaving the visitor with the smallest space possible. By choosing this arrangement, the occupant will, by implication, be asserting his or her territorial imperative. The visitor's chair should be in a direct line of sight across the desk from the occupant, thus making the width of the desk a territorial marker. In a larger office, where the status of the individual can be reflected in more accouterments, Korda suggests that the office be divided into a semisocial and a formal area. The semisocial area would be furnished with perhaps a sofa, a coffee table, and soft chairs. The formal area would consist of visitors' chairs and the occupant's desk and chair. Korda's implication is that the occupant can choose the seating area to be used for any interaction depending on what the objectives for that interaction are. If the interaction is to be informal, with no confrontation foreseen, the semisocial area can be chosen to conduct the visit. If the interaction will involve hard negotiations, the formal arrangement can be chosen to establish and maintain territory, thus providing the occupant with a psychological advantage in the interaction. Korda goes on to suggest that the shape, arrangement, and use of a board-room table and the seating of the persons around it can be used in determining the relative status of each person.

Joiner (1976) offers evidence to support Korda's suggestions. He defines the three physical factors of position, distance, and symbolic decoration as forming a composite statement of territory. Further, the arrangement of territory implies to the visitors and the occupant alike what types of social interaction can be expected. Joiner compared the arrangements of single-person offices in academic, commercial, and governmental settings and simultaneously considered the occupants' status in their organizational setting. He found that persons in academic settings typically arranged their offices so that they did not sit facing the door. Rather, they had their desks oriented toward or against one of the walls, so that a person entering their rooms would be approaching them at an angle perpendicular to their line of sight instead of immediately engaging in visual interaction with them. Commercial and government employees, however, generally arranged their offices so that their line of sight was directed toward the door. In this manner, interactions would be carried out across the desks. (See Figure 4-5.) Joiner found no relationship between occupant status and office arrangement in academic settings. However, in the government and commercial offices surveyed, the status of the occupant was shown to have some relationship to how the room was arranged. Generally, the higher the occupant's status in these settings, the more likely it was that the desk would be oriented toward the door and that formal distinctions would be made between private and public spaces within the office. Neither of these distinctions was found in the offices of lower-status persons in the commercial and governmental settings.

From these results it appeared to Joiner that persons in academic settings were not particularly concerned about strict definitions of territory. On the other hand, the occupants of commercial and government offices did

Figure 4-5. Studies have shown that persons in academic settings typically arrange their desks against a wall, as shown in the top photograph, while government and commercial employees usually arrange their desks so their line of sight is directed toward the door. (Photos by Lars Larmon.)

tend to establish territory by the use of furnishing arrangement, with the implication that they were expressing more of a desire to control the interactions taking place in the rooms. As is indicated by the study discussed next, this desire is not expressed at an unconscious level of behavior.

Preston and Quesada (1974) had managers diagram their offices and the placement of the furnishings within the rooms and then asked them why they chose this particular arrangement. The managers had generally chosen one of the two positions we have been discussing, which result in either more or less control of communications in the office. People whose desks faced the door indicated that they were interested in maintaining total control over the communications taking place in the office. On the other hand, the people whose desks did not face the door were likely to cite their desire to remove barriers to personal communication as the reason for this arrangement.

From the research discussed, it can be seen that office furnishings and their arrangements are subject to many considerations and that the office environment will reflect which criterion is used to design them. If efficiency is the most important variable, there are many mathematical models from operations research concerning optimum work flow, queue-length tolerances, and so on that can be applied to business operations, whether in a plant or in the handling of paperwork. If the problem of designing an office environment were turned over to a team of operations-research specialists, they could provide, from their perspective, a design solution. Similarly, managers have a fairly accurate feel for the objectives of their organizations and certainly have definite opinions on how they would set up the office environment to meet their needs. They also have a concept of how the offices should be arranged to meet social and status expectations. Behavioral scientists have their own ideas on how to arrange the work environment to provide for individuals' needs for comfort and privacy. Architects are naturally concerned with the aesthetic and structural integrity of the office-building environment. Finally, the users of the office environment have, at least at an individual level, ideas on what would be a successful office environment for them, which may involve factors not considered by any of the other groups mentioned. The provision of an office environment that meets all these criteria is a difficult task indeed.

Ambient Environment

Another factor that can affect behavior in offices is ambient environmental conditions. Temperature, humidity, illumination, and noise can produce comfort or annoyance, thus affecting performance. These behavioral effects may be either a direct or an indirect function of some ambient condition. For example, inadequate light may directly affect the efficiency of an office worker engaged in a demanding visual task. If, however, planning for noise reduction was inadequate, a worker may be annoyed and distracted by a conversation between two fellow workers. The noise thus affects not only emotional state but also efficiency. This effect is indirect, the result of an interaction between a physical feature of the office environment and the people in the office.

Providing for at least satisfactory ambient conditions may seem relatively simple, but that impression is erroneous. One reason is that some individuals' preferences in ambient conditions may be different from those of other people. These sets of physical and psychological needs, coupled with the constraints of actual office design, interact with ambient conditions to produce unique behavioral situations in the office setting.

Relatively little attention has been paid to the effect of office temperature on employee behavior. Surveys (Manning, 1965; Nemecek & Grandjean, 1973) have shown that office temperatures are generally comfortable. Nemecek and Grandjean measured the temperatures in several large Swiss office buildings and obtained employees' attitudes on the best temperature. The majority of the temperatures measured (from 71 degrees F to 75 degrees F) were within the range that the employees considered acceptable. They did think, however, that anything above 75 degrees was too warm. Both surveys report some dissatisfaction among the employees with the air-conditioning systems. Although the temperatures supplied by the systems were satisfactory, complaints about the drafts caused by the systems were frequent, even though in some cases measurements by the investigators indicated that air movement was within the range of comfort. Other complaints were directed at the great difference between indoor and outdoor temperatures in summer and the necessity of keeping windows closed during the warmer months. The attitudes expressed in these surveys can be considered behavioral states. Unfortunately, however, nothing can be said about the effects of these ambient conditions on employee efficiency because no performance measures were taken.

The employees' attitudes about air conditioning in the Nemecek and Grandjean study lead to the conclusion that not only temperature itself but also the means used to produce the temperature can result in satisfaction or dissatisfaction. This conclusion had been investigated earlier by Black and Milroy (1967), who conducted a study of occupants of air-conditioned and nonair-conditioned buildings in England. The advantages and disadvantages of air conditioning can be summarized from the respondents' comments. Persons in air-conditioned buildings commented favorably on the quietness and cleanliness but complained about not being able to control the temperature by opening windows. They also made negative comments about the atmosphere of the buildings, complaining that it was stale and dry and did not have enough air movement. Further, they were unhappy about "internal noise" in their buildings, though they did not specify what these noises consisted of. Occupants of nonair-conditioned buildings mentioned outside dust and noise as annoying factors. There were no significant differences in the occupants' judgments of comfort except for the summer months. Discomfort would undoubtedly be more of a consideration in a climate more extreme than that found in England. Black and Milroy offer the opinion that, except for the summertime discomfort, the respondents in the air-conditioned buildings had more unfavorable comments than did the occupants of the nonair-conditioned buildings. However, we do not know whether they would have preferred a nonair-conditioned environment if provided with a choice.

The question of light in office environments has resulted in some controversy even though standards for light levels and the amount of glare (light reflected from work surfaces, walls, and ceilings) are well established and can be met in any office. The argument is over whether the light should be natural or artificial. The results of one investigation (Wells, 1965b) suggest that light obtained from windows is considered an important office feature by employees. Wells obtained estimates from personnel in a large office building of what percentage of the light available at their desks was supplied through the windows. He discovered that the further people were seated from the windows, the more they tended to overestimate the proportion of daylight available to them. Wells also notes that when the subjects were questioned about the quality of daylight compared to that of artificial light, nearly 70% stated that daylight is better to work in than artificial light.

This concern for daylight in an office seems to have little to do with actual lighting conditions; it appears to be a function of a psychological desire for windows. (See Figure 4-6.) Wells reports that almost nine out of ten persons in the offices felt it important that they be allowed to look out of a building regardless of the quality of artificial light. Manning (1965) provides anecdotal evidence obtained from interviews that people do not necessarily want a pleasant view—merely the opportunity to see out.

The apparent need for windows in offices is not particularly surprising. Recall from the previous chapter that the students in the Sommer study did not like the windowless room. Moreover, large buildings almost always have windows even though they are expensive and make insulation and ventilation more difficult than in windowless buildings. Thus, cost reduction is often sacrificed to the common need for windows to look out of. This design decision is, of course, a marked contrast to many other decisions we have encountered in our discussions of the built environment.

Our discussion of noise as an independent variable in the office environment must begin with a qualification. The majority of recent research on office environments that includes noise aspects has been conducted in large, open-plan offices. These offices are quite different from the small, more personal types having only a few occupants. The characteristics of open-plan

Figure 4-6. People working in offices feel that it is important to be able to look out of windows regardless of the quality of artificial light in the offices.

offices probably determine the types of sounds that are ultimately labeled noise and whether these noises are considered disturbing. The same sounds may not be disturbing (or may be more disturbing) in small offices. This qualification should be kept in mind during our discussion.

Two major facts emerge from the investigations of noise in large offices. The first is that noise levels were generally very close to being within acceptable standards in the offices studied. In their survey of several large offices, Nemecek and Grandjean (1973) report background-noise levels ranging from 47 to 52 decibels, with the highest noise levels (defined as "frequent peaks" in noise level) reaching from 56 to 64 decibels. These levels are well within the limits considered acceptable by design engineers. Yet when employees were asked whether they were disturbed by noise in these offices, 35% indicated that they were "greatly" disturbed by noise, with an additional 45% stating that they were slightly disturbed by noise of various types. When these people were further questioned about the specific source of their complaint, nearly half listed conversation as the primary offender and specified that content, not loudness, was the disturbing factor. This contention is a rather surprising contrast to the usual listed sources of office noise— typewriters, key punches, telephones, and so on. The reasons will become more apparent as we discuss the concept of large open-plan offices.

The Landscape Office

A large office with an open-plan design typically consists of one entire floor that has no internal floor-to-ceiling partitions. (See Figure 4-7.) This type of office may encompass an area the size of a football field or larger, and its occupants may range from clerks to upper-level managers. This kind of physical layout has the economic advantages of flexibility, low maintenance, and low initial cost. Moreover, the open-plan office is thought to facilitate interdepartment communication and intradepartment work flow. Finally, the open-plan office is claimed to have social and psychological advantages. Feelings of large-group cohesiveness are supposed to develop because of the lack of walls between managers, supervisors, and clerks, and small-group cooperation is supposedly retained by the provision of low (36 to 48 inches) barriers between defined work groups. Also, the landscape-office design is said to provide greater opportunity for an aesthetically pleasing environment because the designer can use planters as dividers and has greater latitude in color schemes. Thus, besides being economical, the large open-plan office has behavioral advantages in both job-related activities and feelings of well-being and aesthetic satisfaction on the part of all employees.

Because the open-plan office is a relatively new concept in the design of office environments, the success of such offices in achieving these behavioral objectives has not been extensively researched. However, two recent investigations have attempted to provide information about the effects of these offices on job-related and personal behavior.

Brookes and Kaplan (1972) present a relatively rare type of environmental investigation: a before-and-after comparative evaluation. Their study involved evaluations by workers of an old-style office layout and its replacement, a landscape office. Initially, the subjects completed adjective rating scales on the old-style office and on what they considered an ideal office environment. The scales were constructed so that information could be obtained on a number of factors deemed important in assessing the quality of the office environment—for example, functionality, privacy, sociability, and aesthetics. These data were used as suggestions for the design of the new accommodations. After a time in the new office, the employees again evaluated their office design on the adjective rating scales and were also personally interviewed.

Comparisons of the ratings of the old office and those of the new revealed some rather surprising findings. Most surprising was that the landscape design was not judged to be any more functional or efficient than the old arrangement. On a more personal level, the majority of employees stated that privacy had declined on both the visual and the acoustic dimensions; noise of conversations was frequently cited as being annoying,

Figure 4-7. Open-plan offices, such as the one shown here, have a number of economic advantages and may also have social and psychological advantages over the old-style offices. (Photo courtesy of the United Services Automobile Association, San Antonio, Texas.)

and the new, open arrangement was judged to reduce privacy and security substantially. On the other hand, the employees generally judged their new office as being more conducive to social relations and as having more aesthetic appeal than the old. However, the increase in group cohesiveness resulting from the improved sociability was not found to increase efficiency.

Nemecek and Grandjean (1973), in their survey of offices in Switzerland, gave several hundred employees in 15 open-plan offices questionnaires probing their attitudes about their working conditions. The results of the questionnaires revealed that the large offices involved in the survey had both advantages and disadvantages. Most frequently cited as major disadvantages were difficulty in concentrating on work and disruptions in confidential conversations. When questioned on their ability to concentrate in these offices compared to the offices they had previously occupied, more than half the respondents indicated that concentration in the large offices was more difficult. However, this response was found to be a function of the number of people present in the old offices. Persons who had previously worked alone or with few people were the most disturbed by the open-plan surroundings. The reasons for the disturbance (office machines, telephones, office traffic) suggest that these persons were more distracted from their work than hindered because of lack of privacy. The feeling of invasion of privacy was reflected more in the responses of management personnel, who felt that their confidential conversations could be overheard and so felt somewhat hindered in the performance of their roles.

On the positive side, employees in the lower occupational roles indicated that the open-plan offices promoted more social activity than did the old arrangements. Management personnel indicated that job-related communication improved. Averaged over all job classifications, 63% of the respondents felt that their work was accomplished with less effort and more efficiency. This finding is important from the standpoint of the workers' attitudes toward their jobs. One might speculate that a feeling of improved efficiency would promote greater satisfaction. However, this possibility remains to be empirically tested. One last note about employee attitudes toward the open-plan offices is that the majority of the persons initially dissatisfied with the offices stated that they had adjusted to their new working environments enough to feel general satisfaction with them.

An earlier work by Wells (1965a) suggests some ramifications for Nemecek and Grandjean's finding on increased social activity in large open-plan offices. Wells investigated social activity in large and small office spaces by using people's stated preferences for working partners as the dependent measure. The location for his investigation was one large floor in a company that was divided between one very large office area and one smaller, separated area containing smaller work groups. This division was due to the basic design of the building; all the workers had the same general clerical duties and were part of the same working division within the company. Both areas were broken down into organizational work sections. Wells hypothesized that there would be more friendships in the smaller work area than in the more open area. He also thought that more friendship choices would have been made outside the organizationally defined work groups in the open-plan portion of the floor. Friendship choices were obtained by asking all the persons who worked on the floor to list the people they would prefer to work with. His results on social-activity patterns coincide with the Nemecek and Grandjean results and offer important considerations for designing for organizational or managerial objectives.

First, Wells found that the number of social preferences decreased with increasing distance between employees. This finding appears to be fairly logical. He also found, as we would expect, that the age and sex of the respondents predicted working-partner choices. Second, he found a distinction in terms of workmate choices between the large and the small work area. Those persons working in the large area of the floor tended to choose at least one more person they would prefer to work with than those who worked in the small area. People in the small area were more likely to choose their working partners from the same area. Finally, these choices were more likely to be reciprocated than was the case for those working in the large, open area. However, there were more persons who, by not choosing, or by not being chosen as co-workers, were considered social isolates in the small work area.

Wells's data should be taken into consideration by corporate management. The implication is that managers can influence social structure in their work areas through physical design. For example, people who work in smaller, more defined areas would tend to develop more internal cohesiveness. This cohesiveness could be used to enhance small-group performance. Conversely, Wells's results suggest that more informal and larger social networks can be established in the open-plan type of arrangement. This might facilitate interdepartment or intersection communication. Hopefully, if there is a functional interdependence between two departments, such an open area would facilitate work flow. The implications of this study for those involved in shaping organizational processes and outcomes seem quite clear. Intraorganizational-communication networks, organizational competition, and part-versus-whole management philosophies could all be influenced by the provision of either small areas or large open-plan areas in which to work. Thus, during the design process these types of organizational issues should be taken into account.

One last point should be made about office environments. The persons working within them do have distinct opinions about all the factors we have mentioned. In a general survey of office personnel, Johnson (1970) found that they had definite opinions about spatial design, heating, air conditioning, windows, work-area arrangements, type of floor materials, and color schemes. They also had opinions about the provision of privacy, which varied depending on the position they held. They liked to be consulted about office arrangements, especially when their immediate work area was involved. (Many of Johnson's respondents said that they needed more space to accomplish their tasks.) Further, their feelings about office arrangements not directly related to them affected their attitudes toward the office as a whole.

These findings are far from surprising, but they emphasize that user input should be given adequate consideration in the design of office environments. Rapoport (1967) relates an instance in which the architects produced a design that left nothing up to individual users. In fact, the employees of the company were directed not to introduce anything personal into the work spaces. As we would expect, the design and the subsequent order were met with less than wholehearted enthusiasm by the employees. This case certainly stands as the ultimate in exclusion of user considerations from a design and indicates the reactions one could expect to such a practice.

HOSPITALS

The hospital has long been regarded as an institution in its own right. So firmly established and standard is its image that even the mention of the word *hospital* conjures up a picture of a not particularly beautiful building, with long hallways, green-tiled operating rooms, gleaming utensils, and bustling white uniforms, where health care is provided. Even though the hospital is so standardized in its image and activities, it is still of interest to environmental psychologists because it offers innumerable opportunities to study interactions between people and the environment.

Many of the activities in a hospital are highly specialized, requiring great amounts of skill and planning. An obvious example of such an activity is an extensive surgical procedure, such as a major organ transplant. Here the duties of many persons must be performed and coordinated with a high degree of precision if the venture is to be successful. Stringent demands are also placed on the operating-room environment and its various components to provide maximum support. Thus, reliability and efficiency are of prime importance in the design of hospital environments.

A second aspect of the hospital setting is the variety of people there— patients, medical staff, administrative and maintenance personnel, and visitors. Each of these groups makes different demands on hospital environmental features. Moreover, each category can be subdivided. For example, the two categories of patients and staff can be divided according to patient age, type of illness or injury, specialties of the physicians, roles of the nurses, and so on. Similarly, each subcategory of patients or staff may have environmental needs in the stages of diagnosis, treatment, and convalescence different from those of the other subcategories. As will be seen, these needs frequently conflict, resulting in stressful situations for one or more of the people involved.

A prevalent practice in hospital design has been to attempt to maximize medical-personnel efficiency by manipulating the environment. Implied in this effort is an increase in the patients' well-being (Ronco, 1972). The psychological ramifications of such a practice will be discussed later; for the moment we will consider some of the research on medical-staff behavior in different types of hospital layouts and the effects of these layouts on efficiency.

A current controversial issue among hospital designers and medical personnel concerns the relative merits and faults of different ward layouts in such areas as cost, manpower use, and patient satisfaction. In his comparison of various ward plans, Lippert (1971) used nurses' movement about the wards as the dependent variable. Travel was assumed to be an important factor in the evaluation of ward design because a substantial amount of a nurse's time is taken up by travel, and excessive travel has been cited as a source of dissatisfaction by ward nurses. In developing his measure, Lippert constructed what he termed a "tour model." In the model a tour was considered one trip by a nurse from the assigned station to see a patient or patients and the return to the station. Various stops in the tour for fresh linen or other supplies were considered "utility stops" and were included as part of the tour. Thus, a nurse may leave the station, check one patient, make a utility stop, check two more patients, and return to the station, all in one tour.

Lippert then applied his model to four hospital wards, three rectangular and one circular (see Figure 4-8), and attempted to arrive at relative measures of efficiency for each. Two efficiency measures obtained from application of the tour model were average utility stops per patient and average number of patients visited per tour. Lippert suggests that the most efficient ward design is one that allows for the most patients visited per tour, with the fewest utility

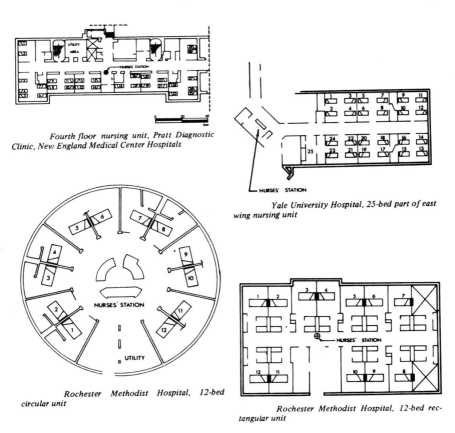

Fourth floor nursing unit, Pratt Diagnostic Clinic, New England Medical Center Hospitals

Yale University Hospital, 25-bed part of east wing nursing unit

Rochester Methodist Hospital, 12-bed circular unit

Rochester Methodist Hospital, 12-bed rectangular unit

Figure 4-8. Hospital-ward layouts used in the investigation of nurses' travel. From Stanley Lippert. Travel in nursing units. *Human Factors*, 1971, *13*(3), 269–282. Reprinted by permission of the Human Factors Society.

stops. Table 4-1 lists the comparative results of the derived measures.

Table 4–1.   Summary of tour-model findings.

Ward in Which Observations Were Made	Number of Utility Stops per Patient	Number of Patients per Tour
Pratt-4	0.375	2.00
Yale	0.500	2.00
Rochester Methodist, 12-Bed Rectangular Unit	0.125	2.67
Rochester Methodist, 12-Bed Circular Unit	0.220	2.25

From S. Lippert, "Travel in Nursing Units." *Human Factors,* 1971, *13*(3), 269–282. Reprinted by permission of the Human Factors Society.

Although Lippert makes no inferences on the superiority of any of the ward arrangements over the others, he does note that, because the circular ward and one of the rectangular ones were in the same hospital, the experimental situation was lent a measure of control in that the nurses were from the same staff, were under the same administration, and dealt with similar types of patients. The nurses did, however, use different tour patterns in these two wards, although the differences were not enough to provide much information on comparative efficiency. Nonetheless, Lippert's method was successful in that it reflected the different behavioral effects of the different wards.

Trites, Galbraith, Sturdavant, and Leckwart (1970) conducted a study similar to Lippert's but made more global comparisons of three basic hospital-ward designs—the radial, the single corridor, and the double corridor. This study also used the wards of the Rochester Methodist Hospital, which was built as a laboratory for conducting efficiency studies of the three ward designs. The investigation centered on determining the effects of these three designs on nurses' activities and their feelings about them. Although the wards were all part of the same hospital and subject to the same administrative policies, the wards were parts of different medical services. To compensate for this, the researchers developed a patient-care index that allowed them to control for the different relative workloads expected in the different medical and surgical wards. They attempted to take as many variables into account as possible—staff composition, patient-census data, the derived patient-workload index, and maintenance problems associated with specific facilities. The dependent measures were work samples that focused on the activities and locations of staff personnel in each of the patient units.

The activities and locational behavior of each staff member were periodically sampled on a 24-hour basis for approximately two months. These work samples were collapsed into categories such as direct patient care, indirect patient care, personal activities, supply activities, and nonproductive activities. The locations used were nursing stations, patient rooms, corridors, and off-ward. In addition to the work samples, the staff members were asked to fill out questionnaires before and after every shift probing their feelings of tension, anxiety, fatigue, perceived workload, and their efficiency at the job on that shift. The staff members were also given a general questionnaire soliciting their opinions about the radial, single-corridor, and double-corridor designs. Finally, an additional experiment was conducted during the study because of an administrative decision to move two of the services from a double-corridor ward to a radial ward and vice versa. The researchers took advantage of the move by constructing a before-and-after questionnaire comparing the efficiency of the wards. This questionnaire was given to patients and staff.

Mean percentages of time spent at the different locations and in the accomplishment of the various activities were calculated from the workload samples. In prior sessions with the staff, the investigators had determined whether a high or a low mean-percentage score was desirable. These judgments were used to construct rankings of the three designs on each activity and location dependent measure. Comparison of the rankings indicated that the single-corridor design was generally considered the least desirable, with no large overall differences evident between the radial and double-corridor designs. However, the radial design was ranked highest in terms of locational variables because the most time was spent in patients' rooms and with patients and the least time was spent on travel. The double corridor received the highest rankings for support of nursing activities; the most time was spent on direct and indirect patient care, and the least time was spent off the ward and in nonproductive activities. When the rankings were collapsed into a composite index of efficiency, the radial-unit design was generally judged to be the most efficient. The data from the first question-naire offered no conclusive distinctions between the designs in staff moods during the shifts. However, the second, general questionnaire given to the staff, as well as the opinions of the staff personnel involved in the exchange between the double-corridor and the radial wards, indicated a tendency to rate the radial unit as contributing more to the quality of patient care. Although only a small number of patients (14) were queried about the relative efficiencies of the wards, 11 of those felt that the radial unit contributed to patient care.

The researchers included in their report a general caution—that in spite of all the measures collected to predict nursing activities in the wards, not much of the actual behavior occurring there could be attributed to any of the variables mentioned. Although such a revelation clouds the immediate applicability of the study results, it points to yet another example of how extremely difficult it is to conduct behavioral research in real-world settings.

In reviewing the two studies just discussed in conjunction with his own research on nursing activities in different wards, Keleman (1975) suggests that very little of a nurse's behavior may be predictable by ward-design factors that can be related to efficiency. Even if behavioral differences can be attributed to design factors, we do not know whether any of the dependent measures used to date are adequate for making design decisions. Further, none of the studies discussed made a concerted attempt to determine patients' opinions on which of the ward designs met their needs best.

As in other environmental settings, social and organizational norms in hospitals interact with features of the physical environment to produce predictable behavior. In fact, the strictly upheld status distinctions among doctors, residents, interns, medical students, registered nurses, surgical nurses, aides, and patients are firmly entrenched in the social structure of any hospital. An individual with any one of these statuses maintains a quite rigid behavioral role. However, this role (and hence behavior) may change with the person's location in the hospital setting.

Rosengren and DeVault (1963) observed the gamut of behavior and activities in an obstetric ward of a large hospital, from the admitting room to the recovery rooms. Their approach was ecological in that virtually every activity was deemed to contribute to the overall behavioral setting. Thus, they viewed behavior not as strictly a result of the environment but as a result of the interaction of social and organizational variables with the persons in particular environmental settings.

Using this approach, Rosengren and DeVault related status to different components of the ward. The labor rooms, for example, were the domain of the nurses attending the patients there, and the nurses knew it and acted accordingly. Once they were in the delivery room, the attending physician was, understandably, the person with unquestioned authority. The researchers note, however, that interactions between the doctors and the nurses were more informal in locations where each person's role was ambiguous—for example, in the hallways. Other locations where status was reflected, both physically and behaviorally, were the respective lounges for residents and practicing physicians. Although both lounges served the same function, there were two of them, and they differed substantially in interior appointments. Moreover, the residents and interns were hesitant to use the private physicians' lounge even though they were entitled to do so at any time. Thus, it was evident to the investigators that something other than the features of the lounge environment was producing the behavior they observed.

We mentioned earlier that the most important design consideration for hospitals is thought to be the facilitation of medical-staff activities, which in turn is thought to promote patient satisfaction and well-being. In other words, the needs of the patients are assumed to be met by fulfilling the requirements of the medical personnel. However, in some situations the needs of the patients and those of the staff conflict, so that one must be favored over the other. Fitch (1965) describes such a situation in the operating room:

> The surgeon and his staff will meet their greatest period of stress during surgery. At this juncture their requirements will be opposed to those of the patient. Where the latter requires warm, moist air (and antiexplosive measures demand even higher humidities), the staff under nervous tension should ideally be submerged in dry, cool air. But since stress for them is of limited duration while any added load might be disastrous for the patient, the room's thermo-atmospheric environment is usually designed in the latter's favor. The staff sweats and suffers and recovers later [p. 713].

Although in this case the decision is made in favor of the patients to protect their physical well-being, to the discomfort of the staff, Ronco (1972) points out that psychological considerations involving the patients are frequently rejected in favor of enhancing staff efficiency. The result of one such decision is the physical and psychological confinement of the patients. Because of the crowded conditions in hospitals, patients are often discouraged from moving about in their rooms or wards even though their illness or injury is such that they are able to do so. Ronco also notes that corridors are frequently so unappealing that patients avoid traveling in them. If they do move about in the corridors, they do so in a rigid fashion, to avoid infringing on other patients' privacy by inadvertently looking at them through the open doors. Moreover, patients have little control over the furnishings in their rooms and are not allowed to rearrange things to their liking.

Lack of privacy is yet another result of designing for function rather than patient need. Ronco cites a study by Jaco (1967) investigating psychological reactions to a radial nursing unit. Many patients reported a lack of privacy, presumably due to the ability of the nurses at their station to look directly into the rooms. The lack of privacy is especially evident during visiting hours; with no private visiting areas, most patient/visitor interaction is around the patient's bed and witnessed by others. As Ronco states, this situation is not conducive to frank or confidential conversations, especially in large, multipatient wards.

Obviously, providing the comforts of home is functionally and financially impossible in any hospital. Yet ignoring patients' needs and denying them the opportunity at least to approximate various normal activities make the patients' burden heavier, which in turn may result in a need for increased care. And any increase in care would be undesirable because of the shortages in medical personnel currently facing many hospitals. Often the most they can do is provide only the rudiments of patient care. Also, staff members vary in their ability to relate to patients. Simply because these persons are engaged in a "helping" profession does not mean that they will be able to provide substitutes for amenities not addressed in the design process as well as cope with their regular duties. We cannot show any observable deleterious effects of hospital design on patient health or behavior. However, to continue to ignore patient needs in hospital design is to invite such effects to occur.

SOCIAL INSTITUTIONS

In this section we will be dealing with mental institutions, nursing homes and housing for the elderly, and penal institutions. Our emphasis will shift from occupational types of environmental settings to settings for special segments of our population. In all instances one function of these special environments is to provide their occupants with a place to live for extended periods. In the case of mental institutions and prisons, an additional purpose is to facilitate behavioral change back toward societal norms. An examination of the rehabilitative methods used and of their recent criticism by sociologists and psychologists is certainly germane to any discussion of mental and penal institutions but is beyond the scope of this text. The following discussion deals with certain physical features of these institutions that may facilitate or hinder the functions the institutions were designed to perform.

These settings offer a unique opportunity for investigating the effects of built physical environments on the people who live in them. They can be considered microcosms, nearly free of any external influence or control. Although the staff members of the institutions have everyday contact with the "real world," the inmates, patients, or residents are relative captives in a single physical and behavioral environment. Thus, aside from occasional visits of family and friends and preinstitution experience, the influence of external variables is negligible. This isolation allows the formation of stable people/environment relationships and makes their observation easier. However, due to the nature of the institutions and the reasons the inhabitants are there, any attempt to generalize the results of an investigation would be met, at best, with skepticism. Nonetheless, any links established between physical features of the institutional environment and occupant behavior can prove extremely valuable in designing for maximum rehabilitation and life support.

Mental Institutions

In our discussion of behavior in mental institutions, their unique nature should not be overlooked. These institutions can be thought of as being entire worlds for many individuals where basic physiological and psychological needs must be met. It must also be kept in mind that prior to their admittance these individuals were engaged in a variety of behaviors. They worked, cared for families, cooked, visited, went shopping, drove cars, and at least attempted to engage in other activities associated with day-to-day living. More than likely, they were accomplishing a number of these things with some degree of competence. It would seem unreasonable to expect that immediately upon admittance these activities should be curtailed. Rather, it would seem more appropriate to allow these individuals at least to simulate as many "real-world" behaviors as their particular condition allows. This spectrum of needs and activities has implications for designing total-living packages for mental institutions.

Unfortunately, few total-living packages, in terms of rehabilitation procedures and physical-site characteristics, are available for study. One reason is that creating a simulated lifestyle in institutions is very much limited by the physical plant. Since the majority of mental facilities are public institutions, it is not economically feasible, or politically realistic, to construct or revamp mental facilities to incorporate all the desirable physical aspects of a simulated-lifestyle environment. Second, the public perception of what mental institutions are and what they should be often limits the application of total-living packages to institutional environments such as the village-model concept mentioned by Isikpinar and Velioğlu (1973). Also, in these environments the administrative philosophies typically are such that more advanced therapeutic programs are being used. Thus, even if we were to find a comparison of rehabilitation rates between a village-model facility, for example, and the more common, state-supported institution, we could not attribute any differences to physical-design factors alone but must consider other salient factors present in each of the institutions. Finally, and possibly most important, the physical aspects of design cannot be positively or negatively related to length of stay in the facility. Any design factors that may serve to detract from the therapeutic process cannot be separated from the individual's condition. A lack of improvement or a worsening in a patient's mental state can simply be attributed to the difficulty of the patient's case.

The extraction of design influence on mental behavior will require planned evaluative programs comparing settings that differ only in their physical aspects. Patients, administrative philosophies and procedures, and therapeutic techniques will have to be subject to some control. Given these constraints, we can offer studies that provide only partial answers to possible design influences on patient behavior.

Patient Needs

The emotional states of patients in mental institutions lead them to behave in ways considered abnormal in our society. Because of their behavioral disorders, these people have needs above and beyond those of a normally functioning individual. Thus, knowledge about these needs is important in the design of mental institutions, whether their ultimate purpose is considered to be rehabilitative or custodial.

In one study on the relationship between patient needs and institution design, Osmond (1970) cites the abnormalities in a schizophrenic's perceptions—visual, auditory, time, and self—and offers suggestions for institutional design that might help to alleviate, or at least not aggravate, these distortions. Sensory-deprivation experiments have shown that a lack of changing visual stimulation may cause even normal people to experience visual hallucinations. Although not as extreme as in the experiments, somewhat analogous conditions exist in the majority of psychiatric hospitals; drab single-color or uniform-color schemes or barren walls, floors, and ceilings present the patient with minimally changing visual stimuli. Although we have no empirical evidence proving that the reduced visual stimulation in institutions causes hallucinations, the visual change in leaving an institution for the outside world has been a source of confusion and trauma in a number of persons (Wildeblood, 1959). This, too, is predictable from data reported by McReynolds (1963) suggesting that withdrawn schizophrenics show a reduction in seeking new stimuli. His implication is that care should be taken in the design of their physical environment not to exceed their threshold and confront them with stimulus situations more novel than they would prefer. Similarly, Izumi (1968) cautions that, for some, complex visual patterns may be too demanding. We might speculate that there may be an ideal gradient of environmental stimulation depending on a patient's position on the continuum of disorder. Such a gradient could be used to avoid the extremes of attenuated stimulation, on the one hand, and the impinging complexity of the real world, on the other.

As will be discussed in Chapter 6, the distorted self-perception of schizophrenics results in an expansion of their personal-space requirements (Horowitz, Duff, & Stratton, 1964). This exaggerated need for personal space, in combination with a mental patient's desire to have a place to hide, leads Osmond to suggest that designers should provide for private spaces, or at least reduce the potential for unwanted personal contacts. These requirements could be met in a number of different ways—single-occupancy bedrooms, small wards, alcoves, and landscaping the institution grounds for solace and seclusion.

Other patient disabilities requiring consideration by designers are the tendency toward rapid mood changes and the difficulty in making decisions. Osmond states that small groups who have had the opportunity to form understanding relationships are more resistant to mood swings than are larger, less cohesive groups. Thus, smaller wards and bedrooms again may serve a useful purpose. To alleviate decision-making difficulties, Osmond advocates reducing ambiguous situations (large dining halls and dormitories and junctions of long, unmarked corridors, for example) by using smaller units to reduce the number of alternatives present in each decision situation.

Throughout his article, then, Osmond contends that avoiding certain features now common to institutions (reduced visual stimulation, for example) and providing for other features (private spaces) may facilitate therapeutic efforts. These efforts may also be enhanced if institutions are designed to require a minimum of adjustment on the part of new patients and so reduce potentially stressful situations.

Social Behavior in Mental Wards

A prevalent notion in the treatment of mental patients is that they need to engage in social interaction both as a means of activity during their treatment period and as a preparation for social encounters once they leave the institution. Although social behavior is a function of many variables, such as therapeutic technique, administrative policy, and patient characteristics, features of the ward environment can be isolated as possible determinants of social activity. Among these features are the size of the ward, the size of ward components (bedrooms and day rooms, for example), and the components' internal arrangements. Typically, psychiatric wards contain all the features necessary to support patient activity: rooms for eating, sleeping, recreation and socializing, treatment, and personal hygiene. Thus, when the other variables mentioned are taken into consideration, the effects of wards differing in physical features can be compared by observing the activities taking place in them. Such investigations are reported by Ittelson, Proshansky, and Rivlin (1972); Wolfe (1975); Gump and James (1970); Sommer (1969); and Barton, Mishkin, and Spivack (1971).

Although the major purpose of the study by Ittelson and his co-workers was to observe the stability of behavior patterns in psychiatric units, the report also provides information about the physical aspects of the wards and potential behavioral relationships. The investigators chose wards from psychiatric units in three hospitals. These wards varied substantially in size (both overall and in their components) and appearance as well as patient population.

The first ward consisted of a converted medical ward in a general hospital. Thus, it retained a hospital appearance, with tiled hallways, bright lights, and bustling activity. The bedrooms had either three or six occupants and were open to direct observation from the corridors. In addition to the standard day room, this ward contained a solarium for patient use.

Two more wards were in a state mental institution. This hospital was typical of many state mental-health facilities in that it operated under rigid financial constraints. Both wards were utilitarian in structure and furnishings. Each contained a few private bedrooms and a mixture of three-bed, six-bed, and 20-bed, or dormitory-type, rooms. Because of administrative policies, the wards did differ in one respect. One of the wards showed evidence of patient cooperation in keeping it neat and attractively decorated; the other had a considerably gloomier atmosphere.

The fourth ward was in a private hospital. The investigators report that this ward seemed more like an attractive hotel than a psychiatric ward. The color schemes were tasteful, and the furnishings were well appointed. All the bedrooms were either one-bed or two-bed rooms and had doors to seal off any corridor activity.

To observe and record the variety of behaviors occurring in these wards, the investigators developed a technique called behavioral mapping. To construct a map of each ward, trained observers were positioned at specific locations in the ward. At predetermined time intervals the observers recorded the types of behavior occurring in their areas and the number and characteristics of the persons involved. For instance, at one time interval an observer in the day room might record that six male patients, two female patients, and one ward attendant were watching television; four male patients were playing cards; three female patients were reading; and one male patient was dozing in his chair. Thus, combining all the observers' data for one time interval gives an accurate description of the behavior occurring in the entire ward. Similarly, combining the data of all the observers at all time intervals establishes the behavioral patterns of the ward patients and the staff. Such behavioral maps of a normal day's activities were constructed for each ward for extended periods.

For the purpose of meaningful explanation, the investigators put the locations of behavior into two major categories—bedrooms and public rooms. Places considered to be public rooms included the hallways, the day rooms, the eating rooms, and the solarium in the city hospital. The behavior was also categorized according to type of activity and types and amount of social encounters involved. These categories were isolated/passive (sitting or lying in bed alone, awake or asleep); active (personal duties, reading, and individual recreation); and social (patients interacting with other patients, visitors, or staff). Analysis of the data in these categories revealed differences among the wards as well as marked differences in the types of behavior as a function of location.

Comparison of the overall activities in the four wards showed that more active or social behavior occurred in the private hospital than passive behavior. In the state and converted city wards, isolated/passive behavior predominated. In the public places of the wards, behavior in the private hospital was again much more active or social than isolated/passive. Behavior in the state and city wards, on the other hand, was relatively equally distributed among all the behavioral categories. However, the researchers felt that these differences were more the result of the differences in patient populations and administrative policies than of differences in physical environment.

The most intriguing findings of the study are the marked differences in behavior observed in the ward bedrooms within each unit. The investigators early noted overall differences among the wards and the behavior occurring in the bedrooms. Although isolated/passive behavior was prevalent in all ward bedrooms, a smaller percentage of the patients in the private hospital engaged in this kind of behavior than in the state and city wards. This difference was quickly traced to the presence of only one-bed or two-bed rooms in the private institution. The researchers then discovered that the percentage of isolated/passive behavior in bedrooms increased in all four wards with the number of beds per room and, consequently, with bedroom size. At first glance one might assume that these results would be expected; the larger the bedroom, the more people occupying it and engaging in isolated/passive behavior at any one time. However, the rate of use of the bedrooms did not increase with size enough to account for the differences. The authors interpret this finding as follows:

> . . . the patient in the smaller room experiences the entire range of possible behaviors as open to him, he feels free to choose from the whole range of options, and he does, in fact, choose more or less equally from among all possibilities. This is [most] dramatically shown in the single rooms of the private hospital, where behavior is equally distributed over all categories.
>
> In contrast, the patient in the larger room is far more likely to be engaged in isolated–passive behavior than anything else and will spend anywhere from two-thirds to three-fourths of his time, while in his room, lying on his bed, either asleep or awake. He seems to see the range of options among which he can choose as severely limited and to be constrained to choose isolated–passive behavior over any other [p. 103].

In a more recent study Wolfe (1975) offers a different interpretation of Ittelson and his co-workers' results. She suggests that bedroom size, in terms of square feet per occupant, is not the sole determining factor in the behavior mapped in their study but that the behavior may have also been influenced by the number of persons in or assigned to the bedroom. Thus, density and not size becomes the issue. Further, she hypothesizes that the manner in which density is achieved is important in determining bedroom use and the behavior taking place there.

Wolfe conducted her study in a state-supported children's hospital. She used a behavioral-mapping approach very similar to the one used by Ittelson and his colleagues in determining the activities and their locations in the children's wards. For the purposes of her report, she concentrated on the activities occurring in the children's bedrooms as they were related to the size of the room, the number of children assigned to the room, and the resultant density.

The facility where the study was conducted had a mixture of one-bed, two-bed, and four-bed rooms, which were designed to allow approximately 80 square feet per child. Because of variations in patient load, the numbers of children occupying different-sized bedrooms varied.

Three indexes of bedroom occupancy were used: the proportion of observation periods in which someone was in the room, the number of children in the room when it was occupied, and the proportion of room usage by each child. Each time a room was found occupied, the type of activity taking place was noted and recorded. Wolfe's results and interpretation provide substantial insight into physical/social interactions taking place within the wards.

First, the results revealed that the bedrooms were occupied only about 13% of the time and that the behavior observed was predominantly isolated/ passive. This was especially true for the bedrooms with single occupants, which is a direct contrast to the results of the earlier study. Wolfe explains these findings as being due to the typical regime in a children's therapeutic setting, which occupies more time and emphasizes social interaction. Thus, a child's free time is more likely to be spent in privacy and solitude to compensate for the extended periods of interaction during programmed activities. A second finding of interest was that the bedrooms were generally occupied by only one person at any given time no matter how many persons were assigned to the room. Also, each child was found to use the room less as the number of children assigned to the room increased. These results were interpreted as indicating that privacy was an objective and that density in terms of the number of people who could use the room decreased the opportunity for solitude. Other findings reflected the influence of density on behavior. For example, it was found that two children sharing a four-bed room were more likely to use the room than two children sharing a two-bed room. The implication here is that the increased space enabled each child to use the room without as many feelings of being interrupted or confronted by the other occupant. Thus, each child was more likely to treat his or her share of the room as private rather than shared territory.

The interpretations of this study can provide information on the importance of the interactions between therapeutic objectives, physical design, and patient activities. For example, if we can assume that both privacy and social interaction are important features of a therapy program, then adequate provision for privacy must be made, especially if programmed time is filled with social interaction, as was the case in this children's hospital. The unconscious denial of privacy, in the case of certain disorders, could conceivably affect patient progress in the therapeutic program.

In the previous chapter we discussed the work of Sommer (1969), who established relationships between the arrangement of furnishings in class-rooms and classroom activity and who showed that persons wanting to converse have strong preferences in seating arrangement and distance.

Sommer's research also provides evidence that the arrangement of furnishings in mental-health facilities is important in determining the extent of social encounters among patients. He points out that the arrangement of chairs in the lounge areas of mental institutions is not unlike that in airport terminals. Typically, the chairs are in straight rows along the walls and back to back in the center of the room, with the distance between the center chairs and those against the walls far exceeding the limit for comfortable conversation. The reasons for this arrangement are ease of maintenance, neat appearance, and the unspoken tradition of what institutions are supposed to look like.

Sommer reports that, in an investigation of such a ward arrangement in a Canadian institution, his observers recorded both one-way social communications (greetings or questions directed by one patient to another, for example) and reciprocal social communications lasting for 2 seconds or more. These data were gathered for use as baseline data for later comparisons with data gathered under different conditions. At the end of the baseline period, several square tables were moved into the lounge, and the chairs along the walls were rearranged around the tables. This new arrangement provoked resistance from maintenance and other personnel, who complained that it disrupted their activities. Initial resistance also came from the patients. After allowing time for adjustment to the new arrangement, the observers again recorded the number of communications and found that both one-way communications and reciprocal communications increased.

The results of these investigations provide relevant information for administrators and planners in the field of institutional design. Although the research is exploratory and a host of other variables may have influenced the results, it at least supplies a basis for alternatives to existing features in psychiatric wards.

Nursing Homes and Housing for the Elderly

In this section we will look at another special segment of the population—the aged. A special problem with this subpopulation is its growth, as Heimstra and McDonald (1973) relate:

> In recent years, there has been a marked shift in the age makeup of our population. Through the prolongation of life by new advances in medical science, the over-65 segment of the population is increasing disproportionately. By 1980, it is estimated that this age group will make up over 10% of the population, or somewhere in the neighborhood of 25 or 30 million people [p. 293].[1]

[1]This and all other quotations from this source are from *Psychology and Contemporary Problems*, by N. W. Heimstra and A. L. McDonald. Copyright © 1973 by Wadsworth Publishing Company, Inc. Reprinted by permission of the publisher, Brooks/Cole Publishing Company, Monterey, California.

Given this expected increase in numbers, it seems important to consider how built environments can be designed to accommodate this very special group of individuals.

Individual is a key word when considering the elderly. Possibly in no other segment of our population can so much variety be found in individual capabilities and needs. We are all probably familiar with at least one anecdotal account of someone near or over the age of 100 who still lives alone and has a rather independent lifestyle. Unfortunately, we also probably can recount instances in which a medical problem, such as a stroke, has rendered individuals in their fifties or sixties unable fully to care for themselves. Finally, our own "senior-citizen" relatives may suffer from a hearing loss, for example, causing them some exasperation with "folks who don't talk loud enough." These examples only serve to emphasize that a wide spectrum of disabilities and needs characterizes the elderly.

There is no fully conclusive or established pattern of deterioration of mental or physical abilities with increasing age. One of the more common effects of increasing age is a general tendency to take more time to react to stimulus situations or to complete laboratory-derived tasks. There may or may not be a decline in intellectual processes, such as problem solving. Vision and hearing losses are common but not inevitable. Psychomotor deterioration is also possible, making fine manipulative skills or simple ambulation difficult.

Also associated with increasing age are sociopsychological problems. Dissociated from work and subject to losses of spouses, friends, and relatives, elderly persons may become lonely and insecure or withdrawn. Their reliance on fixed incomes or on others for support can affect their self-esteem. For unknown reasons they may become cantankerous or childlike in their behavior and refuse extended periods of meaningful social interaction. A "typical" elderly person, then, may be subjected to some, all, or none of the above afflictions. Thus, for reasons that are biological, psychological, sociological, or economic, elderly persons may find themselves living in an extended-care facility, such as a nursing home. Taking each individual composite of capabilities and needs into consideration, what can be said about the interactions of these people with the built environment?

Patients' Needs

We have pointed out that elderly residents of home-care facilities have a wide range of abilities and needs. There are a number of design considerations that can be incorporated into these facilities to enhance the living routine for those who need them without infringing upon the routine of those who do not. Many of these design considerations reflect commonsense approaches and do not have (or need) experimental verification. For example, any printing, such as signs, nameplates, or room numbers, can be made larger and with more contrast than is "normally" necessary to help those who suffer from reduced visual acuity. Similarly, glare is a problem for those who have had cataract operations. Thus, any opportunities to reduce either reflected or direct glare from light sources would be a welcome design feature. Nonslip surfaces can be used to prevent falls. Unnecessary changes in elevation requiring the negotiation of steps should be avoided. Handrails can be included in hallways to facilitate residents' movements to and from their rooms. Such a list of considerations for the elderly with reduced physical and perceptual capabilities could be quite extensive. Our point is that these amenities can and should be included in facilities for the elderly to enhance their daily living.

DeLong (1970) mentions a set of sensory/perceptual problems that need to be addressed when designing social and physical environments for the aged. First, he suggests that, because of reduced sensory capabilities, older persons may find themselves moving closer to individuals in order to communicate with them. A staff member may react to such behavior by withdrawing somewhat; the resident has unconsciously intruded on the staff member's personal space. (The concept of personal space is discussed in Chapter 6.) Room design and furniture arrangement can provide for this need for close contact by creating small alcoves for conversation. Also, DeLong suggests that the elderly, like anyone else, need distinct areas designated as private, semiprivate, or public in order to engage in their full range of behaviors. Finally, DeLong maintains that special attention to design features such as tactile cues (for example, surface textures) should be considered in order to compensate for possible sensory attenuation.

To provide some congruence between elderly individuals with disabilities and appropriate prosthetic environments, Lawton (1970) suggests that an assessment technique be developed to probe capabilities and needs on sensory/perceptual, motor, social, and mental dimensions, so that a profile of the individual could be developed. Ideally, this profile would be matched with an environment meeting those capabilities and needs. Such a procedure could conceivably determine factors from sizes of print in rooms to room assignments to possible part-time occupations.

Social Behavior

In addition to physical needs, nursing-home residents have varying needs for social interaction. Conversely, they should be afforded the opportunity for privacy. Provision for privacy is often economically determined. Private rooms may not be economically feasible for the person's sponsor,

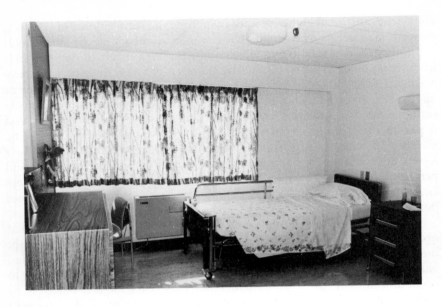

Figure 4-9. Facilities for the elderly vary considerably. In the top photo is a bedroom in a nursing home; in the lower photo is a living room in an apartment that is part of a large complex designed for the elderly. (Photos by Lars Larmon.)

whether it be a government agency or relatives. Therefore, privacy may be thwarted by circumstances beyond a resident's control.

Social behavior has been extensively studied in nursing-home settings, so we could believe that social behavior is an important part of an elderly resident's life. Though it undoubtedly is important, the study of social behavior may have received disproportionate emphasis by default; residents may have little else to do. Thus, social areas such as lobbies, solariums, and courtyards are predominant areas in the facilities, and much research on the arrangements within these spaces is available.

Lipman (1967, 1968) has investigated social interaction in sitting rooms and lobbies with specific focus on the effects of chair arrangement. In both studies he mentions the behavioral phenomenon of residents' staking out claims on particular chairs and subsequently defending their ownership of the chairs. The occupation of the chairs was considered of prime importance. Residents would remain in their chairs even when it proved uncomfortable to accomplish whatever they were doing. For example, they were observed to undergo various contortions in order to converse with people on either side of them rather than move to another available seat (1967). In another instance Lipman found that groupings of chairs were used to establish and maintain strict, status-associated boundaries (1968). In both reports the majority of the behavior reported involved conflict, intrusion, and defense.

In research on other intraresidence variables, proximity has been shown to be an important determinant of friendship. Friedman (1966) found that some 60% of reciprocal friendship choices were made by persons living on the same floor in a home for the aged. It might be assumed that a wide friendship base would be important for elderly residents for at least two reasons—for variety and to lessen the emotional impact of death in a friendship circle.

In considering the results of the Lipman and Friedman studies, it appears that an implicit assumption has been made concerning social interaction. The assumption seems to be that social interaction is good, even if it is conflictual, and that positive and pleasant social interaction in the form of establishing friendships is even better. However, before designing environments to meet a criterion of maximum social interaction, it should be first established that the residents desire social interaction. The elderly persons' definition of social interaction and what types of social interaction are desired should also be established. Much of this is a problem for administrators rather than designers. For example, if a study shows that the majority of patients' time is spent in passively watching others, there may be a number of reasons for this observation. First, the residents may have nothing else to do. Second, that may be all they are capable of doing. Third, that may be what they want to do. Fourth, they may want to be in a socially oriented area and not want to be passive, but certain features of the environment, such as furniture arrangement or distance, may preclude active social behavior.

To summarize, sometimes what is considered best for the residents by administrators, sociologists, psychologists, and medical personnel may not be what the residents perceive as best for them. It would appear that the designers and administrators of nursing homes might benefit from an extensive "consumer study" of resident preferences before embarking on decisions that affect the residents' lives.

Resident Satisfaction

We have discussed features of extended-care facilities for the elderly that may contribute to daily activities or to the establishment of friendship patterns, on the one hand, and may provide a means for social conflict, on the other. Whatever their result, these features can be considered at a micro level, or within the habitat. We might ask whether there are features at a more community-based, or macro, level that affect resident behavior in one form or another. A variety of measures could be used to evaluate housing for the elderly at this level. One measure might focus on the degree of social activity in the community by tabulating the number of visits to others in the community, the distances traveled within the community to visit, or the reported number of friends. A common assumption is that elderly individuals have more desire for security-related features than do other persons. Thus, any behaviors that show feelings of security could prove valuable—for example, the number of people walking around the housing site after dark. It might be easier, though, simply to ask residents how secure they feel and to solicit reasons for their feelings.

If we can assume that leisure or recreational activity is important to the residents, data could be collected on attendance at planned activities or usage of informal-gathering places to engage in these types of behavior. Yet another evaluative measure of housing could deal with accidents or injuries occurring as a direct result of physical features such as slippery walks, lack of handrails, and juxtaposition to high-density, high-speed traffic. These factors, as well as others, are likely to be considered in the evaluation of resident communities for the elderly.

Lawton, Nahemow, and Teaff (1975) have attempted to assess some of the behaviors we have mentioned in their study of resident satisfaction in different housing projects. Their study focused on the site or community variables of sponsorship, size of community, size of building, and building height and their possible influence on resident satisfaction. They summarized the results of more than 2400 questionnaires in a nationwide sample of elderly people living in federally assisted public-housing and nonprofit-housing projects. Items in the questionnaire dealt with friendships in the project, mobility around the project, visits from relatives, participation in project activities, and general satisfaction with the project. The authors were also aware of the impact that personal and social variables can have on satisfaction, as shown in the Onibokun (1976) study discussed in Chapter 3. Consequently, they also collected data on these influences on resident satisfaction.

As was found in the Onibokun study, the personal and social charac- teristics of the respondents accounted for sizable portions of their expressed satisfaction. But even with these social-system variables taken into account, significant portions of the satisfaction could be attributed to characteristics of the housing projects. For example, friendships, as measured by reported number of friends and number of visits, were more numerous in the nonprofit-sponsored projects than in the public housing. More friendships and greater housing satisfaction were also reported in the smaller projects. Housing satisfaction was found to be related to smaller communities and lower buildings. Mobility (the frequency of travel out of the buildings and of travel off the project grounds) was also found to be more prevalent in the lower buildings. Finally, more participation in activities was reported in the nonprofit-sponsored projects and smaller communities.

In reviewing these results, it is surprising to find no relationship between building height and friendship. Although no specific descriptions of the building characteristics were included in the report, it would seem logical from the studies reported by Newman (1973a, 1973b, 1973c) that the high- rise buildings may have had a negative influence on friendships. Such a result would have been supported by the finding of less mobility in the high-rise residents if we consider that elderly persons, as a group, could be more affected by design features that discourage interaction because of their difficulties in negotiating the hallways and stairs of high-rise buildings. Until such a research finding is reported, however, this notion can be considered only hypothetical.

Penal Institutions

The physical features of penal institutions are somewhat similar to those of mental-health facilities. However, there are major differences between the two types of institutions that may affect the manipulation of physical features to help achieve institution objectives. Whereas the aim of mental institutions is to return the individual to society as quickly as possible, in penal institutions mandatory sentences and minimum time spent there before parole eligibility tend to emphasize the custodial function, not the rehabilitative function. Still, providing a physical environment meeting the individual's personal needs may be as important in a prison as in a psychiatric ward. This consideration often conflicts, unfortunately, with society's demand for punishment.

Another difference between the two types of institutions lies in their populations. With the exception of some unusual cases, persons in mental institutions are not considered as being harmful to one another and are encouraged to engage in various types of social interaction. In prisons social interaction must be subjected to much more control for custodial reasons. Certain types of social interaction may also be discouraged for rehabilitative purposes—for example, keeping young first offenders separated from hardened criminals.

This need for control places additional restraints on the design of penal facilities. Obviously, one technique useful in controlling social interactions is the provision for physical separation of inmates. Equally obvious is that the construction of independent mini-prisons for individual inmates is probably far beyond economic limitations. Nonetheless, a general feeling among administrators and social scientists engaged in research on penal institutions is that the provision for inmate privacy is instrumental in rehabilitation. With a room or a cell of their own, inmates can engage in such private activities as reading, writing, and studying without being disturbed by cellmates. It is also desirable to group inmates according to stage in the rehabilitative process. This concept has resulted in the compartmentalization now used in several newer prison systems.

When the contrasts between mental and penal institutions are considered in conjunction with the recommendations for inmate privacy and grouping according to stage of rehabilitation, one factor becomes clear—that administrative policies dominate most considerations involving prison environments. Physical features of prison environments currently change only as a consequence of changes in administrative rehabilitative procedures. For example, the decision to provide private cells for inmates and the resultant behavioral effects have only indirect implications for the physical features of the prison environment. Thus, discussions of the design aspects of prisons should focus on how they can be supportive of positive rehabilitation efforts or how they can be manipulated to lessen the negative impact of more undesirable administrative rehabilitative procedures.

It is easy to understand that various aspects of prison procedures could have negative influences on the inmates. Sommer (1974, pp. 28–32) has summarized a number of these effects under the label "symptoms of institutional care." They include:

> *de-individuation*—a reduced ability of a person to engage in independent thought and action, due to the highly structured behavioral routine in their environment.
> *disculturation*—the acquisition of the values and attitudes of the prison society, rather than society on the "outside."
> *damage*—psychological or social effects in terms of stigma, and reduced self-esteem.

estrangement—removal of the individual physically and psychologically from all group functions on the outside in which he would play a significant role (occupational, family, friendships, relatives).

stimulus deprivation—reduced opportunity for variety in visual, physical or social stimulation; leads to feelings of being overwhelmed when confronted with the real world.

When one considers this list of possible undesirable effects of the prison experience, it is relatively easy to prescribe several changes in rehabilitative policies or procedures to alleviate them. Among those mentioned by Sommer are decentralized work programs, which allow prisoners to spend time in interaction with the outside world; extended vocational-training programs; provision for family-living centers in prisons; increased use of television as an educational and entertainment stimulus; and adoption of flexible security arrangements that are dependent on a prisoner's crime or stage of rehabilitation. Many of Sommer's suggestions also incorporate changes in the environmental settings. However, these changes are needed to support the program objective and would not involve a change in environment as the main variable. Even such changes as providing inmates individual cells or allowing them to use motel or apartment-like facilities for extended living periods with their families are primarily manipulations of social rather than physical-environment factors. Possibly the only institutional symptom listed by Sommer that is subject to change by manipulation of strictly physical features is stimulus deprivation. As has been discussed, the effects of stimulus deprivation could be partially alleviated by the use of variety in color schemes and physical arrangement of spaces within the prison. However, it is unlikely that a simple change in color scheme or arrangement could offset the other negative influences of prisons on inmate behavior.

One physical feature of prisons that can have distinctly positive or negative behavioral consequences is space, in terms of the number of square feet allocated per person in living and recreational areas. Although, as discussed in Chapter 6, space per person is not the sole determinant of the experience of crowding, it is an important contributor. The dimension of space and the related concepts of privacy, territoriality, and crowding are important concerns in prison design. For example, we have already mentioned that privacy is considered an important feature in inmate rehabilitation. Crowding also is of concern to prison administrators because of its suspected contribution to outbreaks of violence.

One reason for such outcomes in crowded situations can possibly be traced to higher individual spatial needs in prisoners, especially those with tendencies toward violence. This notion is supported by Kinzel (1970), who discovered that the violent prisoners in his study had body-buffer zones (explained in Chapter 6) nearly four times as large as those of nonviolent prisoners. Such a finding, if replicated, would appear to have definite implications for designers in terms of cell size, fixed-furnishings arrangement, and space allocated for shared activities, such as lounge and recreation areas.

Space in prisons may also have medical consequences as by-products of crowding-induced stress. McCain, Cox, and Paulus (1976) found significant differences in reported illnesses between inmates living in dormitory-style units and those living in single-person or two-person cells in county-jail and prison settings. The inmates who were living in the dormitory units in both locations had more illness complaints than did the inmates who were living in the cells. Illnesses that would be expected to spread more readily because of physical proximity, such as colds and influenza, were *not* used in the analysis. The investigators contend that the social experiences of crowding may have more influence on stress than the spatial dimension does. However, this notion remains to be validated.

Up to this point, we have concentrated on the more negative aspects of prison environments and their possible consequences for inmate behavior. During the course of this discussion, it was mentioned that privacy and the rehabilitation stage of the inmate are important considerations. As a final and more positive note, we will consider observations made by Glaser (1972) that provide some information on expected results when these factors are taken into account.

In a study of the use of separate cells as a deterrent to criminogenic influences, Glaser conducted a survey of inmate activities in single-occupancy cells and in dormitories in five institutions. Data were collected on the number of hours each inmate spent in everyday activities, such as working, eating, sleeping, talking with fellow prisoners, recreation, and reading. Although each institution differed from the others in administrative policy and treatment programs, time spent in reading and eating was consistently greater for occupants of single cells. Glaser attributes the increased time spent eating to the single-cell inmates' need to socialize or to be away from the isolation of their cells. The results of this survey suggest that although occupants of single cells do have more opportunity for privacy, they do not take advantage of it as much as they might.

Glaser also obtained the same types of information for separate housing units in one prison setting. The housing units were organized according to different stages in the rehabilitative process and thus varied in physical features as well as in administrative policies on inmate supervision. Basically, the units at the bottom of this honor system consisted of dormitories, each with a supervisory officer. As inmates advanced up the honor scale, their physical environment changed as well as the amount of supervision. The first significant change was from a dormitory to a single room, which was not locked in the "semihonor" units. From there the inmates' rooms increased in size, and in the "top honor" unit they could have their lights on any time they wished. Associated with the changes in environment was decreasing supervision, which in the top honor unit was virtually nonexistent.

Although Glaser's activity analysis in these units reflects little influence of their physical characteristics on inmate behavior, some of the findings may provide grounds for future decisions in the design of penal institutions. One rather unexpected finding leads one to question the success of the honor system. Glaser's analysis of work and play activities of the inmates across housing units showed that work time increased while recreation time decreased until the inmates reached the two highest honor units. At that time the trend reversed, with play activities occupying substantially more time than in the other units and time spent working decreasing accordingly. In addition, the "intellectual quality" of the recreation activities seemed to decrease in the two top honor units. Records of enrollment in and completion of correspondence courses taken by the inmates also indicated that participation in courses decreased dramatically in the top honor units. Glaser thus concludes that "the 'honor units' may often contribute more to the comfort of both the inmates and staff than to the reformation of the inmates" (p. 112).

COLLEGE DORMITORIES

In this section we will focus on yet another type of living environment that is familiar to many readers of this text—the college dorm. As a living environment, dormitories differ substantially from mental institutions, nursing homes, and prisons in that dormitories are not total-living environments, or microcosms. However, dormitories are important contributors to a student's total college experience in terms of the quantity of time spent in them, the functions performed there, and the qualitative results of the various activities that take place within them. Thus, dormitories deserve and have received the attentions of several researchers.

As with other parts of the built environment, dormitories are designed and constructed to fulfill certain objectives. These objectives are different depending on whose point of view is being considered. For the administrator, the dormitory is designed to be a reasonable-cost living alternative for students. From a long-term standpoint, dormitories may be a source of income for the institution. From the parents' viewpoint, the dormitory may be thought of as an environment where some means of guidance, control, or security for their children is provided. Finally, as far as the student/user is concerned, the college dormitory may be considered an environment where academic, social, and personal needs can be fulfilled. For the purposes of our discussion, we will focus on the student/user and on how adequately dormitories have fulfilled this objective from a student perspective.

One function of dormitories is to provide an environment that facilitates the student's part of the academic process—studying. A common issue throughout the years has been whether the institution-controlled dormitory setting is more conducive to studying and hence better academic performance than noncontrolled living environments. In recent years administrative policies requiring students to reside in college dorms have come under fire. Administrative officials have often cited better academic achievement of dormitory residents as sufficient justification for the policies. Grant (1968) investigated the possible influences of on-campus versus off-campus residence on student grade-point averages. In conducting her study, she also took into consideration age, past academic performance, and measures of intelligence. Her summary indicated no relationships between any of the locational or personal variables and academic performance other than previous performance. Unfortunately, a full report of her investigation is not available, so it is difficult to make any broad inferences from her results.

Regardless of location, a certain amount of privacy would seem necessary in order for students to study effectively. Student respondents to questionnaires sent out by Van Der Ryn and Silverstein (1967) indicated that dormitory residents were quite emphatic in their desire for privacy in order to study, in addition to desiring privacy for sleeping, personal activities, and entertaining. A study by Stokes (1960) also supports the need for privacy as well as emphasizing the importance of dormitories in providing places for study. The data revealed that 55 to 78% of studying was accomplished in dormitory rooms. It was also found that 80% of the students surveyed preferred small spaces to large ones for studying and that 85% preferred to study alone. The study also has implications for policies and designs concerning multiple-person dormitory rooms or suites, as time spent studying in rooms generally declined as the number of roommates increased. These data are similar to those reported by Wolfe (1975) on multiperson bedrooms in mental institutions, where the amount of time each individual spent in the room decreased with the number of persons assigned to that room. It appears that for students, as well as mental patients, privacy is a need that must be filled, although the activities they engage in while isolated differ. Essentially, a multiperson room forces people to seek other spaces in which to fulfill their needs. What remains to be investigated is whether those needs can be satisfactorily met by alternative locations. For students, this is particularly relevant, especially if the alternative spaces for studying, such as libraries and lounges, do not offer benefits comparable to the relatively private spaces of the dormitory in terms of either quality or quantity. Therefore, if the needs of the student cannot be met by either the multiperson rooms or the alternative locations, it seems that the potential for poor academic performance is increased.

In previous discussions we mentioned the influence of common walls and ceilings/floors on feelings of auditory privacy and annoyance in residents of multiple-family dwellings. These same architectural features are present in dormitory construction and probably have similar influences on residents' perceived privacy and annoyance. Another feature of many dormitories is the long single or double-loaded corridor, with its attendant noise of traffic and conversation. Feller (1968) has reported that, if a low noise level in corridors is desirable or conducive to rest or study, it can be controlled by varying the illumination level of the halls. Specifically, a reduction of candlepower in hallways from 5.4 to .5 resulted in a significant reduction in hallway-noise level in the majority of situations tested. Thus, at least on the auditory dimension, it may be possible to provide more privacy by putting such findings to use.

Privacy, or the lack of it, for student residents may have either positive or negative effects on their academic performance. Lack of privacy may also affect social interactions. Conditions in which students are sharing studying, sleeping, recreational, and hygiene facilities can result in close friendships, a cooperative and supportive social atmosphere, and very cohesive informal group relationships. However, the lack of private space and the sharing of territories may result in feelings and behavior associated with crowding—that is, more stress, decreased cooperation, and involvement in the preferences and problems of others. (See Figure 4-10.)

Valins and Baum (1973) investigated possible differences between residents of corridor-style dormitories and those living in suite-style dorms. Although the space allocated to the residents was very similar in both cases, some 34 corridor residents shared bathroom and shower and lounge facilities, as compared to four to six students sharing the same facilities in the suite arrangement. The investigators hypothesized that the corridor arrangement, with its heavy sharing of facilities, could influence the residents by causing feelings of crowding because of too many interactions with others and the inability to avoid some contact with others with whom they did not get along. Further, they felt that these conditions could cause the residents to engage in avoidance behaviors in other social situations because of a perceived overload in their living environments. (This concept is discussed in detail in Chapter 5.) The investigators collected data from the corridor and suite residents in a number of ways. First, they questioned both groups and found that residents of the corridor-style dormitories felt that there were too many people on their dorm floor, that there were too many situations in which they met others where interactions were not desired, and that their dormitory was crowded. In all cases these feelings were significantly less predominant in residents of the suite-type arrangement.

Given these results, Valins and Baum then conducted a series of laboratory investigations involving residents from both groups. In these experiments the residents were given the opportunity to engage in social interaction with another person already seated in a room under apparently

Figure 4-10. Dorm rooms provide positive benefits in that they offer conditions in which close friendships can develop in a cooperative and supportive social atmosphere. The lack of private space and the necessity of shared territories, however, are disadvantages. (Photos by Lars Larmon.)

normal conditions and under conditions that were purported to be either cooperative or competitive. The residents were observed during these situations, and data were obtained on how closely they approached the other person, how much they interacted with the other person, and how uncomfortable they appeared to be.

The researchers found that, generally, residents of the corridor-type dormitories tended to choose seats further away from others, engage in less conversation and visual contact, and appear more uncomfortable than the subjects from the suite-type dormitories. Valins and Baum interpret these results to mean that the perceived effects of crowding and more intense social encounters in the dormitories were influencing the way the residents from corridor-type dorms were handling themselves in other social situations. Findings such as these are of great potential importance and should be replicated. If further efforts in the area prove reliable, it appears that dormitories with both a corridor layout and much sharing of facilities could prove less than conducive to the social adjustments of their residents.

Even if corridor arrangements with high densities in common facilities prove to have a somewhat negative influence on resident social adjustment, several points still remain to be resolved before suite-type dormitories can be completely endorsed. For example, some suite-type arrangements have used smaller private or semiprivate sleeping areas and provided a room to use for group study. According to Stokes' (1960) data, however, such a plan may be in contradiction to the stated desire of students to be alone while studying. The net effect could be to negate the perceived positive aspects of suite-type arrangements—that is, lower density in shared areas. It appears that students perceive studying to be an activity that has a lower threshold for feeling crowded than other activities, such as sharing bath and shower facilities. If this is true, it is possible that the traditional two-person room in the corridor arrangement could offer more relative privacy for studying than a shared study area in a suite arrangement.

Another potential negative feature of suite-type arrangements is the creation of stressful social relationships by the arbitrary assignment of suitemates who do not mesh well. The underlying rationale as stated by students is that the possibility of being placed with someone they cannot get along with is increased, since from three to eight others are assigned to the same living area. Students feel that it is easier to adjust to only one other person's lifestyle (Corbett, 1973).

All the features mentioned do have solutions or positive corollaries. If suite bedrooms are large enough, many students feel they have more privacy than could be obtained in other situations. Also, the idea of sharing living areas with three to eight others is exciting to those who desire many social relationships. Finally, if choices of roommates are possible, the potential for negative social relationships can be reduced. In summary, though we cannot offer an optimal design solution for student residency, we can state that the needs for privacy and the establishment of positive social relationships must be heavily emphasized when design alternatives are considered.

SCHOOLS

Obviously, much of the influence on behavior in schools can be traced to the process of education, not to features of the physical environment. As we have mentioned in other examples of the built environment, however, the physical environment of schools can be structured to support the purposes of this educational process. Conversely, inadvertent design features may be counterproductive.

Because schools have a great impact on a child's early life, much of the research currently available is concerned with elementary and middle-school settings. Our research examples will follow this trend and will concentrate on two specific environmental features—ambient temperatures and windows—and the more general concept of the open-plan schools and their potential for influencing student behavior.

Temperature and Learning

The ambient environment in schools has been shown to affect the behavior of students, notably those in the elementary grades. This is in contrast to our earlier discussions of the ambient environmental features of rooms and office buildings. In schools student performance has been shown to be related to the ambient feature of temperature. Lofstedt, Ryd, and Wyon (1969) conducted a study involving a variety of elementary-school children in four different experimental settings: a climatic chamber, a language laboratory, an observation classroom, and an ordinary classroom. The students were required to perform a number of different school-related tasks in each of the settings at varying temperatures. The students in the climatic chamber solved addition and multiplication problems and completed tasks involving memorizing. The language-lab students learned words from lists. The students in the observation classroom engaged in reading, vocabulary lessons, and math operations. The students in the ordinary classroom were also tested with arithmetic problems. The temperatures in the settings ranged from 21 to 27 degrees C.

The results indicated a general tendency for performance on the tasks to decrease as a function of increasing temperature. The most significant differences in performance occurred at the higher temperatures. Also, in some cases, poorer students were more adversely affected by the higher temperatures than were the better students.

Windows

Recall that in studies of office buildings windows were perceived as being quite important by the workers. No mention was made, however, of windows possibly causing decreases in worker production by acting as a distraction. This concept has been given consideration in the design of school buildings; that is, the distractions windows offer may outweigh the positive benefits of "free" light and outside environmental stimulation. Larson (1965) conducted a study to determine any positive or negative effects of removing windows in classrooms. To conduct his study Larson used two similar schools serving kindergarten through grade 3. The study was conducted for three years. One school was designated the control school and was left with its windows intact for the entire period. The experimental school had regular windows the first year and the third year of the study. In the second year, however, the windows were replaced with opaque panels. Each year, students and teachers were asked about the school as an environmental setting and how satisfied they were with it. In addition, class-performance records were kept for comparisons.

The students were generally not concerned about the presence or absence of the windows, but younger children did show a preference for windows. Teachers, on the other hand, were more satisfied with the window-less condition and commented on the lack of distractions and increased flexibility with windowless walls. Student performance was virtually un-changed across the conditions. The author's conclusion was that no learning deficits were in evidence due to windowless classrooms. He states that, when taking the performance data into consideration with the teachers' and pupils' comments, if windows are not relied on for light or ventilation, it should be safe to do without them. Such a practice would be initiated with much hesitancy on the part of school planners and administrators, however, and probably would be met with criticism by others, such as Sommer (1974), who would maintain that the removal of windows is yet another way of de-humanizing buildings.

Open-Plan Schools

An important issue confronting present school administrators and teachers is the concept of the open-plan school. From an architectural standpoint, the open-plan school is similar to the open-plan office and offers the same advantages of internal flexibility to meet the shifting requirements of school loads and incorporation of curriculum offerings and staff personnel. The open school, however, is not simply a concept for ease of manipulating internal structure but is also an incorporation of significant changes in teaching philosophy. For example, *open* refers not only to spaces but to the internal social structure of the classroom. To support this philosophy, the traditional row-and-column seating arrangements have been done away with, and the classroom area is arranged functionally by providing separate areas for reading stories, arts and crafts, and individual study. The apparent philosophy is that the child should be able to use these areas in a much less structured manner than in the traditional classroom. These design features, in terms of both the education program and the environment constructed to support it, conceivably lead to an enriched educational experience and hopefully to higher achievements at the individual level.

The open-plan school has not been without critics. Some individuals feel that younger children need the more formalized, structured activities offered by the traditional educational philosophy and design until they master basic educational and behavioral skills. In addition, specific features of open-school environments could have negative behavioral results. One such feature that may be a source of annoyance, at least from the teachers' point of view, is the possibility of increased disturbance due to noise. Although sound-absorbing materials, such as corkboard, may be incorporated into the partitions—and the partitions in many cases are more than 8 feet high—there still exists the distinct possibility of noise intrusion from one area of the school to another. This can be especially so in elementary schools, where periods of relatively noisy physical activity and conversation in one area may be impinging upon a time of relatively quiet study or individual work in another area. Another feature in totally open schools is the partial absence of door and wall control. Doors and walls in classrooms can serve two purposes: (1) control the entrance and egress of students into the area and (2) screen individuals occupying the spaces from the possible distractive influences of passers-by and their conversation in the passageways or in high-traffic areas of the spaces. If doors and walls are absent, these two control functions are not fulfilled.

There has been some research dealing with the open-plan school. Stebbins (1973) noted possible negative characteristics of open-plan schools in his study of disruptive or disorderly behavior in the classroom. The schools in which he conducted his observations were not designed for the specific objectives of the open-classroom or open-school concept. Nevertheless, they had walls that did not reach the ceiling and were sometimes made of ornamental brick rather than solid brick. They did not have doors and, in some cases, had only three walls. These features were provided to facilitate ventilation within the school. Although these features were provided for different purposes than those in open-plan schools, the results can be considered very much the same in terms of the absence of walls and doors. In his study Stebbins observed that students would carry on conversations with friends while in different classrooms. Although such behavior could be considered uncharacteristic and could certainly be thwarted by policies on classroom discipline, the possibility of noise intrusion from one classroom to another has at least been anecdotally documented.

Hurt (1975) also offers a comment that the vast open spaces of the "educational hangar" may prove slightly overwhelming or confusing to the younger students and result in their not being able to orient themselves satisfactorily to rooms, restroom facilities, and the different centers available to them. She suggests that, for the younger students, various cues be provided to allow differentiation of their territory from other territories in the building. This could be accomplished through the use of differentiation of scale, focal points, different colors in furnishings, equipment, and room partitions, and possibly directional signals in the form of built-in graphics.

Sanders and Wren (1975) noted that students from open schools do at least as well as students in traditional classrooms. Also, there is preliminary evidence reported by Schnee and Park (1975) that elementary-student scores in reading achievement were associated with remodeling a building to use the open-school concept. However, this is an associative relationship, not a cause-and-effect relationship. Thus, there is no guarantee that the improved student achievement in reading was due to the physical attributes of the open-school plan. It may have been due to the teaching orientation usually associated with the environmental arrangement of the open school. It also may be possible that simply having a new school has a temporary positive influence on student performance. As we mentioned earlier, these and other factors must be considered in order to develop a reliable data base from which to evaluate open-plan school environments.

COMMERCIAL ENVIRONMENTS

Commercial environments differ in many respects from the built environmental settings we have discussed up to this point. Most important is the purpose they are designed to fulfill. Commercial environments are designed, constructed, and evaluated in terms of their success in promoting or providing a suitable location for various consumer behaviors—eating, drinking, purchasing goods, services, or recreation. These behaviors are quite different from those expected in the environments previously discussed.

Second, the circumstances that bring a person to interact with features of the commercial environment are quite different. The customers in commercial establishments are there on a voluntary basis and are engaged in active pursuit of meeting their consumer needs. Although possibly influenced by marketing strategies and advertising campaigns, they have made a definite commitment to be there and will even endure some amount of environmentally induced stress in order to accomplish their buying mission. Anyone who has witnessed or participated in the shopping crush during the holiday season can attest to the doggedness of many consumers in achieving their purchasing goals. Finally, because of the nature of the differences between commercial and previously discussed environmental settings, the period of time individuals interact with commercial environments is relatively circumscribed and may be on the order of magnitude of minutes, versus years in some other settings.

These differences have implications for the type of research undertaken and the behaviors investigated. First, the commercial environment is a privately sponsored setting, in contrast to the public funding present in the institutional environments. Since the users of public-supported institutions are in many instances part of the public domain and relatively captive subjects, they make for more convenient populations for researchers to study. Also, since in these cases public funds are committed and are thus accountable to the fund providers, investigations of satisfaction and efficiency are relevant research topics. In contrast, commercial establishments are run by the profit motive and have no control over their consumers. Therefore, research investigations are not nearly so convenient. Further, satisfaction with the commercial environment is measured in terms of sales, not in terms of questionnaire results. For these reasons, research of the type we have seen in previous sections is not readily available for restaurants, bars, and department stores. We will present one research example that underscores the relative *unimportance* of design features in shopping situations, and we will report on an exploratory study dealing with ecological behavior in shopping centers.

Dimensions of Consumer Choice

In a methodological study Hudson (1974) investigated the images used by persons in reconstructing retailing environments, the dimensions used to describe them, and the relative importance of those dimensions in choosing in which business they would do their shopping. The commercial setting chosen by Hudson was grocery stores, something that is not too exciting but should have generalizable principles and possibly results. After questioning his subjects, he defined 24 dimensions they used in discriminating between grocery outlets. Among the most important in terms of proportion of subjects specifying them as attributes were convenience to home, price, service, selection and quality of goods, and hours open per day. In contrast, attributes that could be related to physical factors—atmosphere, organization, and physical size—were mentioned far less frequently than the other attributes. Also, when the subjects were asked to rank the attributes according to their importance, the dimensions that could be associated with physical design did not receive any meaningful rankings.

Results such as these do not lend much importance to physical-design factors in any equation predicting consumer behavior. However, Hudson's method could be applied to any retailing environment to determine whether these results are generalizable to other types of establishments.

Since Hudson's subjects were relatively homogeneous (college students), their choices may have been influenced by social or marketing factors, as discussed by Mehrabian (1976). His premise is that commercial establishments are often designed with a particular clientele in mind, most often defined by age, income, and, to some extent, social status. Thus, for example, a clothing or department store projects a certain image. If the store's image matches the self-image of a particular individual, that person will more than likely attempt to shop there. At that point the individual may consider the dimensions reported by Hudson: convenience, price, service, and selection and quality of goods.

Shopping Malls

The gathering of dozens of stores in one enclosed environment appears to be a retailing trend that will continue in the foreseeable future. It is less costly in terms of construction, energy consumption, and maintenance than separate buildings for each retail establishment. Also, by providing a judicious mix of stores, mall operators can appeal to a broad spectrum of individuals, although the collective image of the stores may still exert some influence on the sorts of people who go there.

If we can assume that shopping malls will continue to be constructed, it would appear that evaluations by consumers of the features they are dissatisfied with *may* have implications for renovations or future projects. Preiser (1973) supplies some brief recommendations based on an exploratory study conducted in a shopping mall. Shoppers commented on the absence of food stores, hardware outlets, drugstores, and newsstands. They also commented on the seating areas in the mall and indicated that they preferred them to be removed from main traffic areas and that the seats have some sort of backrest. Finally, young mothers indicated that informal play areas for children adjoining the seating areas would be desirable. These recommendations are quite relevant because they are based on perceived needs of mall customers. However, given the orientation of business toward profit, they would be important only if the customers felt strongly enough about them to avoid the mall in the future. In this case, since the customers were interviewed while shopping, it is apparent that they had not yet chosen to avoid the mall for these reasons.

ENERGY AND THE BUILT ENVIRONMENT

As the first edition of this text was being prepared, North America was immersed in an energy crisis. Long lines at gas stations and pleas to lower winter and raise summer thermostats were commonplace. However, there was a feeling that the immediate crisis and the associated concern would gradually subside, and they did. At the present writing the question of adequate energy has again become a national-priority issue both in Canada and the United States. The full impact of the initial energy crisis is now being realized as the governments of these countries have increased funding for alternatives to conventional energy production, such as solar and wind devices. Simultaneously, national measures aimed at reducing energy consumption are being constantly developed and implemented. Thus, it appears that present and future supplies of energy will continue to be an issue of national importance.

Granting that energy concerns will be here for the foreseeable future, one might be led to ask, "What does the energy issue have to do with environmental psychology, especially in built environmental settings?" As it turns out, the built environment is highly related to energy, especially to energy consumption. Using figures supplied by the National Bureau of Standards, Caudill, Lawyer, and Bullock (1974) state that buildings account for approximately 30% of the energy consumed in the United States. Further, it is estimated that about 40% of the energy consumed by buildings is wasted. A proportion of this energy loss can be attributed to building-usage practices, such as overheating and overcooling. However, a substantial proportion of the consumption is also related to design/construction practices in use when energy supply and cost were not prime concerns. The design practices related to energy consumption are primarily concerned with illumination, heating, and cooling. Given this, the behavioral perspective on energy consumption and buildings begins to have relevance. Specifically, if the physical features of buildings are changed to reflect the new concern over energy consumption in providing illumination and temperature control, what are the potential behavioral results? Our discussion will focus on several aspects of building design and their implications for satisfaction, comfort, and performance.

Glass and Windows

One of the factors considered in an energy-conservation program for buildings is the use of glass. Engineers often think of glass in terms of the BTUs (British thermal units) transmitted through it to the outdoors by heating systems in winter and cooling systems in summer. Conversely, glass can be considered in terms of BTUs of heat gained indoors as a result of its orientation to the sun. Finally, engineers can think of glass in terms of providing natural illumination for buildings. For environmental psychologists, behaviorally oriented architects, and consumers, glass is a window providing daylight and a view of the outside world. In our earlier discussions, windows were found to be very important to the occupants of buildings. They considered daylight superior to artificial light and tended to overestimate the daylight received from windows. Building occupants also wanted windows to see outside. Given the importance of glass from both an energy-engineering and a behavioral standpoint, it appears that design manipulations of windows could have consequences for the satisfaction of building occupants.

Caudill and his co-workers (1974) discuss several design options available to reduce energy consumption through glass. Although their work is aimed at preserving windows for human use, each of their suggestions prompts questions that require answers. For example, one strategy to reduce solar heat gain through windows is to recess them into the building rather than place them flush with the exterior surface. Recessed windows can reduce both the view and, naturally, the amount of daylight available through them. A practical question from a behavioral standpoint might be "Is the view or perceived available daylight more important to building occupants?" Other questions can be directed at other design strategies. If overall window area in a building is reduced to cut down on energy loss or heat gain, to what extent can the window area be reduced before occupant satisfaction is affected? Another strategy is to construct the building with windowless walls on the exterior surfaces and to arrange the building around a courtyard and provide windows oriented to this interior view. However, it is not known whether such "constructed" views offer the same degree of satisfaction as windows that are oriented to the outside world. Answers to such questions would offer design teams a behavioral-data base to use in considering the relationship of glass and windows to energy consumption.

Illumination

Interior lighting can be supplied by either natural or artificial means. In our discussion of windows, the trade-offs between solar gain, light distribution, and a view were briefly considered. When artificial-lighting systems are discussed, energy consumption again is a topic worth consideration.

In North America the general lighting supplied in offices is quite high because, in most cases, the designers do not know what the exact office configuration will be. Office configurations are also subject to change. Thus, the general illumination level is made high enough to support almost every configuration and work situation. Quite naturally, such a practice may consume more energy than is needed to supply adequate illumination to every office user. Liljefors (1973) notes that the use of general lighting to increase the illumination level at a work surface is an expensive proposition. The cost of providing additional lighting increases disproportionately to the amount of increased footcandles made available at the work surface. Also, the cost of energy to produce the additional lighting increases. Finally, increased lighting causes heat gains that must be offset by even more energy consumption to keep the building at a stable temperature. Caudill and his colleagues (1974, p. 46) state that heat generated from lighting systems can account for as much as one-half of the cooling load. Both Liljefors and Caudill's group advocate a decreased emphasis on general lighting by providing higher illumination in local, task-related areas. This has been practiced for quite some time in factories with no reported negative effects. Therefore, any efforts at energy conservation in this area should be met with positive total results.

Temperature and Comfort

The task of providing a shirt-sleeve indoor climate in the face of seasonal variations has been accomplished by relying on increasingly larger heating and cooling systems. Confronted with energy concerns, designers and engineers have responded with a variety of structural strategies for reduced consumption. Increased use of insulation, incorporation of more mass into the structure itself, and judicious choice of building materials have all been suggested as solutions. The incorporation of these features conceivably will have little, if any, impact on human behavior. However, one suggestion that could have behavioral implications is the idea of locating parts of buildings underground. From our discussions about the importance of seeing the outside world, it would seem that people living and working in buried environments would be dissatisfied unless some attempt was made to provide simulated outside environments by using courtyards or partially exposed outside walls. Thus, comprehensive evaluations of user satisfaction should be undertaken as underground buildings begin to be used more extensively.

A strategy to reduce energy consumption in already existing buildings is to control the indoor temperature by voluntary reductions in winter and increases in summer. Recall that Nemecek and Grandjean (1973) reported that most persons interviewed were comfortable in temperatures ranging from 71 degrees to 75 degrees F (21.6 to 23.8 degrees C). Their study was done in Western Europe, where typical indoor temperatures are 2 to 3 degrees F lower than in North America. It is interesting to note that the lower end of the temperature range in their study (71 degrees F) is 3 to 6 degrees higher than that suggested as a temperature to be used in voluntary energy-control measures during our recent energy pinches.

Similarly, Caudill and his co-workers (1974) suggest that temperature controls be adjusted so that the high side of the comfort envelope is used in summer and the low side is used in winter. Individuals would then be expected to adjust their clothing to compensate for any discomfort. But in spite of personal adjustments, following the guidelines and suggestions may still cause individuals to perceive these temperatures as uncomfortably hot or cold. The extent to which this may affect their attitudes and job performance is yet to be determined but should be kept in mind.

Because of the relative recency of energy concerns, many of the relationships we have mentioned among conservation measures, building design, and human behavior are at best tentative or hypothetical. However, if designers, engineers, and social scientists are at least aware of potential relationships, possible behavioral consequences can be considered in the design/construction/evaluation process. The process can and should be viewed as an opportunity for creativity, not as an additional design constraint (Eberhard, 1976). Caudill and his co-workers sum up the problem and the prospects most appropriately: "We can learn how to save energy. . . . We have the technology. Can we learn to fulfill the needs of the human being at the same time?" (p. 87). Taken in a more general context, their statement also serves to underscore the whole point of studying human behavior in the built environment.

CHAPTER 5

THE BUILT ENVIRONMENT: CITIES

We have seen in previous chapters how various aspects of the built environment—rooms, houses, buildings, neighborhoods, and so forth—may affect behavior. These kinds of built environments can be thought of as subsystems of the ultimate built environment, the city. Although in this chapter we will be discussing studies dealing primarily with the urban environment and behavior, the reader should remember that, directly or indirectly, the behavior studied is influenced by all the subsystems that make up a city.

LIVING IN THE CITY

As pointed out earlier, environmental attributes may elicit either approach or avoidance responses (Wohlwill, 1970; Mehrabian & Russell, 1974). Nowhere is this more apparent than in cities. The individual living in a city is continually exposed to a tremendously diverse array of environmental attributes, some of which may have great appeal while others serve as a source of threat. Thus, although the urban environment may impose major restrictions on some types of behavior, it offers the opportunity for a variety of other kinds of behavior that no other environment permits.

It is impossible, of course, to begin to list all the environmental attributes that characterize life in the city and to discuss which of these serve as sources of satisfaction or dissatisfaction for those living there. This is due to the fact that city dwellers are an extremely heterogeneous population, differing tremendously in virtually every characteristic—economic, educational, motivational, and so forth. Consequently, what a wealthy executive living in an expensive house in a suburb and commuting to a plush downtown office would consider satisfying or dissatisfying about life in the city might be quite different from what a welfare recipient living in a slum area would consider satisfying or dissatisfying. Because of this heterogeneity, researchers conducting environmental studies in urban areas must be careful to spell out the characteristics of the persons being studied.

Some features of urban environments, however, do have some effect on the majority of city dwellers. Unfortunately, these features are negative aspects of the urban environment and, in combination, have resulted in what has become known as the *urban crisis*. The complexity of the urban crisis is cogently spelled out by Arthur Naftalin (1970), whose background includes not only a Ph.D. in political science but also eight years as mayor of Minneapolis. He says:

> The subject is so broad and wide and deep, affecting us in so many different ways, it has come to be all things to all men. It involves concerns that are at once governmental, economic, social, psychological, technological, moral, and philosophical, and it covers all aspects of community life and individual behavior: human relations, law enforcement, housing, sanitation, health services, education, income distribution—name it and you name a part of the urban crisis.
>
> . . . It involves the full sweep of our physical environment: growing congestion and pollution, the waste of our natural resources, especially our land, the critical lack of adequate housing, the failure to preserve open space, the growing problems of water supply, drainage, and waste disposal, and the baffling explosion of technology that has introduced speed and movement and change at a pace that confuses and bewilders almost everyone.
>
> On the social side the crisis is not only a matter of poverty although this is certainly its single most critical element. It involves a changing value structure that is fundamentally altering the nature of family life and the overall pattern of human relationships. It also involves an alarming increase in the use of alcohol and drugs and mounting tensions that derive from growing insecurity and our inability to control or discharge hostility. It involves a general weakening of our major institutions of social control, especially the family and education [pp. 108–109].

Although these comments were made in 1970, the factors mentioned as well as others still contribute to the urban crisis and have a profound impact on the lives of millions of city dwellers. Nonetheless, we know very little about the behavioral responses associated with urban problems. Environmental psychologists have investigated only a few of these problems, so in most cases we can only speculate about the effects of a particular aspect of the urban crisis on behavior.

Although we have little data linking a specific urban problem with specific types of behavior, we do have data showing that the problems associated with the urban crisis contribute greatly to most persons' feelings of dissatisfaction with urban living. Survey results differ according to the characteristics of the particular segment of the urban population sampled, but nearly everyone lists the same environmental attributes as important contributors to dissatisfaction with city life. High population density, leading to overcrowding, is on most lists, as are crime, aggression, and violence, poor housing, and virtually all the other urban problems listed by Naftalin. Thus, determining what factors appear to be important in contributing to dissatisfaction with city life is not particularly difficult. It is more difficult to investigate the factors contributing to satisfaction.

Sources of Satisfaction with City Living

Obviously, cities appeal to a great many people for a great many reasons. Cities offer varieties of experience that can be found nowhere else, and many of these can serve as a source of intense personal satisfaction. As Milgram (1970a) suggests, "cities have great appeal because of their variety, eventfulness, possibility of choice, and the stimulation of an intense atmosphere that many individuals find a desirable background to their lives" (p. 1461).

More research has been conducted on the urban environmental factors that contribute to dissatisfaction than on those contributing to satisfaction. In addition, much of the research that has dealt with the satisfactory aspects of urban living focuses on the factors in the immediate neighborhood in which an individual resides and does not deal with attributes of the larger area—the community and region—that may be satisfying or dissatisfying. In other words, most of the concern has been with features of the microresidential environment as sources of satisfaction rather than with the attributes of the city of which the residential area is a part. Although it seems reasonable to assume that eliminating the problems associated with the urban crisis would result in a higher percentage of people being satisfied with urban life, there is little systematic research in this area.

In attempting to determine the satisfying aspects of a microresidential environment, researchers have generally concentrated on (1) the physical characteristics of the residences and the surrounding area and (2) the social interactions of the residents. Actually, of course, it is not feasible to separate the two; the physical characteristics to a large extent determine the types of social interactions. In previous chapters we discussed a number of studies that demonstrated the importance of such physical factors as location of doors and windows in determining friendship patterns and social interactions among residents of various types of housing developments. Also important are personal space and privacy in determining level of satisfaction or dissatisfaction. Although we will not consider these factors here, it should be kept in mind that they are important sources of satisfaction with city living. In this section we will discuss studies dealing with characteristics of neighborhoods that are found satisfying by two distinctly different populations, one made up of residents of high-income suburban neighborhoods and the other of residents of a slum area.

Resident Satisfaction in an Urban Slum

In recent years a great deal of attention has been focused on urban slums and the problems associated with them. Residents of these areas have called attention to themselves not only by demonstrations and riots but also by becoming much more vocal and making themselves heard at local and national governmental levels. The result has been a number of government programs, such as urban renewal. Although funds for these and other programs are more limited than in the past, interest in slum areas and the behavior of their residents continues.

Unfortunately, the available data do not present a very clear picture of slum areas and their populations. One reason, of course, is that no two slum areas are alike. As Fried and Gleicher (1972) point out:

> Slum areas undoubtedly show much variation, both variation from one slum to another and heterogeneity within urban slum areas. However, certain consistencies from one slum area to another have begun to show up in the growing body of literature. It is quite notable that the available systematic studies of slum areas indicate a very broad working-class composition in slums, ranging from highly skilled workers to the nonworking and sporadically working members of the "working" class. Moreover, even in our worst residential slums it is likely that only a minority of the inhabitants (although sometimes a fairly large and visible minority) are afflicted with one or another form of social pathology [pp. 137–138].

Keeping in mind, then, that there are major differences among slum areas and that the findings of studies of one area may not be completely applicable to other areas, let us consider the study by Fried and Gleicher (1972) dealing with residents of Boston's West End. The data in this investigation were based on a probability sample of residents and included only households with a female between the ages of 20 and 65. Of the residents in the sample, 55% had either been born in the area or had lived there for at least 20 years. The authors report that there was a marked residential stability and that the majority of the residents had changed housing within the West End little if at all. This finding, of course, is contrary to the commonly accepted view of a slum area as having a highly transient population. Fried and Gleicher also found that, contrary to the popular view of slum dwellers' feelings about the area in which they live, 75% of the sample liked living in the West End while only 10% disliked living there.

In the exploration of the reasons for such a high rate of satisfaction, two major factors emerged. One is that the physical area has considerable meaning as an extension of the home, and various parts of the area are delineated and structured on the basis of a sense of belonging. In other words, the local area around the dwelling unit is viewed as an integral part of the home. The strength of a feeling of belonging in an area—that is, a sense of localism—was an important factor in determining whether the residents liked or disliked living in the area.

The second factor is that the residential area provides a framework for a vast and interlocking set of social ties, which serve as an important source of satisfaction. Fried and Gleicher found a strong association between the respondents' satisfaction with living in the West End and the social relationships they had established. The study revealed a variety of social relationships, but kinship ties (those involving the nuclear families of both spouses) appeared to be even more important than relationships with neighbors; "the more extensive these available kinship ties are within the local area, the greater the proportion who show positive feeling toward the West End" (1972, p. 144). However, Fried and Gleicher stress that the absence of these kinds of relationships does not necessarily mean that negative feelings about the area will be expressed. In many instances, residents without strong social ties reported very positive feelings about the West End, so that alternative sources of satisfaction must exist for some people.

This study also revealed the importance of physical space and the special uses of the area made by the residents. A complete discussion of these factors would again involve us in such concepts as personal space, privacy, territoriality, and so forth. Basically, however, in working-class areas, such as the West End, home is viewed as the local area rather than just the dwelling. The boundaries between the dwelling unit and its immediate environment are usually much more "permeable" in slum areas than in middle-class areas. In the slum a great deal of activity occurs outside the dwelling: children play in the streets, women go out in the street to talk with friends, families gather on steps and talk with neighbors, street corners serve as meeting places for social exchanges, and so forth. The external environment, in a sense, becomes an extension of the dwelling. Fried and Gleicher state:

> In conjunction with the emphasis upon local social relationships, this conception and use of local physical space gives particular force to the feeling of commitment to, and the sense of belonging in, the residential area. It is clearly not just the dwelling unit that is significant but a larger local region that partakes of these powerful feelings of involvement and identity. It is not surprising, therefore, that "home" is not merely an apartment or a house but a local area in which some of the most meaningful aspects of life are experienced [p. 151].

Apparently, then, life in a slum area furnishes enough sources of satisfaction that a high percentage of the residents like living there. This fact has important implications, particularly for urban-renewal projects. It has typically been assumed that altering the physical characteristics of slum areas by means of new dwellings or relocation of residents benefits not only them but the city as a whole. Perhaps so; we still know very little about the behavioral consequences of living in a slum. However, we also know little about the behavioral effects of massive changes in the physical characteristics of slums or of forced relocation. Yet it would appear that the local area provides the framework for an extensive social integration that slum dwellers find highly satisfying. Programs that dislocate people and destroy social relationships may have deleterious effects that outweigh the expected benefits.

Resident Satisfaction in Suburbs

In an effort to determine the sources of community appeal, Zehner (1972) studied four suburban locations, each within 15 to 18 miles of a major metropolitan area and having primarily affluent, well-educated residents. The median home value was more than $33,000 in each of the four areas, and the median family income was more than $17,000. (Keep in mind that these home values are now probably closer to $60,000 and the median income closer to $30,000.) In two of the areas, the proportion of married couples with both husband and wife having at least a B.A. degree was more than 40%; in the other two areas it was 17% and 20%. Obviously, the residents of these areas differed greatly from the respondents in the study done by Fried and Gleicher.

When asked to rate the community in which they lived as excellent, good, average, below average, or poor, more than 80% of the residents in each of the suburbs rated their community as excellent or good. Among the reasons given for positive evaluations were well-planned and accessible physical facilities; good schools; friendly neighbors; relative safety from crime; good access to stores, jobs, and so on; good environmental quality in that trees, lakes, hills, and so on were available; plenty of space; and little congestion.

In addition to investigating the factors contributing to community satisfaction, Zehner gathered data on the factors involved in neighborhood satisfaction. (See Figure 5-1.) He grouped these factors into five general categories: neighborhood density, accessibility of facilities, respondent's home, social compatibility, and neighborhood maintenance level.

Zehner found that the respondents in the least dense neighborhoods, which are the quietest and furnish the most privacy, expressed a high level of satisfaction with the neighborhood. The lack of noise in neighborhoods with low densities seemed to be the most important variable in the neighborhood-density category. Accessibility of facilities was not found to be highly associated with neighborhood satisfaction, although in families with children the adequacy and accessibility of playgrounds were important.

Social compatibility was a source of neighborhood satisfaction, just as it was in the slum study. However, Zehner found that his respondents felt it

Figure 5-1. Resident satisfaction is high in neighborhoods like this one; they meet the criteria of privacy, high maintenance level, low noise level, and so forth. (Photo by Lars Larmon.)

more important to have neighbors they felt were compatible than neighbors with whom they frequently interacted.

Neighborhood maintenance was most highly related to satisfaction in the communities studied. Maintenance level of the neighborhood had a correlation coefficient of .56, friendliness of .44, and similarity of neighbors .36. Neighborhood density, as it related to noise level, had a correlation of .34. The factors least related to neighborhood satisfaction were those involving accessibility of various community facilities.

The Fried and Gleicher and Zehner studies, as well as several others that have not been discussed, indicate that a significant percentage of city dwellers report being satisfied with life in the city. These studies have isolated several attributes of the urban environment that serve as sources of satisfaction. It should be kept in mind, however, that other attributes of the urban environment are viewed as threatening. Perhaps the surveys conducted to determine the sources of satisfaction with city living do not sufficiently take into account the unsatisfactory aspects of city life in the questions asked of the respondents. That several surveys show a high percentage of city dwellers reporting that what they would most like to do is to move to more rural areas may indicate they are not as satisfied with city life as one might assume.

Some Dimensions of Urban Environmental Quality

As pointed out by Carp, Zawadski, and Shokrkon (1976) in their study of the quality of urban environments,

> investigations into the nature of environmental quality have not defined the concept in terms of its dimensional properties. Many of the studies in this area have not been directed toward analysis of the global concept but rather toward understanding a selected aspect of it. Most have relied heavily upon expert judgment, but recent evidence indicates that experts' judgments do not coincide with those of the residents [p. 246].

Carp and her associates designed a study involving a large number of items that are descriptive of urban environmental quality and that were largely developed by residents. The items were rated by a large sample of adults who represented a major portion of the population of one metropolis. The ratings were then subjected to a factor-analysis procedure that, basically, combines or groups items together because of common properties, or "factors." Thus, in this study the 100 items on the questionnaire, when factor-analyzed, yielded 20 factors that could be interpreted meaningfully as dimensions of residential environmental quality.

It was found that five dimensions emerging from the analysis reflect some aspect of *noise* as an important feature of environmental quality. Although noise had previously been identified as an important aspect of residential quality, this analysis showed that noise is not a single dimension but rather several separate factors. For example, noise disturbing indoor activities is distinguished from that disturbing outdoor activities. The source of the noise—for example, in one's own or a neighbor's home, outside one's own or a neighbor's home, or from aircraft and trains—makes up the other dimensions.

A second cluster of factors is related to *aesthetics* or, more specifically, the aesthetic quality of the physical environment of the neighborhood. This cluster also contains five dimensions. An important factor has to do with the general appearance of the neighborhood. Air quality, maintenance by residents within one's own block, and maintenance service (by others, such as street crews) are other factors. The last factor, labeled "environmental correlates of alienation," includes evaluations of one's own block as close or cramped versus open or spacious; cold versus warm; active/busy versus quiet/tranquil.

A third cluster consists of three factors concerned with various descriptions of *neighbors,* such as unfriendly/friendly, not helpful/helpful, snobbish/not snobbish, nosey and gossipy versus tending to mind their own business, and so forth, as well as with the residents' feelings about being in the area, such as feeling lonely, that would be influenced by the respondents' perceptions of their neighbors.

A fourth cluster is labeled *safety* and involves two dimensions—traffic safety and safety/security of self and property. In the latter dimension are included concern over personal injury and loss of property due to house-breaking, concern over being attacked on the street, being injured in a construction zone, or having to walk where there are no sidewalks, and a general feeling about the safety of the area around the home.

The fifth cluster, *mobility,* refers to two types of mobility—automobile and nonautomobile. Important aspects of automobile mobility include traffic conditions on freeways, access to freeways from the home, ease of getting around local areas, and parking conditions. In the case of the nonautomobile factor, convenience of public transportation and ability to get around by walking are important.

Finally, a cluster labeled *annoyances* was identified. It includes three dimensions: solicitors, lack of privacy, and animal nuisances.

This study demonstrates the usefulness of a factor-analysis approach for determining the various dimensions of urban residential environmental quality. In discussing the various dimensions delineated in the study, the researchers point out: "Some of them resemble dimensions previously discussed in the literature, but this analysis more finely differentiates some previously proposed dimensions, merges others, and uncovers new dimensions" (Carp, Zawadski, & Shokrkon, 1976, p. 249). They add: "The clean and meaningful dimensions produced suggest that the approach should be used in future efforts to clarify the meaning of environmental quality and to refine methods for its measurement" (p. 262).

The Image of the City

Studies such as those by Fried and Gleicher, Zehner, and Carp and her co-workers give the investigators some idea of how their respondents view the neighborhood or community in which they live. Other researchers have been more specifically concerned with the image that cities hold for their inhabitants or for visitors and have designed some ingenious techniques for studying these images. Typically, these methods are based on the assumption that inhabitants of a city acquire a "cognitive map" of the city and that this map results from both the personal characteristics of an individual and the physical characteristics of the city. The problem for the investigator, then, is to develop ways to "read" the maps carried around in the heads of the inhabitants. In this section we will discuss several of the procedures that have been developed and used by researchers interested in these cognitive maps of the city.

The Urban Atmosphere

One of the factors important in forming an image of a city has been referred to as the *urban atmosphere.* (See Figure 5-2.) Psychologists have found it hard to define just what an urban atmosphere is and to isolate its components. However, Heimstra and McDonald (1973) point out some of the components that may be important:

> Obviously, the look, or physical layout, of a city will have an effect on its atmosphere; some would argue that the look of Paris or London or New York can be equated with their atmospheres. There are undoubtedly many visual components of a city that contribute and are therefore of interest to anyone who is concerned with urban atmosphere.
> For example, the tempo, or pace, of a city contributes to its atmosphere. A visitor to a city is immediately impressed with the apparent hectic quality of the life. This may be an erroneous impression (empirical data are lacking), but it is certainly part of the atmosphere. Similarly, the density of the population, the types of people represented in the population, and the attitude and behavior of the people toward each other and toward visitors all contribute. It is a complex interaction of the inhabitants' characteristics and the city's characteristics that forms the "urban atmosphere" [p. 46].

Because the interaction between the inhabitants' characteristics and the characteristics of the city is complex, the urban atmosphere is difficult to quantify. For example, consider some of the personal characteristics that will determine an individual's impression of a city. Milgram (1970a) suggests that three personal factors can affect an individual's response to a city. First, a person's impression of a particular city will depend upon his or her standard of comparison. A Parisian who is visiting New York may have an impression of a frenetic city; to a native of Tokyo, New York may look relatively leisurely. Second, the perception of a city is affected by the status of the perceiver. A tourist, a newcomer to the city, an old-timer, and someone who is returning to the city after a long absence all may have different perceptions of the city. Finally, a person comes to a city with preconceived ideas and expectations about it. Even though these preconceptions may not be accurate, they contribute to the impression of the city.

Milgram (1970b) also describes a study he conducted dealing with "the atmosphere of great cities." Questionnaires were developed and administered to 60 persons who were familiar with at least two of three cities—London, Paris, and New York. The questionnaires were designed to elicit descriptions of the cities and, in general, to illuminate the character of the cities. For example, one item on the questionnaire asked the respondents to list several adjectives that they felt applied to a particular city. Analysis of these adjectives showed that New York elicited more descriptions concerned with its physical qualities, pace, and emotional impact than did Paris or London.

Figure 5-2. Many factors contribute to the atmosphere of a city, including the characteristics of the inhabitants and the characteristics of the city. Among the characteristics of the city are its cultural and artistic components. (Photo of Oslo, Norway, by Lars Larmon.)

For London, the respondents placed greater emphasis on social interactions than on physical surroundings. For Paris, the respondents were about equally divided in the emphasis placed on interactions with the inhabitants and on its physical and sensory attributes.

Another approach to studying the impressions created by a city is exemplified by the research of Lynch (1960).

The Lynch Studies

Kevin Lynch's book *The Image of the City* describes studies conducted in Boston, Massachusetts; Jersey City, New Jersey; and Los Angeles, California. Although we cannot begin to summarize Lynch's discussions of the characteristics of these cities and the findings of his studies in the space available, we will consider in some detail the methods used in his research. Lynch's book provides a detailed rationale for his approach, and his findings have important implications for urban designers.

Lynch used two principal methods in studying the image of these cities. In the first method a sample of citizens were interviewed about their image of the urban environment. In the second method trained observers made a systematic field reconnaissance of each city. Using information that had proved significant in the analysis of pilot studies, these observers mapped the presence of environmental elements, their visibility, their image strengths or weaknesses, and so forth. This approach allowed for a comparison of the data from the interviews with the data from the field analyses.

The interviews were lengthy, each taking about an hour and a half, and were tape recorded. According to Lynch, the subjects were greatly interested in the interviews and often displayed emotion. The subjects were asked to:

1. Tell what came to mind when they thought about their city and give a broad description of it.
2. Draw a quick map of the central area of the city as though they were sketching for a stranger the location of some point.
3. Describe in detail their trip from home to work. They were also asked to do the same for an imaginary trip along a route given by the interviewer. Their emotional reactions to each trip were requested together with the physical description.
4. Give what they thought were the distinctive elements of the central area of the city.

Essentially, then, the interview consisted of asking the subjects to sketch a map of the city, to give a detailed description of several trips through the city, and to give a brief description of the parts of the city they felt to be most distinctive or vivid. The analysis of the images obtained through these questions was limited to the effects of physical, perceptible objects, although Lynch points out that there are other influences on the development of an image of an area, such as its social meaning, its history, its functions, and even its name. Lynch found that the physical elements of the city images could conveniently be classified into five types: paths, edges, districts, nodes, and landmarks.

Paths are streets, walkways, transit lines, railroads, and so forth. They are channels along which the observer moves and for many people are the predominant elements in their image of a city. *Edges* are the "linear elements not used or considered as paths by the observers." They may be shores, railroad cuts, borders of developments, and so forth, but each serves to separate one region from another or to relate and join two regions. Edges are also important organizing features of a city for many observers. *Districts* are the "medium-to-large sections of the city, conceived of as having two-dimensional extent, which the observer mentally enters 'inside of,' and which are recognizable as having some common, identifying character." *Nodes* are important or strategic areas that a person can enter and that are foci to and from which the person is traveling. These areas are junctions, places of a break in transportation, crossings or convergences of paths, and so on. They may also be such features as street-corner hangouts and enclosed squares. As

Lynch suggests, "Some of these concentration nodes are the focus and epitome of a district, over which their influence radiates and of which they stand as a symbol." In their image of a city, people almost always have nodal points, which in some cases are the dominant features of the image. Finally, *landmarks* are, like nodes, points of reference. However, landmarks typically are physical objects, not areas. Examples of landmarks are towers, signs, and stores (pp. 47–48).

The analysis of the images also showed that the five elements did not exist in isolation; typically, districts were structured with nodes, defined by edges, penetrated in various ways by paths, and often had a number of landmarks sprinkled throughout. As Lynch points out, however, although his method allows for collection of adequate data about single elements, it does not yield much information about element interrelations, patterns, sequences, and wholes. He stresses that other methods must be developed to study these vital aspects of images of cities.

Other Kinds of Psychological Maps

The psychological-mapping technique used by Lynch is relatively unstructured; the persons interviewed responded to questions or instructions in an open-ended fashion. A method of psychological mapping used by Milgram (1972) is more structured. He showed his subjects color slides of a variety of scenes in New York and asked them to identify the locations. The scenes were selected in an objective fashion by means of a coordinate-grid system, with each intersection of a latitude and longitude line defined as a scene. For economy purposes the viewing points were narrowed down to 25 in the Bronx, 22 in Brooklyn, 31 in Queens, 20 on Staten Island, and 54 in Manhattan. The subjects were recruited through an advertisement in *New York Magazine.* Most of the 200 subjects obtained were in their twenties (mean age of 28.9), and a slight majority were women. The "median" subject held a job at the minor professional level and had lived in his or her neighborhood five to ten years and in New York City more than 20 years.

The subjects, who were tested in groups, were each given an answer booklet and a neighborhood map and told to become familiar with the map. They were informed that the primary purpose of the study was to discover how well people can recognize various scenes of the city. The color slides of the various scenes were then projected on a screen. The subjects were asked to imagine that they were seeing the scenes from the window of a bus touring the city and to indicate in the answer booklet the borough where each scene was. They were also asked to identify the neighborhood and the street of each scene. The entire testing procedure took about an hour and a half.

By summing the percentage of correct responses for all the scenes in a borough and dividing this figure by the number of scenes, Milgram determined the "index of recognizability," or mean, of the borough. The means of the boroughs were as follows:

Manhattan	64.12%
Queens	39.64%
Brooklyn	35.79%
Staten Island	26.00%
Bronx	25.96%

In considering these results, the reader should bear in mind that the scenes used were not selected because of the likelihood they would be recognized but were randomly sampled.

Milgram also found substantial differences according to borough in the proportion of scenes placed in the correct neighborhood. A scene in Manhattan was five times more likely to be placed in the correct neighborhood than was a scene in the Bronx or on Staten Island and about three times more likely to be placed correctly than was a scene in Brooklyn or Queens. A similar pattern was found in street-location identification. Thus, as Milgram states:

> New York City, as a psychological space, is very uneven. It is not at all clear that such world cities as London, Paris, Tokyo, and Moscow have comparably uneven psychological textures. It would be extremely interesting to construct a similar psychological map of other cities of the world to determine how successfully each city, in all its parts, communicates to the resident a specific sense of place which locates him in the city, assuages the panic of disorientation, and allows him to build up an articulated image of the city as a whole [p. 200].

Among other studies of city images is that by Rand (1969), who used an approach similar to Lynch's. Rand interviewed airplane pilots and taxi drivers and found that the images of cities known to both groups were markedly different. In another study Rozelle and Bazer (1972) interviewed residents of Houston, Texas, to determine how they assigned meaning and value to elements of their city by asking them what they regarded as important about the city, how they saw the city, and how they remembered it. Each type of question yielded a different response. Rozelle and Bazer concluded that such verbal tasks can elicit the same kind of information as Lynch's sketch maps and have greater flexibility. Studies using photographic techniques include those of Honikman (1972), who showed his subjects photographs to determine the relationship between qualitative evaluation and physical characteristics of an environmental display, and Kaplan and

Wendt (1972), who studied urban environmental preference by means of a series of slides.

The findings of these and similar studies might have important implications for urban design, but, unfortunately, little use has been made of them. As pointed out by Bell, Randall, and Roeder (1973) in discussing the work of Lynch:

> The original work by Kevin Lynch has had a significant effect on designers only because of the usefulness of his analytical methods as a tool of description. Because Lynch has been required reading for every design student for a decade, and because of the value of his work in creating a framework into which personal observations can be placed, he has been successful. This is a tool for visual awareness, but not a design methodology [p. 22].

In an article dealing with "designing for people," Porteous (1974) suggests that cognitive-map studies may be useful in the design process "as a basis for the reconsideration of urban esthetics, and as a means of analyzing the underlying dynamics of human behavior" (p. 49). He also points out that further development of the methodology is necessary. Similarly, Beck and Wood (1976) argue that coherent theory is lacking in the cognitive-mapping field and "that the map as method has been thrown into some doubt" (p. 198). These investigators discuss, in some detail, the mental operations involved in the creation of a cognitive map. It is apparent that this is an extremely complex process and that many factors are important in creating and interpreting a cognitive map. Beck and Wood point out that the creation of a cognitive map involves subject variables, in that the subject brings to the mapping situation a complex store of information prior to receiving instructions. It also involves variables concerned with orienting in or touring about the urban environment—for example, tour routes and schedules, guide information, travel mode, and so on. There are also variables dealing with the nature of the field itself, such as regular versus irregular street-grid patterns, landscape features, density, and so forth. Finally, there are variables associated with the nature of the experiments themselves, "principally with regard to the kinds of maps employed by investigators in retrieving or recapturing information about the field" (p. 205). Possibly, with a better understanding of the nature of cognitive maps and the variables important in creating these maps, they will become more useful tools for those in the design field.

CITY LIVING—A PATHOGENIC EXPERIENCE?

It is a common belief that factors associated with living in the city cause a variety of forms of social pathology as well as several types of physical pathology. In the limited space available, we cannot begin to discuss all the types of social pathology that in all likelihood are caused by aspects of the urban environment. Take, for example, crime in urban areas. This form of social pathology receives a great deal of attention and has been extensively researched. Studies of the relationship between certain kinds of built environments and crime were discussed in some detail in an earlier chapter. In these studies the urban environment was considered to be the independent variable and crime rates or types the dependent variable. Other researchers have used the crime rate as the independent variable and determined the effects of high crime rates in an area on the behavior of noncriminals living in that area. Thus, investigators have reported not only changing attitudes toward crime and criminals with increasing crime rates but also more overt behavior changes, such as buying watchdogs, installing new locks and burglar alarms, and carrying tear-gas pens and other weapons. Although crime is certainly a factor that is viewed as a threat by most city dwellers and may have pronounced effects on their behavior, a discussion of this topic is beyond the scope of this book. We will restrict our discussion here to several topics of more direct interest to environmental psychologists.

Only relatively recently has widespread interest been shown in the possible pathological qualities of city dwellers' everyday behavior. The numerous articles on this behavior—often based on no more than casual observation—suggest that urbanites do not care, that they lack spontaneity, that they have withdrawn behind a critical facade, that they exist in a perennial state of distrust and reserve, and on and on. As we shall see later in this chapter, such conclusions are often the result of comparing the behavior of urbanites with that of persons living in rural areas. However, what must be questioned is the interpretation of the behavior of city dwellers as patholog-ical. Michelson (1970) points out in discussing the behavior of urbanites and the tendency of observers to label this behavior pathological:

> In glorifying the assumed open, trusting, and spontaneous posture of nonurban peoples, they treat what may well be a different pattern in cities as a harmful one. And harmful it may be, both absolutely and in certain circumstances, but labeling it as pathological is nonetheless a value laden decision, which may say as much about the labelers as those labeled [p. 149].

Regardless of whether such behavior patterns are pathological, investi-gations have suggested relationships between certain characteristics of the urban environment and mental illness, heart disease, hypertension, and some types of behavior patterns. Frequently, the common element in these relationships is stress. Because of the importance of the concept of stress in considering the causes of some of the assumed pathological effects of city living, we will discuss this concept in some detail.

The Concept of Stress

Such terms as *stress* and *stressor* are part of our everyday vocabulary. Unfortunately, however, they mean different things to different people, not only laymen but also researchers. Where one researcher uses the term *stress*, another might use *anxiety*, still another might use *frustration*, and a fourth might use *conflict*. All may be referring to the same phenomenon (Lazarus, 1966, p. 2). Since there is no agreed-upon terminology in the study of stress, any definition of terms here will necessarily be somewhat arbitrary.

In the literature in this field, two kinds of stress are often distinguished—*systemic* and *psychological* stress. The concept of systemic stress was first introduced into the biological sciences by Hans Selye in 1936, and since that time thousands of articles and numerous books have been published on this topic. Basically, systemic stress is a situation in which an organism's tissue systems react to or are damaged by certain types of noxious stimulations. Selye (1976) refers to these noxious stimulating conditions as *stressors; stress* is the reaction of the organism's system to the stressors. In much of the research on systemic stress, some type of aversive stimulus, such as a chemical agent, heat, or cold, is introduced and manipulated and the effects of this manipulation on various of the subject's biologic systems determined.

Many types of stimulus situations do not, however, involve physical stressors, such as those typically used in systemic-stress studies, but will also result in responses considered to be reflections of a *stress state* in the organism. These stimulus conditions often involve psychological factors that serve as stressors. Although people may encounter situations involving physical stressors and systemic stress, they are much more likely to encounter psychological stressors. Whereas in systemic-stress conditions the stress response is physical changes in the organism's biologic systems, the response in psychological-stress situations is often quite different (though physical changes may also occur).

Let us briefly consider the conditions that produce psychological-stress reactions and the nature of these reactions. Appley and Trumbull (1967) point out that the stimulus conditions involved in psychological stress are

> characterized as new, intense, rapidly changing, sudden, or unexpected, including (but not requiring) approach to the upper thresholds of tolerability. At the same time, stimulus deficit, absence of expected stimulation, highly persistent stimulation, and fatigue-producing and boredom-producing settings, among others, have also been described as stressful, as having stimuli leading to cognitive misperception, stimuli susceptible to hallucination, and stimuli calling for conflicting responses [p. 5].

Obviously, then, many situations can be thought of as involving psychological stress. Although, as we have pointed out, there is a great deal of disagreement among researchers in this field, all the above have been used by investigators as operational means for defining and producing psychological stress.

Possibly a simpler way of viewing the complex of stimulus situations that result in psychological stress is in terms of a characteristic common to nearly all these situations. As Lazarus (1966) points out, "Psychological-stress analysis . . . is distinguished from other types of stress analysis by the intervening variable of threat. Threat implies a state in which the individual anticipates a confrontation with a harmful condition of some sort" (p. 25). Thus, many investigators feel that a stimulus situation involving the threat or anticipation of future harm may result in psychological stress. It should be pointed out that whether the situation actually is or can be harmful to the individual is irrelevant as long as the individual perceives it as threatening. It is also important to keep in mind that the term *harm* does not imply only physical damage of some sort. A situation can be seen as threatening and potentially harmful if it may involve embarrassment, loss of face, financial loss, and so forth.

In research on psychological stress, a number of types of responses have been used as indexes of stress. Lazarus suggests that these dependent variables fall into four major categories: reports of *disturbed affect, motor/ behavioral reactions, changes in the adequacy of various types of cognitive functions,* and *physiological changes.* Disturbances in affective states, such as anxiety, anger, and depression, are common stress responses, as are certain types of motor behavior, such as increased muscle tension, disturbances in speech, changes in facial expression or bodily posture, and loss of sphincter control. Changes in cognitive functioning are another response to stress; there "is an extensive literature on the effects of stress on perception, thought, judgment, problem solving, perceptual and motor skills, and social adaptation" (Lazarus, 1966, p. 7). A wide range of physiological and psycho-physiological measures have been used as indexes of stress states. Among these indexes are changes in blood composition, particularly in regard to eosinophils; increases in 17-ketosteroids in the urine; changes in adrenal-gland functioning; increases or decreases in the weight of various glands; and changes in heart rate, galvanic skin response (GSR), and critical flicker fusion.

It cannot be overemphasized, however, that the capacity of any situation to produce such stress reactions is very much dependent upon the characteristics of the person or persons involved. Situations that are perceived by some as threatening will be perceived quite differently by others. Moreover, the past experience of individuals with a particular situation will determine, to a great extent, their perception of the situation. Thus, with repeated exposure to a situation, *adaptation* may occur; the situation is no longer seen to be as threatening as it once was, and either no stress reaction takes place or it is considerably modified.

That individuals differ in the ways in which they perceive specific situations or stimulus conditions often makes research on psychological stress difficult. One cannot assume that all subjects perceive the stimulus conditions in the same way. Yet even if all subjects did perceive the situation similarly, personality factors and past experiences would determine to a great extent the stress reaction shown.

Stressors in City Living

Earlier in this chapter, some of the negative features of the urban environment that may have an effect on city dwellers were briefly mentioned. As Naftalin (1970) has pointed out, these negative features contribute to what has become known as the urban crisis, and any or all of them could be perceived as threatening by city dwellers. Crime, violence, aggression, overcrowding, deteriorating neighborhoods, excessive traffic, and so forth are perceived as threats by some city dwellers and, consequently, can be thought of as stressors. As previously discussed, any situation in which the individual perceives threat—whether real or imagined—can result in psychological stress. Obviously, the situations to be found in cities that might be perceived as threatening to someone are numerous, so the potential stressors are practically unlimited.

Recognizing, then, that there may be a variety of possible stressors depending upon a person's perception of the world, what sorts of situations have environmental psychologists been most concerned with? What have they considered the most relevant stressors to be researched and studied?

Crowding

One aspect of city living that has often been assumed to be stressful is high population density, which leads to the experience of crowding. Probably no other area of environmental psychology has received as much study as that concerned with crowding, territoriality, personal space, and privacy. These topics will be discussed in detail in Chapter 6. However, at this point we will briefly consider crowding as a possible stressor.

There is no shortage of "expert" opinion on the effects of crowding, and articles about its many expected adverse effects appear frequently. These articles, generally, are scantily documented or are based on animal-study data, correlational data, or opinion. Zlutnick and Altman (1972) reviewed *The Reader's Guide to Periodical Literature* for a ten-year period and, from a number of articles, derived 17 propositions concerning overcrowding or overpopulation that have been cited in the popular literature. The investigators grouped these popular conceptions in three categories on the basis of the types of undesirable effects attributed to crowding:

1. *Physical effects.* Starvation, pollution, slums, disease, physical malfunctions.
2. *Socidl effects.* Poor education, poor physical and mental health facilities, crime, riots, war.
3. *Interpersonal and psychological effects.* Drug addiction, alcoholism, family disorganization, withdrawal, aggression, decreased quality of life [p. 49].

Although there are a few controlled experiments on the effects of crowding (these will be discussed in the next chapter), most of the data supporting the popular conceptions of crowding effects come from animal and correlational studies. Animal studies have a number of limitations, and it is dangerous to generalize from these studies to human behavior. Correlational studies attempt to establish relationships between population density and such indexes of social disorganization as crime rates, frequency of physical and mental illness, and so forth. As noted earlier, a number of studies have found high population densities to be associated with high crime rates. Other studies have shown that certain types of physical illness are more frequent in high-population-density areas. However, Hay and Wantman (1969) compared the rate of such diseases as hypertension and heart disease (both presumably associated with stress) in New York City with national samples and found that hypertension rates were only slightly higher in New York. Heart disease was found to be lower in New York than in the United States overall. As Srole (1972) states, "the assumption that the city is inherently pathogenic for certain degenerative somatic disorders apparently may have to be rejected" (pp. 578–579).

Of the number of investigations attempting to link population density with mental illness, most report a positive correlation (Chombart de Lauwe, 1959; Faris & Dunham, 1965; Hollingshead & Redlich, 1958; Lantz, 1953). However, Srole questions the view that a heavily populated urban area is necessarily less "mentally healthy." He reviews research in this area and points out that differences between urban and rural mental-health figures are often not statistically significant and can be explained on the basis of factors other than population density. Srole concludes that the available data suggest:

1. For *children* under certain special combinations of conditions, both the metropolitan and rural slums are more psychopathogenic than are the adjoining nonslum neighborhoods.

2. For *adults* seeking a change in environment, the metropolis under most (but not all) conditions is by and large a more therapeutic milieu than is the small community, especially for the many troubled escapee–deviants among them [p. 583].

Apparently, then, we cannot state with certainty that the high population density of urban areas leads to such pathological conditions as mental illness, hypertension, and heart disease.

Information Overload

It has become convenient to think of our complex technological society in terms of systems in which industries, organizations, machines, and even people are considered to be interdependent components (subsystems) working together to achieve some objective. Systems analysts study the relationships among the subsystems and the ways in which these relationships contribute to the purposes of the system. These analysts tend to think in terms of *inputs* to the system and *transformations* of the inputs into *outputs.* If we think of a person in these terms, environmental stimuli are inputs; transformations are effected by a number of behavioral subsystems (perception, cognitive functions, memory, motivation, and so on); and outputs are behavior (Heimstra & Ellingstad, 1972).

If there are too many inputs for the system, either human or nonhuman, to cope with, we then talk about *system overload.* For humans, information overload can serve as a source of stress and may modify their behavior in a number of ways. Because information overload cannot always be avoided in people/machine systems, or in any other systems of which people are an integral part, research has been conducted to determine how people handle information overload and how it affects behavior. In a summary of some of this research, Miller (1964) lists the following adjustment processes that humans tend to use in response to information overload:

1. Omission, which is not processing information if there is an overload.
2. Error, processing incorrectly and failing to correct for it.
3. Queuing, delaying responses during heavy load periods and catching up during any lulls that occur.
4. Filtering, systematic omission of certain types of information usually according to a priority scheme.
5. Approximation, a less precise response given because there is no time for details.
6. Multiple channels, making use of parallel subsystems if the system has them at its disposal.
7. Decentralization, a special case of multiple channels.
8. Escape, either leaving the situation or taking other steps which cut off the input of information [p. 93].

Although the research dealing with these mechanisms has been conducted in laboratories, Milgram (1970a) suggests that somewhat similar adaptive mechanisms are involved in the behavior of city dwellers. He feels that city life is made up of continuous encounters with input overload and argues that this overload "deforms daily life on several levels, impinging on role performance, the evolution of social norms, cognitive functioning, and the use of facilities" (p. 1462). He discusses a number of responses adopted by city dwellers to deal with system overload. These include:

1. *Allocating less time to each input.* One way to adapt to some kinds of overload, such as encountering vast numbers of people each day, is to allow little time for these kinds of inputs. Thus, urban dwellers "conserve psychic energy by becoming acquainted with a far smaller proportion of people than their rural counterparts do, and by maintaining more superficial relationships even with these acquaintances" (p. 1462).
2. *Disregarding low-priority inputs.* Urban dwellers become selective; they invest their time and energy in carefully defined inputs while disregarding others. Thus, the urbanite walking down a street ignores such inputs as panhandlers and drunks.
3. *Redrawing boundaries in certain social transactions.* In this adaptive mechanism the burden of an overload is shifted to the other party in a social exchange. For example, "harried New York bus drivers once made change for customers, but now this responsibility has been shifted to the client, who must have the exact fare ready" (p. 1462).
4. *Blocking inputs.* Milgram uses as an example of this process the tendency of city dwellers to have unlisted phone numbers or to leave their phones off the hook. He also points out that a more subtle example of this response is when a city dweller discourages other persons from initiating contact by wearing an unfriendly expression.
5. *Diminishing the intensity of inputs.* The person responding in this way establishes "filtering devices" to avoid developing deep or lasting involvements with other people.
6. *Creating specialized institutions.* Various kinds of institutions are developed by city dwellers to "absorb inputs that would otherwise swamp the individual" (p. 1462). An example is the welfare departments that handle the needs of individuals who "would otherwise create an army of mendicants continuously importuning the pedestrian" (p. 1462).

Milgram's system-overload concept is an interesting theoretical framework for explaining the behavior of the urbanite in a wide range of situations. In his article Milgram deals with a number of specific consequences of responses to system overload and discusses how these responses make for differences in the behavior seen in cities and in towns. Although several of the investigations he cites will be discussed in this chapter, readers who are interested in pursuing this topic in more depth should read Milgram's article.

Noise Pollution

When we use the term *sound,* we are referring to both a form of physical energy and what we hear. In other words, sound can be thought of as having both physical and psychological dimensions. As physical energy, it consists of variations in air pressure caused by some type of vibrating body that has set air molecules in motion. We can measure this energy with various types of meters and specify, with considerable accuracy, the physical makeup of a particular sound. As what we hear, sound can also be studied as a psychological phenomenon. Measurement in this case is much less precise. Though the physical attributes of sound are related to its perceived attributes—that is, what we hear or experience when exposed to a sound—how the sound is perceived depends upon a variety of factors. We will discuss some of these factors later in this section.

Among the countless sounds to which we are exposed on a regular basis are some that are unwanted. They may be unwanted because they produce physiological or psychological damage or because they interfere with such activities as communication, work, rest, recreation, and sleep. When for these or other reasons a sound is unwanted, we refer to it as *noise.*

Noise pollution is becoming an increasingly serious problem in our society for several reasons. First, each year the number of new noise sources increases tremendously. Although transportation noise is the major source of complaint—and this problem grows yearly—numerous other new sources of noise, ranging from washing machines to construction equipment, appear each year. A second reason that noise pollution is becoming more of a problem is that demographic changes are causing more of the population to be exposed to noise sources. As more and more people move into urban regions, increases in population density significantly increase the number of people exposed to noise pollution.

Noise pollution promises to remain a serious problem. We have noise pollution because it is generally cheaper to produce noisy products by noisy means than quiet products by quiet means. Thus, the noise producers lack economic incentive to lessen their noise output. However, there is increasing public concern about noise pollution. Thus, as Goodman and Clary (1976) point out: "At the present time, environment problems such as air, water, and noise pollution are producing highly visible citizen activism" (p. 441). As we shall see, however, this activism is not always easily translated into meaningful action.

The nature of sound. When we talk about noise, we are, of course, talking about a particular type of sound that for various reasons is unwanted. As we have indicated, sound can be considered in terms of its physical characteristics and its psychological characteristics. Physically, sound has two characteristics, frequency and intensity.

Vibrating bodies cause air molecules to be alternately pushed together (positive pressure) and pulled apart (negative pressure), resulting in a wave of positive pressure moving through the air immediately followed by a wave of negative pressure. This is the sound wave that is the physical stimulus for hearing. The back-and-forth movement of the air molecules can be represented graphically with sine waves, as shown in Figure 5-3.

The *frequency* of a sound wave is indicated in cycles per second (cps) or, in more recent usage, *hertz* per second (Hz). In Figure 5-3 the middle sine

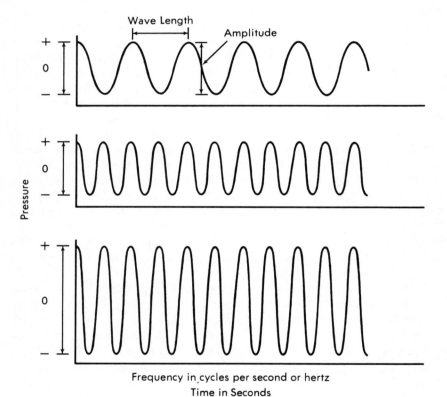

Frequency in cycles per second or hertz
Time in Seconds

Figure 5-3. Three sine waves that have different frequencies and amplitudes. The amplitude is the same for the top two sine waves, but the frequencies are different. The bottom sine wave has the same frequency (cycles per given period of time) as the middle wave, but it has twice the amplitude. From Heimstra, N. W., & Ellingstad, V. S. *Human behavior: A systems approach.* Monterey, Calif.: Brooks/Cole, 1972.

wave has a frequency twice that of the upper sine wave. Frequency, in cps or Hz, is a physical quality of sound. The frequency of a sound wave is primarily responsible for the psychological dimension of hearing that we refer to as *pitch*. In other words, how high or low a sound is perceived to be is primarily due to its frequency.

The *intensity* of a sound wave is the amplitude of the wave (see Figure 5-3). Note that in the figure the middle and bottom sine waves have the same frequency but the amplitude of the bottom wave is twice that of the middle wave. The psychological correlate of intensity (amplitude) is *loudness*. Thus, a particular sound wave will result in the auditory sensation of pitch, which is related to its frequency, and loudness, which is related to its amplitude.

The physical and psychological dimensions of sound are more complex than indicated here. For example, a change in intensity may also produce a perceived change in pitch, and a change in frequency may result in a change in perceived loudness. Moreover, we rarely encounter the pure tones illustrated in Figure 5-3. Normally, tones are complex and made up of a number of frequencies. This mixture of frequencies leads to a third psychological dimension of sound, called *timbre* or *tonal quality*.

The range of sound intensities to which people respond is so great that intensity is measured on a very large scale called the *decibel scale*. The decibel is a ratio indicating the relative difference in intensity between two sounds. However, this ratio has meaning only if everyone uses the same reference value. The reference value selected is .0002 dynes per square centimeter (a dyne is a unit of pressure), which is about the lowest change in pressure to which the ear is sensitive. It should also be kept in mind that the decibel scale is a logarithmic scale, which means that if one sound is 100 decibels more intense than another sound, it is 10 billion times more powerful. The sound-pressure (decibel) levels of a number of sounds are shown in Figure 5-4. On this scale the pain threshold is reached somewhere around 125–135 decibels. In other words, sound pressure around this level actually causes a person to experience a painful sensation.

When is sound unwanted? The manner in which a sound is perceived depends upon a number of factors. As mentioned previously, the psychological dimensions of sound—pitch, loudness, and timbre—depend upon the physical attributes of frequency and intensity and the mixture of different frequencies. When certain physical characteristics are present in a sound, it is more likely to be perceived as unwanted than when these characteristics are absent. However, other factors, such as situational variables, are also important. Thus, a particular sound might be considered unwanted in a church but not in a bar. Similarly, a sound may not be unwanted in the afternoon but may be considered noise at 2 A.M. Personality and past experience are also

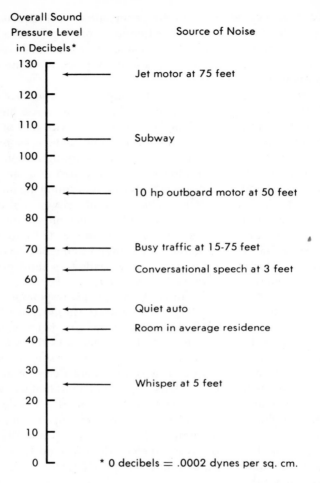

Overall Sound
Pressure Level   Source of Noise
in Decibels*

130 ──── Jet motor at 75 feet

120

110

100 ──── Subway

90 ──── 10 hp outboard motor at 50 feet

80

70 ──── Busy traffic at 15-75 feet
──── Conversational speech at 3 feet
60

50 ──── Quiet auto
──── Room in average residence
40

30 ──── Whisper at 5 feet

20

10

0   * 0 decibels = .0002 dynes per sq. cm.

Figure 5-4. Sound-pressure levels for a number of different sounds. From Heimstra, N. W., & Ellingstad, V. S., *Human behavior: A systems approach.* Monterey, Calif.: Brooks/Cole, 1972.

important variables in determining how a sound is perceived. A good deal of research has been conducted on all these variables.

As Kryter (1970) points out, the use of the word *noise* for unwanted sound sometimes results in confusion because there are two general categories of unwantedness. Very often, it is not the sound itself that is unwanted but the information that the sound conveys. For example, if we were awakened at night by a sound that we knew indicated the presence of an intruder, the information, not the sound, would be unwanted. Thus, we would not consider these sounds to be noise in the way we consider other kinds of sounds unwanted in a particular situation to be noise. People quite consistently judge the latter types of sounds to be unwanted, annoying, or objectionable, and it is these kinds of sounds that cause noise pollution.

Of the physical characteristics of a sound that result in its being perceived as noise, *loudness* appears to be most important. However, *frequency* is also a factor; high-pitched sounds are more likely to be considered unwanted than sounds with a lower pitch. Similarly, an *intermittent* sound is usually considered unwanted more often than a continuous sound of the same frequency and intensity. Duration, increases and decreases in intensity, frequency characteristics, and other physical characteristics are also associated with the degree of perceived noisiness of a given sound.

As one might expect, a variety of situational factors are important in determining whether a sound is perceived as noise. It would be impossible to list all the situational factors, but we can make some generalizations. When a sound interferes with some ongoing activity, the sound tends to be perceived as unwanted even though its physical characteristics may be such that normally it would not be considered noise. When some sound interferes with speech communication, for example, the sound is highly likely to be viewed as unwanted. When sleep is disturbed by a sound, the sound is even more likely to be considered unwanted. Sounds may interfere with a person's concentration, relaxation, work, and so forth. In general, then, when a sound interferes with some activity, it becomes a noise.

The individual's personality and past experience also interact with the situation and the characteristics of a sound to determine whether it will be considered unwanted. Research indicates, for example, that extroverts and introverts respond to sounds in a different fashion. There is some evidence that complaints about noise come disproportionately from neurotic people and that the individuals who are most annoyed by noise may have difficulties in personal adjustment. Attitudes, which are based on the past experience of the individual, play an important role in perceived noisiness. The attitude of the listener toward the source of a sound is critical in determining whether the sound is perceived as noise. Thus, the sound of a neighbor's lawn mower may not bother a person, while the sound of a motorcycle might.

Obviously, then, whether a sound is perceived as unwanted and, consequently, as noise is a complex affair and dependent upon a variety of variables that have just been touched upon in this section. Engineers are increasingly called upon to predict whether the sound of a piece of equipment, a new highway, or a new airport will be perceived as noise by the persons exposed to the sound. These predictions, at best, are often educated guesses, since the data needed to make the predictions with a high degree of accuracy are unavailable.

Noise pollution and behavior. A considerable amount of research has dealt with the effects of noise on human behavior. Much of this work has concerned the already discussed relationship between the physical characteristics of sound, situational variables, and personality variables and the perceived noisiness of various sounds. Typically, in these studies the variables listed above serve as the independent variables; the dependent variable is some indication of the annoyance or perceived noisiness elicited by a particular sound. The dependent variable is generally measured by a rating scale of some type.

Other studies have been concerned with community reaction to noise, generally that associated with aircraft or other types of transportation. These studies have usually measured attitudes toward the noise and the "bother" that is generated. Some investigations have attempted to correlate exposure to noise with hearing impairment, psychological disturbances, and various other health problems. Finally, a large number of laboratory studies have been conducted to determine the effects of noise on the performance of a variety of tasks. We will briefly summarize the findings of each of these types of studies.

Studies on community reaction to noise have shown that it is difficult to predict community response to noise because so many variables are involved. A significant percentage of people in a community exposed to high noise levels will indicate that they consider noise a problem. They will generally give as a reason that the noise interferes with their talking, sleep, and so forth. Typically, however, they do not try to have something done about the noise unless it is very loud. If the noise level reaches 90 decibels or thereabouts, most people will react vigorously with complaints and threats of action.

Investigations of community attitudes toward noise and the factors that will modify the attitudes have been relatively numerous. As might be expected, when the noise source is a major economic factor in the community, attitudes toward the noise are more favorable than when it is not. Many other situational and personal factors, such as the type of annoyance developed by the noise and the time when the noise occurs, will determine the attitude toward noise pollution. Research also suggests that more favorable attitudes toward noise can be established, sometimes by rather simple methods. For example, letters to citizens explaining a noise source and discussing its necessity were shown, in one study, to reduce significantly the percentage of people who considered the noise an inconvenience. Similar findings have been reported near military air bases when the public was made aware of the importance of the base and the efforts being made by the pilots for the comfort and safety of the citizens.

Even though studies do show that most members of a community often have negative attitudes toward noise pollution, only a few members make any effort to do something about it. This was shown in a detailed investigation conducted by Goodman and Clary (1976) of community attitudes and action in response to airport noise. They concluded, "While a majority of the persons living in the communities is bothered by aircraft noise at one time or another, only a small proportion actually has tried to do anything about it" (p. 466).

A large number of studies have dealt with the effects of noise on the performance of various types of tasks, but the findings are ambiguous. Some investigations show that noise has a detrimental effect on performance, other studies show no effect, and still other studies reveal that noise facilitates performance. What has become apparent is that the effects of noise on performance depend upon the characteristics of the noise, of the task, and of the individual. The frequency and intensity of the noise, as well as other physical characteristics, help determine the effect of the noise on behavior. Intermittency appears to be a particularly important physical variable; in several studies in our laboratory (Warner & Heimstra, 1971, 1972, 1973), intermittent noise with a 30% on/off ratio (1.5 seconds on, 3.5 seconds off) facilitated performance on a number of tasks. Task variables important in determining noise effects include how difficult the task is, whether it requires constant alertness, whether it is largely psychomotor or primarily mental, and how long the task takes. Personal variables include both transient and relatively permanent factors. A person's mood or motivation at a particular time is an important determinant of noise effects, as are personality, age, sex, and attitudes. The predictability of the noise and whether a person can control its termination influence the annoyance level of the noise and its effect on behavior (Glass & Singer, 1972; Reim, Glass, & Singer, 1972).

Most investigations have been concerned with the immediate effects of noise on performance. Glass and Singer (1972) were also interested in the behavioral aftereffects of exposure to noise. They report, "Tolerance for frustration, quality of proofreading performance, and ability to resolve cognitive conflict (i.e., response competition) were all impaired following exposure to high-intensity noise, providing the schedule of stimulation was aperiodic or unsignaled" (p. 156). Behavior following exposure to noise was most impaired if the noise had been unpredictable rather than predictable.

A number of studies have been conducted in real-world situations rather than in the laboratory in an effort better to understand the relationship between noise and behavior. In a study in a natural environment, Cohen, Glass, and Singer (1973) found that schoolchildren who lived on lower floors of buildings and were directly exposed to expressway noise showed greater impairment of auditory discrimination and reading achievement than did children who lived in apartments on higher floors and were less exposed to the noise. In a study by Bronzaft and McCarthy (1975) dealing with the effects of elevated-train noise on reading ability, it was found that the reading scores of children on the noisy side of the school buildings involved lagged behind the scores of children on the quieter sides of the buildings.

In an interesting variation on the usual type of noise/behavior study, Mathews and Canon (1975) investigated environmental noise level as a determinant of helping behavior. Two studies were conducted—one in a laboratory setting and one in a field setting. In each condition an "incident" was staged in which a subject could come to the assistance of another person (a confederate) who dropped materials that the subject, if he or she so desired, could help pick up. The dependent variable was the presence or absence of helping behavior, while the independent variable was the ambient noise level. The results showed that in both settings the subjects in the noise condition were less likely to offer help than the subjects in the quiet condition. The authors suggest "that the presence of high levels of noise may be an important factor not only in helping behavior but in other social interactions as well" (p. 576). It should be kept in mind, however, that the relationship between noise and behavior is complex and that all the variables associated with the noise, the tasks, and the person interact in unpredictable ways and make it difficult to state accurately the effects noise will have on performance.

Numerous studies have explored the relationship between noise and health. Long exposure to high-intensity noise does result in hearing loss. Because this fact has been well established, the U.S. government has set standards for permissible noise exposures. For example, under these standards the permissible sound level for an eight-hour workday is 90 decibels. A person may be exposed to 100 decibels for only two hours per day and to 110 decibels for only one-half hour. Though most people are now protected when they are at work, they are often exposed to noise levels that exceed the permissible exposure limits in other settings. For example, in discotheques and at rock concerts, music is often played for long periods at levels of around 110 decibels and sometimes as high as 120 decibels. Several studies have shown that persons who spend a good deal of time listening to music in these settings suffer either temporary or permanent hearing damage.

There have been reports that long exposure to noise may result in mental-health problems for some persons, but this conclusion is not well documented. There is also some evidence that there may be health differences among groups subjected to different noise exposures. A European study reports correlations between cardiovascular irregularities and intense occupational-noise exposure, and a study in Russia found that adults living near airports had a higher morbidity rate than did persons living some distance away. Additional European studies suggest that long exposure to noise may have still other effects on health (Antigaglia & Cohen, 1970).

In the United States the prevailing view among noise experts is that people's tolerance for noise is high and that they can usually adapt to present noise conditions without harmful physical effects. This view has been challenged, however, by researchers in the U.S. Public Health Service. Antigaglia and Cohen (1970) state:

> There is no question that noise or sound can cause physiologic changes. At issue is whether long-term repetitive exposures to noise can induce physical changes that are eventually degrading to the health of the individual. The position of the United States experts that noise has no ill effects is difficult to defend at this time in view of the absence of systematic study and objective data in this area. For example, epidemiological surveys concerned with the incidence of acute and chronic ailments in different work groups have never been undertaken in this country and are greatly needed. Such information could corroborate or refute findings from the European literature which . . . suggest apparent associations between noise and adverse health effects [p. 280].

Adaptation to the Environment

We have seen in this and previous chapters that certain characteristics of the physical environment are perceived as threatening by some individuals and, consequently, serve as stressors. Though we have emphasized the characteristics of overcrowding and noise pollution in the present chapter, the concept of a stressful environment has been discussed at various other points in the text. For example, certain types of housing areas have high crime rates, which are stressful for many residents, as are various geographic environments where the probability of natural disasters is quite high. A question of some interest to environmental researchers is how people are able to adapt to the various environmental conditions, many of which are stressful, in which they exist.

Psychologists and other scientists have known for many years that a sensory system is modified by the continuous presentation of stimuli. This process of modification is called *adaptation.* Although the physiological mechanisms underlying adaptation vary depending upon the sensory modality involved, adaptation as a general process occurs in all the senses when they are exposed to constant stimulation. However, some of the senses adapt much more than others. Though we usually think of adaptation as resulting in a lowering of the sensitivity of the receptors involved, adaptation is a two-way process that can involve either a heightened or a lowered performance of the receptors. For example, when the eye becomes dark-adapted, the receptors become much more efficient during the course of adaptation. A light that would not be detected before adaptation is easily detected after adaptation has taken place. However, in the case of cutaneous adaptation, the receptors become less efficient. Thus, we may feel a sweater on our bodies when we first put it on, but in a short time we will no longer feel it. Taste and smell also adapt rapidly.

Most research on adaptation has involved simple dimensions of sensory intensity, such as brightness of light, temperature, and odor, and has been conducted under carefully controlled laboratory conditions. Adaptation to a real-world environment is undoubtedly much more complex because of the multidimensional characteristics of the stimuli involved. When attempting to generalize from the findings of laboratory studies on adaptation to the real world, a question raised by Wohlwill (1970) must be kept in mind: "How do they apply with reference to such stimulus attributes as complexity, incongruity, ambiguity, or to the multidimensional character of such workaday experiences as that to which a commuter on the New York subways or the Los Angeles freeways is subjected?" (p. 307). Although we know that people are endowed with an excellent adaptive physiology and that they do adapt to many kinds of built and natural environments, there are a great many questions about this process to which we do not have answers.

One question has to do with the characteristics of dimensions of the stimuli that are important in the adaptation process. Intensity of stimulation is, of course, an important dimension and has been of concern to designers for some time, as shown by their attempts to provide specified levels of noise and illumination. Wohlwill (1966) points out other dimensions of stimulation that may be important: complexity, variation, surprisingness, and incongruity. But how does an investigator measure and manipulate such dimensions as surprisingness and complexity to study adaptation to them? Because this task is so difficult, we do not have a great deal of information about these aspects of the physical environment and about adaptation to them.

Another key question has to do with the limits of adaptability. Both common sense and some empirical data indicate that there are limits, but as yet we know relatively little about them or about the behavior to be expected when the limits are reached. It is generally assumed that there is an optimal level of stimulation along the stimulus dimensions listed above and that too little or too much may have detrimental effects. Indeed, sensory-deprivation research, in which subjects are deliberately deprived of much of their normal sensory experience, has shown that under these conditions hallucinations and other behavioral effects occur. Typically, however, environmental conditions are such that excessive stimulation occurs rather than too little. When these excessive limits are reached, in some cases physical or mental illness may occur. In other situations more subtle effects—nervousness, irritability, and so forth—are likely to occur. Undoubtedly, there are significant individual differences in level of tolerance to stimulation, but, again, relatively little is known about this topic.

A last question is that of long-term adaptation effects. Wohlwill (1966) asks: "What are the long-range effects of exposure to a given environment featured by a particular level of intensity, complexity, incongruity, etc. of stimulation?" (p. 36). He then goes on to question "whether, in spite of the individual's capacity to adapt to an astonishingly wide range of environmental conditions, such prolonged exposure to stimulus environments falling near the extreme of the complexity or intensity dimension, for instance, may not leave its mark nevertheless" (p. 36). This type of exposure probably does have a variety of behavioral effects. Recall, for example, our earlier discussion of system overload encountered by persons living in cities and the adaptive responses that are thought to develop to reduce the overload. According to the system-overload theory, many of the types of behavior thought to characterize urbanites can be considered to be adaptive responses that have developed because of long exposure to excessive stimulation.

Adaptation to the environment, then, is a process that obviously does occur, but we know very little about it. Since adaptation may result in a wide range of behavior, this topic should be an important area of research for those interested in behavior/environment relationships. Although various researchers are beginning to pay some attention to the problem, questions like those asked above still do not have answers.

THE BEHAVIOR OF URBANITES

It has been suggested that the conditions existing in urban areas may affect the behavior of people living there. It is usually assumed that, since many of the conditions encountered in urban areas do not exist in more rural areas, there should be differences in the behavior of rural and urban dwellers. Thus, one would not expect the same adaptive behaviors on the part of rural residents that Milgram suggests occur with urban residents as a response to system overload. Consequently, some of the research dealing with the behavior of urbanites has been aimed at comparing their behavior with that of residents of more rural areas. In this section we will discuss a few of the variety of approaches and techniques involved in the study of the behavior of urbanites.

It should be kept in mind, however, that investigations described in other parts of this text would also be appropriate for consideration here. For example, the studies dealing with the effects of high population density on behavior, which are covered in Chapter 6, are relevant, as are several of the studies discussed in previous chapters. The reader should keep in mind that the point in the text where a particular study is discussed is a somewhat arbitrary decision on the part of the authors and does not mean that the study would not be equally relevant elsewhere in the book. For example, although it might be convenient to discuss a certain behavior/environment interaction under the heading of "Multiple-Family Dwellings," that these dwellings are probably located in an urban area and their inhabitants' behavior affected by the urban environment would justify discussing the interaction under "The Behavior of Urbanites." Much environmental-psychology research is directly or indirectly concerned with the behavior of urbanites although usually not labeled as such.

Some Studies of the Behavior of Urbanites

As suggested, if system overload, resulting from the conditions existing in cities, brings about adaptive behavior, then persons living in small towns should not be overloaded and consequently should not show the adaptive forms of behavior supposedly characteristic of city dwellers. Studies comparing the behavior of urbanites with that of small-town residents under a number of different conditions would reveal whether differences in behavior do in fact exist. Unfortunately, though speculation about differences abounds, very little empirical research is available. Milgram (1970a) cites two unpublished investigations illustrating this kind of research and suggests that additional research along the lines of these studies might be profitable.

One of these two studies is by Altman, Levine, Nadien, and Villena (1969), who compared the behavior of city and town dwellers in agreeing to extend a type of aid that increased their personal vulnerability and required some trust of strangers. In this study the investigators (two males and two females) each rang doorbells in New York and in small towns, explained that he or she had lost the address of a friend living nearby, and asked to use the telephone. The researchers made 100 requests in the city and 60 in the small towns.

The investigators had much greater success in gaining admittance in the small towns than they did in the city. Although the female researchers were admitted more often in both the city and the towns than were the male researchers, all four were at least twice as successful in gaining admittance in the small towns as in the city. Besides recording the number of admissions, the investigators observed qualitative differences in the behavior of the rural and urban residents. They reported that the small towners were much more friendly and less suspicious than the city dwellers, who, even if they did allow the investigators inside, appeared suspicious and ill at ease.

The other unpublished study, by McKenna and Morgenthau (1969), was designed, in part, to compare the willingness of urbanites to do favors for strangers with that of small towners. The favors requested entailed a small amount of time and inconvenience but, unlike the requests in the other study, could in no way be interpreted as posing any personal threat. The researchers telephoned a number of people living in Chicago, New York, and Philadelphia and in 37 small towns in the same states as the three cities. Half the calls went to homemakers and the other half to saleswomen in women's apparel shops. The investigator phoning represented herself as a long-distance caller who had been mistakenly connected with the respondent. The investigator began asking for information on various topics and then said "Please hold on" and put the phone down. After nearly a minute she picked up the phone and asked for more information. The investigator assigned scores to the respondents on the basis of how cooperative they had been.

The results of the study showed that the homemakers were less helpful than the saleswomen in both the cities and the towns. Milgram (1970a) points out, however, that "the absolute level of cooperativeness for urban subjects was found to be quite high, and does not accord with the stereotype of the urbanite as aloof, self-centered, and unwilling to help strangers" (p. 1465).

The results of these two studies can be discussed in terms of Milgram's system-overload concept. One possible reason for the urbanite's reduced social involvement seen in these studies is the need to reduce system overload. Milgram points out that the "ultimate adaptation to an overloaded social environment is to totally disregard the needs, interests, and demands of those whom one does not define as relevant to the satisfaction of personal needs" (p. 1462). One example of this type of adaptation is the failure of urban bystanders to help a person in distress. A similar adaptation can be seen in less urgent situations, as illustrated in the study by Altman and his co-workers, in which many urbanites failed to lend a hand to a stranger at their doors. The McKenna and Morgenthau study also reveals adaptive behavior in that cooperation with the caller was a matter of social responsibility.

Milgram (1970b) stresses that we have very little objective documentation of the differences between urbanites and town dwellers. However, his urban-overload concept does provide a theoretical framework for further study of these differences. He states:

> The concept of overload helps to explain a wide variety of contrasts between city and town behavior: (1) the differences in *role enactment* (the urban dwellers' tendency to deal with one another in highly segmented, functional terms; the constricted time and services offered customers by sales personnel); (2) the evolution of *urban norms* quite different from traditional town values (such as the acceptance of noninvolvement, impersonality, and aloofness in urban life); (3) consequences for the urban dweller's *cognitive processes* (his inability to identify most of the people seen daily; his screening of sensory stimuli, his development of blasé attitudes toward deviant or bizarre behavior; and his selectivity in responding to human demands); and (4) the far greater competition for scarce *facilities* in the city (the subway rush, the fight for taxis, traffic jams, standing in line to await services). I would suggest that contrasts between city and rural behavior probably reflect the responses of similar people to very different situations, rather than intrinsic differences between rural personalities and city personalities. The city is a situation to which individuals respond adaptively [pp. 161–162].

There are, of course, other studies that have, for one reason or another, compared the behavior of persons living in urban and rural areas. For example, Martin and Heimstra (1973) tested children in rural and urban areas on a perception-of-hazard test to determine the degree of risk perceived in a number of scenes depicting different levels of hazard—a child holding a gun, loading a gun, swallowing aspirin, and so forth. Children living in urban and rural areas perceived different amounts of hazard in different scenes. For example, children in rural areas saw more hazard in the gun scenes, in street scenes, and in scenes depicting various types of power tools than did children in urban areas. Lowin, Hottes, Sandler, and Bornstein (1971) compared the "pace of life" in urban and rural settings and reported that there is a consistent tendency for a number of activities to be carried out more rapidly in an urban setting than in a rural setting. In another study dealing with the pace of life in cities, Bornstein and Bornstein (1976) observed the rates of pedestrian locomotion over a constant distance in a number of cities and towns in Europe. Their conclusion was that "city dwellers move at significantly greater speeds than their smaller town compatriots" (p. 558). They further concluded that city life is carried on at an increased tempo.

In addition to studies dealing with differences in behavior between urban and rural residents, some investigations have been aimed at identifying differences in behavior between residents of different cities. One such investigation was conducted by Feldman (1968), who studied the behavior of residents of Boston, Paris, and Athens toward compatriots and foreigners. This study, which was quite complicated, consisted of five situations, or experiments, in which "native" or foreign experimenters (a Frenchman in Boston, for example) were involved in situations with residents of each of the cities. The situations were (1) asking a resident of the city for directions; (2) asking a resident to do a favor for a stranger by mailing a letter (half of the letters were unstamped); (3) asking a resident whether he or she had just dropped a dollar bill (or the foreign equivalent) to see whether the resident would falsely claim money from a stranger; (4) deliberately overpaying a clerk to see whether the mistake would be corrected; and (5) determining whether cab drivers overcharged strangers or took longer routes to obtain higher fares.

Feldman found that the more than 3000 subjects in the five experiments showed consistent differences in treatment of compatriots and foreigners. In the experiment in which directions were asked for, both the Parisian and the Athenian samples gave help more often at the request of fellow citizens than at the request of foreigners; in Boston there was little difference. In the experiment in which the subjects were asked to mail a letter for a stranger, there were no major differences in the way compatriots and foreigners were treated in Boston and Athens. Surprisingly, in view of the U.S. stereotype of Parisians' behavior, the Parisian subjects treated foreigners significantly better than their own compatriots. Moreover, the Parisians were significantly more honest in resisting the temptation to claim money falsely and, again, were less likely to make the false claim if a foreigner was involved than if a compatriot was involved. However, the stereotype of the typical Parisian cab driver held up; they overcharged foreigners more often than their compatriots. This was not the case in Boston or Athens.

The studies described were primarily concerned with comparing the behavior of urbanites with that of residents of rural areas or with comparing the behavior of residents of different cities. Other studies are investigations of a particular type of behavior thought to be associated with urban living. We will consider two studies of this type—one dealing with bystander intervention and the other with behavior in waiting lines.

We have already pointed out that one adaptive response to urban overload is to disregard the needs of others in circumstances ranging from intervening in an emergency to lending a hand to a stranger. An often-cited example of bystanders' refusing to become involved in the needs of someone else even if the person urgently needs assistance is the 1964 Genovese murder case in Queens. A young woman was stabbed repeatedly, and, even though her cries for help were heard by many persons, not one came to her assistance or even called the police until after she was dead. This murder, as well as other instances in which bystanders failed to help someone in serious trouble, has led to a series of controlled investigations of bystander intervention.

Probably the best known of these studies are those by Latané and Darley (1969). These studies involved a number of different experimental conditions. However, they all involved situations that were contrived in such a way that the researchers could observe the reactions of "bystanders" (who were actually subjects in the studies although they were not aware of it) to various kinds of "emergencies." For example, in one study the subjects were in a supermarket, where they were under the impression that they were to assist in a survey. They were placed in a room under a number of conditions. Some subjects were alone; some were joined by one or two other persons. The others were friends or strangers, in on the experiment or not, and so forth.

Shortly after the subject entered the room, a loud crash occurred in an adjacent room, together with moans and cries, as though someone had been injured. The dependent variable in this study was whether the subjects went to the assistance of the "injured" person and, if they did, how long it took them to do so. When the subjects were alone in the room, 70% of them intervened. However, under all the conditions in which more than one person was present, the percentage who intervened dropped sharply. Other studies involving faked emergencies and bystander intervention had the same results. The general conclusion drawn from these investigations is that the larger the number of bystanders, the less likelihood that any one of them will intervene in an emergency.

One characteristic of life in the city is the need to spend considerable time waiting in lines of one kind or another. Although operations researchers have recognized for some time that queues are inefficient and time consuming and have conducted research aimed at shortening and speeding up all kinds of waiting lines, only recently have psychologists become interested in the behavior of persons forced to wait in line.

Mann (1970) and his co-workers investigated the unique set of social rules and behavioral regularities associated with waiting lines. In a series of field experiments, they studied a number of waiting lines for tickets to football games, plays, and so forth. In other studies they formed their own queues experimentally in libraries and in other settings. They considered a number of aspects of waiting lines—social structure, line jumping, and other kinds of behavior. The researchers found that the social structure of a waiting line is focused on preservation of people's right to leave the line momentarily without losing their place. If they do not follow a clearly defined protocol when leaving, they may not be allowed back in the line. Mann points out that brief leaves of absence from the queue are accomplished by two universally recognized procedures:

> One technique is the "shift" system, in which the person joins the queue as part of a small group and takes his turn in spending one hour "on" to every three hours "off." . . . A second technique for taking a time out is designed especially for people at the end of the queue who came alone. They "stake a claim" by leaving some item of personal property such as a labeled box, folding chair, or sleeping bag. Indeed, during the early hours of queuing . . . the queue consisted of one part people to two parts inanimate objects [p. 392].

Although queue jumpers violate the basic norm of the queue, physical violence is rarely used to punish or eject the violator. Interestingly, the favorite hunting ground of the queue jumper is the rear of the waiting line rather than the front.

Another interesting form of behavior was noted in some lines. When it was known that there was a limited number of items available (100 tickets for a football game, for example), many more than 100 people typically lined up. In one study Mann asked every tenth person in a line to estimate how many people were ahead of him or her. Up to the point where the tickets were likely to run out, the person tended to overestimate the number ahead. In other words, if 100 tickets were available, people up to about 100 in line would estimate that there were more people ahead of them than there really were. After the critical point of 100, the mood of the queuers began to change, and people constantly underestimated the number of persons ahead of them. The investigators called this the wish-fulfillment hypothesis. The researchers also found that the longer the line, the stronger was its drawing power and that a rapidly growing line tended to draw bystanders into it.

Activity Patterns of Urbanites

The studies on the behavior of urbanites that have been described are concerned, for the most part, with a particular type of behavior demonstrated by residents of urban areas and, in some cases, of rural areas. Obviously, an almost infinite range of behavior occurs, and researchers have focused on only a very small segment of this range. In a somewhat different approach, Chapin (1974) attempted to study activity patterns in the city and to describe a broad range of activities engaged in by urbanites. In this investigation, about 225 activities were classified into 12 main behavioral categories. The 12 classes involved activities associated with principal job, eating, shopping, homemaking, family activities, socializing, participation (church and organization), recreation and other diversions, watching TV, rest and relaxation, miscellaneous, and sleeping. Essentially, the measures obtained dealt with: (1) the kinds of activities people engaged in, with the proportion of the sample engaging in each activity and the time allocated to each; (2) when people were engaged in these activities (for example, by different hours of the day or night for weekdays, Saturdays, and Sundays); and (3) where people engaged in these activities. A number of variables, such as sex, race, and work status, were considered. The survey was conducted in Washington, D.C., and in two residential areas near Washington—one predominantly Black and the other largely White.

Space limitations do not permit a thorough discussion of Chapin's findings, which are presented in detail in *Human Activity Patterns in the City.* In brief, the results show that activity patterns vary according to work status, social status, racial or ethnic group, age, sex, and other variables and that activities change during the course of the week. Although these findings are not particularly startling, this study does represent a systematic effort to obtain a more comprehensive picture of what urbanites do and emphasizes that our studies on the behavior of urbanites touch only a small segment of their behavior.

CHAPTER 6

SOCIAL BEHAVIOR AND THE PHYSICAL ENVIRONMENT

In the previous chapters we discussed the relationships between features of the physical environment and human behavior. In those chapters we were concerned with many different kinds of behavior; in this chapter we will focus on social behavior in relation to the physical environment. The topic of social behavior is, of course, a broad one, and there are a number of textbooks dealing only with this subject. Our concern in this chapter will be with several specific kinds of social behavior that have been of particular interest to environmental psychologists.

The social-behavior concepts of crowding, personal space, territoriality, and privacy are central to environmental psychology, and the first three have been subjected to considerable research. In fact, although we have emphasized the lack of theory in environmental psychology, it is in this general area that enough research exists to provide at least the beginnings of a theoretical framework. In discussing this lack of theory, Proshansky, Ittelson, and Rivlin (1976) point out that these concepts have the oldest history and firmest foundations in the field and that "The most advanced theorizing is proceeding in these areas, and if a generally accepted and unifying theory has not yet emerged, one is nevertheless quite clearly in its developmental stages" (p. 7).

Environmental psychologists' interest in these concepts is reflected in the number of recent publications dealing with them. In addition to numerous articles in journals and chapters in books concerned with research in this area, several books have been published presenting literature reviews as well as theoretical formulations on the environment and social behavior (Altman, 1975; Freedman, 1975; Saegert, 1976). The journal *Environment and Behavior* published a special issue on privacy, territoriality, personal space, and crowding (Vol. 8, No. 1, 1976).

These reviews, however, tend to emphasize that our understanding of this type of behavior is still at an early stage and that much more research is needed to unravel the complexities of the relationships between social behavior and the environment. For example, there is considerable evidence that, when animal populations reach a certain level, physiological and social pathologies develop. The relationships between high population levels and human behavior, however, are not so clear. Some investigations suggest an association between high-density living and various social and physiological pathologies, while other studies have not found negative consequences of high densities. Despite such contradictory results, Saegert, Mackintosh, and West (1976) state: "Increasingly, studies are leading various investigators to the conclusion that the level of density in a situation can have psychological and social effects" (p. 34). However, they also emphasize the complexity of the density/behavior relationships by pointing out that the effects depend upon such variables as the characteristics of the space involved and the characteristics of the people in the situation, such as sex, socioeconomic level, social norms, and other factors.

Crowding and *personal space* are two concepts that have generated considerable research, and in recent years the concept of *territoriality* has interested researchers working with humans as well as those working with animal populations. *Privacy* is another concept that has assumed increased importance in the theorizing of some researchers (Altman, 1975), although there is almost no empirical research on this topic. We cannot cover all four concepts in great detail, but we will present representative studies and current thinking on each. First, however, it is necessary to define the terms *density* and *crowding*.

A DEFINITION OF TERMS

In the literature dealing with the relationships between physical settings and social interactions, the terms *density* and *crowding* sometimes are used interchangeably and sometimes are used to mean quite different things. In addition, different investigators often attach somewhat different meanings to these terms. Because this lack of uniform usage results in some confusion, researchers in the field (Rapoport, 1976; Choi, Mirjafari, & Weaver, 1976) have recently been reexamining and redefining the two concepts, and a more consistent interpretation is beginning to emerge.

Basically, density is a physical concept, while crowding is a psychological concept. Stokols (1972) and Altman (1975) limit *density* to a physical meaning—that is, the number of people or animals per unit of space. In their view, *density* has no inherent psychological meaning. Crowding, on the other hand, is a psychological state, a personal, subjective reaction that is based on the feeling of too little space. Although density is a necessary condition for the development of the feeling of crowding, density alone is not always sufficient to create the feeling. For example, in many situations, such as a party consisting entirely of friends, the density level is high, but there is no feeling of crowding. However, in another situation with the same density level but with strangers present, crowding will be experienced. Whether a situation is perceived as crowded depends not only on the number of people present (that is, density) but also on a variety of personal, social, and environmental variables. Much of the research on crowding has been concerned with the identification and study of these variables.

Although this distinction between crowding and density is the commonly accepted one, it should be emphasized that not all researchers feel it is adequate. For example, Rapoport (1976) states that "while density begins with the number of people per unit area, it must go beyond that" (p. 9). He suggests that density has at least two components: people per unit of physical space and what he refers to as perceived density. He argues that density itself is a perceived experience and involves both the physical and the social factors in a situation. Thus, areas with the same number of people may have very different perceived densities based on "qualities such as a high degree of enclosure, intricacy of spaces, high activity levels, many uses, and so on" (p. 10).

Perceived density, then, is basically a psychological process. Though it might appear that this view of density confounds the concepts of density and crowding, according to Rapoport it does not. He states:

> The difference is the following. Density is the perception and estimate of the number of people present in a given area, the space available, and its organization, whereas crowding or isolation (which we could call affective density) is the evaluation or judgment of that perceived density against certain standards, norms, and desired levels of interaction and information [p. 10].

In other words, crowding can be thought of as a condition in which there is a discrepancy between perceived density and some ideal that the individual has established for a particular situation. Rapoport feels that nothing in this redefinition of *density* changes any of the findings on crowding; instead, it adds an intermediate step that allows for cultural and personal differences (p. 28).

Several other investigators have also used somewhat different definitions of *density*, and some interesting comparisons of definitions can be made. However, in this chapter, unless otherwise indicated, we will use the traditional definition of *density*—the number of people or animals per unit of space.

Our definition of the concept of crowding can also be expanded. Zlutnick and Altman (1972), in a more detailed analysis, list the variables associated with crowding under three main headings. In the first group are *situational variables*, which include factors associated with a particular setting, such as the number of people per unit of space within a room or residence (inside density); the number of people per unit of space outside the room or residence, as in the neighborhood (outside density); the duration of exposure to the situation; and the characteristics of the setting, such as the type of room, the way in which the space is laid out, and so forth. These and other situational variables help determine whether the experience of crowding takes place.

The second category consists of *interpersonal determinants* of crowding. One of these, which is probably of primary importance, is the ability of a person to control interactions with others. People control interactions with others in a variety of ways, ranging from locking themselves in a room in order to avoid interacting with others as completely as possible to subtle nonverbal behavior, such as turning away or assuming some type of bodily posture that may discourage interactions. As Zlutnick and Altman point out, "a whole spectrum of techniques is used to pace relations with other people. One hypothesis is that when these control mechanisms break down, especially in high-density situations, a condition commonly described as crowding may exist" (p. 52).

The third group of variables is *psychological factors.* We have already stated that the past experience and the personality of a person are important in determining whether crowding is experienced in a particular situation. Among the many additional factors that may help to determine whether a person feels crowded are expectations about a particular situation in what is considered an optimal density and the perceived ability to control interactions.

Choi, Mirjafari, and Weaver (1976) feel that the concept of crowding "is so inadequately developed that students involved in its study seem to confront serious problems and confusion in the process of developing their conceptual framework" (p. 345). These authors examine several current conceptualizations of crowding and then propose an alternative model. Their model is based on seven propositions that summarize basic assumptions about the concept of crowding, the variables affecting crowding, and the types of responses occurring in crowded situations. Although the model is too elaborate to examine here, we will consider these seven propositions in some detail because they present an excellent framework for the discussion of crowding presented later in this chapter.

1. Crowding is not just people per unit of space. Rather, it is an "experiential state of a psychological phenomenon which accrues from the interaction of a relatively high density of people with other social, personal, and physical environmental variables" (p. 353).
2. There are two kinds of experiential states. One is a cognitive state in which crowding is perceived but in which there are no emotional or physiological changes. In the second type of experiential state, emotional or physiological

change occurs. This state is more likely to elicit reactions than the cognitive state.

3. "Crowding is determined in a relative rather than an absolute context" (p. 354). In other words, a person's experience of crowding in different situations with the same density depends on emotional and physical state, type of interactions occurring, and so on.
4. Crowding does not have to be an unpleasant experience; it can be enjoyable.
5. The time factor is important in the experience of crowding. Longer exposure to a single crowding condition will increase the degree of crowding experienced.
6. Adaptation to crowding occurs. Repeated exposure to crowding conditions will increase adaptability.
7. Crowding, per se, cannot be measured. Rather, it must be inferred through indirect behavioral measures of some sort.

It should be apparent that there is some question about just what is meant by the concepts of density and crowding in the field of environmental psychology. Hopefully, however, at this point the reader has some understanding of the meaning of these terms while recognizing that not everyone agrees on just what they do mean.

RESEARCH ON SOCIAL BEHAVIOR AND THE PHYSICAL ENVIRONMENT

In this section we will discuss research on crowding, personal space, territoriality, and privacy. Because there is relatively little research on the last two concepts, we will concentrate on crowding and personal space. However, since the concept of privacy does play a key role in an important theoretical position in this field (Altman, 1975, 1976), we will begin with a brief discussion of this concept.

Privacy

Although there is virtually no research on privacy, this concept does appear in the literature of a number of disciplines, and several definitions have been presented. Altman (1975) suggests that these definitions fall into two general categories. In the first category the definitions tend to emphasize seclusion, withdrawal, and avoidance of interaction with other individuals. The second group of definitions "puts less emphasis on exclusion, but implies that privacy involves control, opening and closing of the self to others, and freedom of choice" (p. 8). Altman's (1976) own definition is that privacy is *"selective control of access to the self or to one's group"* (p. 8).

Altman (1975, 1976) presents a detailed theoretical analysis of privacy as well as a discussion of the mechanisms employed by people to maintain privacy. He is particularly concerned with this concept because his theory on the relationships between the environment and social behavior stresses the interrelationships among privacy, personal space, territoriality, and crowding.

In his conceptual analysis of privacy, Altman emphasizes its interpersonal-boundary properties and shows how it regulates and controls social interactions. Privacy is seen as having a range above and below which the amount and quality of social interaction are unsatisfactory, where there can be feelings ranging from wanting to be accessible to others to wanting to be alone, where privacy needs differ in different social units, and where there is a "desired" privacy that may differ from an "achieved" privacy. People implement desired levels of privacy through a variety of behavioral mechanisms, including verbal behavior, paraverbal behavior (voice intensity, pitch, and so on), nonverbal use of the body, and such mechanisms as personal space and territoriality.

A complete discussion of Altman's theoretical formulation on the environment and social behavior is beyond the scope of this book. However, an idea of his views can be obtained from the following quotation, which was taken from the introduction to his 1975 book *The Environment and Social Behavior:*

> A major idea to be set forth is that the concept of *privacy* is central—that it provides the glue that binds the four concepts together. It will be proposed that privacy is a central regulatory process by which a person (or group) makes himself more or less accessible and open to others and that the concepts of personal space and territorial behavior are *mechanisms* that are set in motion to achieve desired levels of privacy. Crowding will be described as a social condition in which privacy mechanisms have not functioned effectively, resulting in an excess of undesired social contact [p. 3].[1]

In brief, for Altman, privacy provides a critical link among the concepts of personal space, territoriality, and crowding. Personal space and territoriality can be thought of as mechanisms that function to achieve desired levels of privacy, while crowding will result when there is a breakdown in the achievement of the desired level of privacy. Although not everyone agrees with this theoretical formulation, it does provide a framework that has been lacking. The reader might keep Altman's views of the environment and social behavior in mind during the following discussion of crowding, personal space, and territoriality.

[1]From *The Environment and Social Behavior,* by I. Altman. Copyright © 1975 by Wadsworth Publishing Company, Inc. This and all other quotations from this source are reprinted by permission of the publisher, Brooks/Cole Publishing Company, Monterey, California.

Crowding

Earlier we spent some time attempting to define the concepts of density and crowding. Recall that density is considered a physical concept that refers to the number of people or animals in a given unit of space. Crowding, on the other hand, is defined as a psychological state that is experienced under certain conditions—generally when the density level is high, or, put another way, when one's demand for space exceeds the supply. Whether one feels crowded depends upon a number of situational, interpersonal, and psychological variables.

Theories of Crowding

Although theoretical underpinnings are lacking for much of environmental psychology, we have pointed out that there has been some effort at theory development in the area of crowding and the associated areas of territoriality, personal space, and privacy. We will briefly consider several theoretical approaches to crowding before discussing research approaches and findings.

Stokols (1976), in an article dealing with the experience of crowding, states, "At least three theoretical perspectives have been proposed as a basis for understanding the antecedents, psychological experience, and behavioral manifestations of human crowding: (1) *stimulus overload*, (2) *behavioral constraint*, and (3) *ecological* orientations" (p. 51). The stimulus-overload model, as the name implies, suggests that the experience of crowding and the resulting behavior are brought about by the excess physical and social stimulation encountered in high-density situations. Close proximity to another person requires that we process more information than usual, which results in overload. This model underlies much of the research on crowding.

We considered this model in some detail in Chapter 5 when we discussed Milgram's (1970a) views on system overload. Overload was defined as a situation in which the amount and rate of input to the system were greater than the individual could handle. According to Milgram, urban dwellers use a number of adaptive behaviors to reduce the input to a manageable level. The Zlutnick and Altman (1972) and Altman (1975) view of crowding, which emphasizes the ability of individuals to control their interactions with others, "reflects an overload perspective" (Stokols, 1976, p. 53).

Although the stimulus-overload model is popular, it is by no means a completely satisfactory explanation for the experience of crowding. Evans and Eichelman (1976) present a detailed critique of the stimulus-overload model and discuss several lines of evidence against the overload hypothesis. They conclude: "We believe that this model represents an oversimplification of the manner in which the human organism operates in its environment" (p. 98).

The behavioral-constraint model is based on the view that in some situations people perceive that their freedom to perform a particular act or behave in a certain way has been threatened or curtailed. For example, Proshansky, Ittelson, and Rivlin (1970) discuss crowding in terms of a situation in which the presence of other people will either place restrictions on an individual's behavior or cause the individual to perceive these restrictions, whether or not they exist. A number of variables may interact to determine whether actual or perceived constraint takes place. Stokols (1976) writes: "According to this model, the experience of crowding develops through an interaction of physical, social, and personal variables, all of which combine to sensitize the individual to the actual or potential constraints of limited space" (p. 54).

The ecological orientation to crowding stems from the work of Barker (1968). Recall that in Chapter 2 we discussed environmental psychologists' increased interest in Barker-type research. In the ecological perspective on crowding, behavioral settings are thought to require a specific number of persons for the functions available. Thus, a setting can be undermanned, can have the right number of persons, or can be overmanned. Undermanning or overmanning results in an unstable condition and pressures to achieve an adequate or optimal manning. Limited resources in the overmanned situations lead to the experience of crowding.

The theories of crowding just discussed—restriction of privacy, plus stimulus overload, behavioral constraint, and scarcity of resources—continue to be refined. However, new constructs are also being developed. According to Stokols (1976), "Many psychologists have become disenchanted with theoretical approaches that overemphasize person variables while giving little attention to environmental determinants of behavior" (p. 72).

Stokols's own analysis of crowding stresses the situational dimensions although recognizing the significance of personal variables. He distinguishes between what he terms *primary* and *secondary environments.* The former are environments in which the "individual spends much of his time, relates to others on a personal basis, and engages in a wide range of personally-important activities" (p. 73). Stokols considers residential, classroom, and work environments to be primary settings. Secondary environments are those in which a person's encounters are transitory, inconsequential, and anonymous. Examples of secondary environments are transportation, recreation, and commercial areas.

Although we will not discuss Stokols's analysis in detail, his basic assumption is relatively straightforward. In primary environments, conditions of high density are perceived as more threatening than in secondary environments; consequently, experiences of crowding will be more intense and persistent. Stokols says:

> This prediction is based on the assumption that an individual's expectations for control over the environment are associated with a wider range of personal needs and goals in primary settings than in secondary ones. Hence, social interferences arising from conditions of high density or proximity will be potentially more disruptive and frustrating in the former environments than in the latter [p. 73].

Consideration of the importance of the situational variables in the experience of crowding makes the models of crowding discussed earlier more meaningful. The conditions of stimulus overload, resource scarcity, and behavioral constraint would result in a more intense experience of crowding in a primary environment than in a secondary environment.

Research on Crowding

Research dealing with crowding has tended to fall into two broad categories. In one category are correlational studies that attempt to determine whether relationships exist between high population density, which supposedly results in crowding, and the occurrence of a variety of physical, mental, and social pathologies. The second category includes studies that can be considered experimental or laboratory oriented. In these studies some aspect of the environment—usually density—is manipulated (the independent variable) and the effects of this manipulation on some form of behavior (the dependent variable) observed.

Research relating population density to crime levels and to physical and mental disease was discussed in Chapter 5. Such research is sometimes suggestive and indicates that relationships do exist, but these relationships appear to be much more complex than was once thought to be the case. Essentially, we cannot be certain that the high population density associated with urban areas *causes* social, physical, or mental pathologies. Although there may be a demonstrated relationship between density and, for example, higher crime rates, a number of other factors, such as poverty, educational level, and ethnicity, may be involved. As Freedman (1975) points out, when these factors are controlled the relationship between density and crime disappears entirely.

Typically, in the laboratory studies that have been reported, the subjects are exposed to varying degrees of crowdedness and then asked to rate their feelings while under these conditions. The subjects may be asked to complete an anxiety scale, a stress scale of some type, a hostility scale, or one of a variety of other scales designed to measure their affective state. The differences among the ratings obtained under the various conditions of crowdedness are then compared. Measures of performance on tasks are seldom obtained.

Smith and Haythorn (1972) used 56 naval enlisted men as subjects in a study of the effects of long-term isolation on behavior. The subjects were isolated in groups of two or three for 21 days. Although the primary independent variable in this study was the group size, the investigators were also interested in a number of other variables, including crowding. Thus, a number of the groups were tested under conditions of isolation and confinement that allowed about 70 cubic feet of usable space per man, while other groups were confined in test rooms with 200 cubic feet per man. The design, then, involved two-man groups under high-crowding and low-crowding conditions and three-man groups under high-crowding and low-crowding conditions. A variety of dependent variables were employed, both physiological and psychological.

Among the psychological measures were several tests designed to measure stress, anxiety, and hostility. The measure of stress indicated that the groups were highly similar during the first nine days of confinement. However, during the remainder of the time in confinement, crowdedness appeared to have a greater effect on the three-man groups than on the two-man groups. The three-man groups in the high-crowding condition showed the highest level of stress, while the three-man groups in the low-crowding condition showed the least stress. The two-man groups scored somewhere in between. Measures of anxiety showed that the two-man groups under both conditions of crowding and the three-man groups under the low-crowding condition were considerably less anxious than the other groups. A surprising finding of this study is that greater hostility toward partners was revealed by subjects in less crowded groups than by crowded subjects.

One unavoidable problem in laboratory studies of crowding is individuals' expectations about their ability to terminate crowding conditions. These expectations are probably instrumental in determining reaction to crowding. For this reason Paulus, McCain, and Cox (1973) suggest that a prison environment is a good place to conduct crowding research. Two conditions make prisons attractive for doing research. First, prison living conditions expose inmates to various degrees of crowding over relatively long periods (days or months). Second, the living arrangement enables researchers to analyze the independent effects of social interaction and spatial density.

Paulus, Cox, McCain, and Chandler (1975) gave inmates at a federal corrections institution a human-figures placement task to determine their criterion of what constitutes overcrowding. The researchers found that the inmates who were housed under highly crowded conditions exhibited less tolerance of overcrowding than did those who were housed under less crowded conditions. Higher crowding also yielded higher negative affective responses to the physical environment.

Studies by Baum and co-workers (Baum, Harpin, & Valins, 1975; Baum & Valins, 1973; Valins & Baum, 1973) were also conducted in a seminaturalistic environment and attempted to explore the long-term implications of living in crowded environments for later behavior. However, instead of prison inmates, these researchers used residents of dormitories with crowded corridor arrangements or uncrowded suites. The subjects from both environments were individually directed to sit in a waiting room where a confederate was seated. Measurements of the interaction between the two persons indicated that the crowded residents sat farther away from the confederate and spent less time looking at or talking with the confederate than the uncrowded residents. Valins and Baum (1973) suggest that this finding indicates that dense living is associated with avoidance of social interaction.

An investigation by Baxter and Deanovich (1970) was designed to determine the anxiety-arousing properties of inappropriate crowding. The subjects in this study were 48 female volunteers from a psychology class. They were tested under two conditions. Under the crowded condition the subject was seated in a chair, and the experimenter (another woman) placed her chair very close to the subject's. Under the spaced condition the experimenter placed her chair at the end of a table at some distance from the subject's.

The subjects were presented with the Make a Picture Story Test, consisting of eight settings containing two doll figures and accompanied by a brief narrative describing each of the settings. The subjects were asked to rate the amount of anxiety felt by the dolls in the different settings. The results indicated that the crowded subjects projected more anxiety in their ratings of the scenes than did the uncrowded subjects. The effects became more pronounced during the latter half of the experimental period.

Griffith and Veitch (1971) investigated the effects of hot and crowded conditions on behavior. They tested subjects in an environmental chamber under a normal-temperature condition and under a hot condition. The subjects were also tested under different population densities (small or large groups of subjects together in a test room). Several behavioral measures were used. Under the high-temperature and high-population-density conditions, the subjects who were asked to evaluate a stranger on the basis of responses on a questionnaire indicated more dislike for the stranger than did the subjects under the other conditions. The mood of the subjects was also found to be negatively affected by the high-temperature and high-population-density conditions.

Although studies such as these suggest that crowding affects how a person feels, the results are far from clear-cut. There is some indication that increased density results in feelings of anger or hostility toward others, but the results are not in one direction. Thus, in the Smith and Haythorn (1972) investigation greater hostility was demonstrated toward partners in less crowded groups.

Studies dealing with the effects of crowding on feelings such as anger or hostility do not tell us much about the possible effects of crowding on performance. Though it has often been assumed that crowded conditions have a negative effect on performance, this has not been demonstrated. The lack of any effects of crowding on task performance is particularly apparent when its effects on short-term performance are studied. For example, Freedman (1971) and his co-workers gave subjects a variety of intellectual tasks to perform that varied in complexity and took several hours to complete. The subjects performed these tasks under different conditions of crowding. The findings revealed no performance differences on any of the tasks as a result of crowding. Similar findings have been reported for several other laboratory studies in which subjects performed various tasks under different density conditions.

Some research suggests that crowding, even though it does not appear to have any immediate effects on performance, may have some long-term effects. Recall from Chapter 5 that research by Glass and Singer (1972) found that exposure to noise affected not immediate but later performance. The existence of a similar situation with crowding is supported by the findings of a study by Sherrod (1974). The subjects were placed in either an uncrowded or a crowded situation and given several different types of tasks. There were no immediate effects of crowding. However, when tested later (in an uncrowded room), the subjects who had been exposed to the crowded condition performed worse than the other subjects. Although more research needs to be conducted in this area, certainly Sherrod's findings have important implications.

The studies reported in this section by no means exhaust the research literature on crowding. It is a rapidly expanding field, and we have presented only representative investigations in an effort to acquaint the reader with the approaches used by researchers in this area.

Personal Space

We have seen that, according to Altman's (1975) theoretical framework, the concepts of privacy, territoriality, personal space, and crowding are closely interrelated. Privacy is viewed as a dynamic boundary-regulation process, and "privacy regulation is achieved through a series of behavioral mechanisms, including verbal and paraverbal behaviors, nonverbal behaviors involving use of the body, and environmentally oriented behaviors of personal space and territory" (p. 54). Thus, personal space is one mechanism used to regulate interaction with others and achieve desired privacy.

Personal space is not as difficult to define as some of the other concepts we have been dealing with. Basically, personal space can be thought of as an envelope or a bubble surrounding a person. The intrusion of someone else upon this personal space leads to some type of response, generally a feeling of displeasure or an urge to withdraw. Although individuals carry this personal space about with them, it is not fixed in the sense that it remains the same in every situation and with all other individuals. In other words, the dimensions of personal space for an individual will vary according to a particular situation.

An anthropologist, Edward Hall (1966), proposes a theoretical approach to personal space suggesting that there are four personal-space zones used in social interactions. The first zone is termed *intimate distance* (0 to 18 inches). At this distance, sight, sounds, smells, body heat, and the feel of breath all combine to create an unmistakable involvement with another person. This zone is generally associated with very close, intimate interactions, such as lovemaking. The second zone is called *personal distance* (1.5 to 4 feet) and is the common spacing used for most interactions with another person. Moving closer than this distance—that is, entering the intimate zone—will result in discomfort for the other person. Hall also feels that, within the personal-distance zone, a close phase (1.5 to 2.5 feet) is reserved for intimate friends. In general, Hall sees this zone as a traditional area between intimate and formal public behavior. The third zone is referred to as *social distance* (4 to 12 feet) and is generally used for business and social contacts, such as discussions across a desk or conversations at a cocktail party. Finally, the fourth personal-space zone, *public distance* (12 to 25 feet), is used for formal occasions, public speaking, or interaction with high-status persons. In this zone communication channels are much more restricted than in any of the other zones.

Hall stresses that the physical distances themselves do not make these zones important. Rather, the zones are milieus within which certain interpersonal-communication possibilities are available, creating a variety of behavioral options. Hall is careful to note that the zones are not necessarily the same for all cultures and that the distances defining different zones may differ from culture to culture. Some research on cultural differences in personal-space zones will be discussed later in this chapter.

Research Approaches

Altman (1975) lists three general methods that are used in the study of personal space. These are *simulation* techniques, *laboratory* studies, and *field* studies. Simulation techniques are the most common, then laboratory studies; field studies are used least frequently.

In simulation studies, figures or symbols representing people in particular situations are shown to subjects. The task of the subjects is to arrange these figures in some fashion or to make judgments about the distances that separate the figures or symbols. In some cases the subjects are told to reconstruct arrangements that were shown to them for brief periods. There are numerous variations on this technique, but they all have the obvious advantage of being easy to administer. Laboratory and field studies are often much more complex.

Laboratory studies of personal space have the same advantages and disadvantages of laboratory studies in other areas. Although tight control can be maintained over the variables in the laboratory situation, typically the subjects are aware that spatial behavior is being studied even when deception is involved. Moreover, as we have stressed, generalizations from laboratory findings to real-world situations must be made with some caution.

Many different approaches have been used in laboratory studies. For example, sometimes the subjects physically approach other subjects, and the distances at which they halt or report feeling uncomfortable are measured. A variety of factors have been used as independent variables in these investigations. Typically, the dependent variable in these studies, as well as in the simulation studies, has been some measure of distance.

Personal-space research in natural settings has just recently begun to appear in the literature and offers great promise. With the naturalistic-observation technique, described in Chapter 2, behavior in many different settings can be observed and distances maintained by persons in various situations can be determined without the subjects' knowledge.

Regardless of the approach used, researchers have typically been interested in the effects of certain kinds of factors on personal space. A number of studies have been concerned with the relationship between personal space and such subject variables as sex, age, socioeconomic status, ethnic and racial characteristics, mental factors, and so forth. Other studies have dealt with social relationships between individuals and the effects of these relationships on personal space. Still another class of studies includes those concerned with physical factors in the situation—for example, the effects of seating arrangements on personal space. We will now turn to the results of some of these studies.

Some Studies of Personal Space

Age and sex are two variables that have been shown to be important in determining personal space. For example, using simulation techniques, it has been found that young children place figures marked as strangers farther apart than figures that are labeled as friends. Young children also tend to place figures differing in sex farther apart than figures representing differences in race, while older children tend to place figures differing in race farther apart (Koslin, Koslin, Pargament, & Bird, 1971). In a study in which children selected a circle of a particular size to represent themselves, the size of the circle that was selected increased with the children's age (Long, Henderson, & Ziller, 1967).

In a study by Tennis and Dabbs (1975), the effects of age, sex, and setting upon personal-space preferences were examined. The subjects consisted of students from grades 1, 5, 9, and 12 and college sophomores. They were tested in same-sex pairs in corners and centers of the test room. Corner and center locations were used because previous work by Dabbs, Fuller, and Carr (1973) showed that subjects in a corner of a room who were approached by another subject maintained a greater personal space than did subjects standing in the center of a room.

The Tennis and Dabbs study showed, in general, that a greater distance was maintained by older subjects than by younger subjects, that it was greater among males than among females, and that it was greater in the corner setting than in the center setting. However, sex differences were less marked among the younger children than among the older subjects. Also, younger and older subjects reacted somewhat differently in the corner and center settings, with the youngest children maintaining a closer personal distance in the corner setting and all other subjects maintaining a closer distance in the center setting.

Studies on sex differences suggest that men have larger personal-space areas than women, although, as pointed out by Altman (1975), sex differences in personal-space requirements must be considered in terms of whether males or females are interacting with males or with females. Thus, a number of studies have reported that male/female combinations are generally in closer proximity to each other than members of pairs made up of the same sex. There are other sex differences besides the dimensions of the personal-space zone. Research suggests that males are more upset than females when their personal space is invaded, although both sexes are bothered. The direction of the invasion is also a variable, with women responding more negatively than men to side-by-side invasions of personal space, while men respond more negatively to face-to-face invasions (Fisher & Byrne, 1975). Age and racial differences also interact with sex differences in determining what is perceived as appropriate personal space in any particular situation.

There is considerable evidence to suggest that personal-space behavior is affected by social/emotional disorders. For example, Horowitz, Duff, and Stratton (1964) explored the possibility that the personal-space requirements of "normal" persons are different from those of persons in mental institutions. The mental patients, who were classified as schizophrenics, were asked to approach an object and other persons at three different angles—walking forward, walking backward, and walking sideways. After each subject had stopped moving toward the object or person, the distance between the subject and the object or individual was measured. The same experimental conditions were used for the unhospitalized subjects. The investigators then plotted their data around a drawing of each subject's body. The lines connecting these points were determined to be the boundaries of the subject's zone of personal space. By comparing the average size of these plots for the two groups of subjects, the researchers found that the schizophrenic patients possessed a greater zone of personal space than did the nonpatient subjects.

Personality correlates of various kinds have been shown to be related to personal space. Thus, persons who tend to be anxious have larger personal-space zones than less anxious individuals, and extroverts tend to maintain closer personal space than introverts. Cultural factors may also be important, although substantial evidence to support this view is lacking. Studies comparing different nationalities have had conflicting results. However, there is some indication that some nationalities may maintain closer personal space than others.

The above findings are from studies concerned with subject variables and personal space. Recall that other investigations have been concerned with the effects on personal space of social relationships between persons or of situational factors. Altman (1975) reviews a number of studies dealing with interpersonal relations and personal space. In general, these studies found that when positive relationships are involved, such as those with friends in contrast to strangers, smaller personal-space zones occur. Positive relationships may also involve certain types of behavior, such as a favorable social interchange. In studies dealing with forms of behavior perceived as positive or negative, again perceived positive relationships lead to smaller personal-space zones.

There is not a great deal of research on the effects of situational variables on personal space. However, it has been found that more formal settings tend to increase the size of the personal-space zone (Bass & Weinstein, 1971; Little, 1965). Familiarity of settings can also influence personal space. Altman (1975) reports that when people are in familiar places they tend to be more willing to be in close contact with others.

When we discussed Hall's (1966) spatial zones, we noted that he qualified his observations by stipulating that his spatial zones may be culturally dependent. Altman and Vinsel (1977) suggest that two hypotheses can be stated from Hall's observations. First, there are likely to be differences in spatial distancing in different cultures, with the differences paralleling use of space and social-interaction styles. Second, certain cultures, such as the Arabic, Mediterranean, and Latin American societies, are likely to exhibit smaller distancing than Northern European and Caucasian North American groups.

Hall observes that Arab cultures expect high levels of contact with others. This is accomplished through crowding, rich smells, and close physical contact. People in Arab cultures seldom have feelings of intrusion or getting too close to others. Hall notes that Westerners react negatively to Arabic peoples' casual use of what Westerners consider zones of intimate and personal space. At the other extreme, he notes that Germans are extremely sensitive to invasion of personal space and go to great lengths to maintain privacy through private rooms, closed doors, heavy walls, fences, and so on. According to Hall, German students indicated that the approach of anyone closer than 7 feet would be an inappropriate intrusion.

Most of Hall's observations about cultural differences are general and directed toward supporting the existence of the four spatial zones. In a more recent publication (1974), he also alludes to possible differences in the use of space among Black, White, and Hispanic Americans and emphasizes the inappropriateness of viewing the U.S. culture as homogeneous.

One new area of personal-space research concerns the effects of personal-space invasion on individuals' perception of others. Konecni, Libuser, Morton, and Ebbesen (1975) found that violation of an individual's personal space affects subsequent interactions with the violator. They found that individuals were less likely to return lost objects to persons who had violated their personal space than to persons who had not. The researchers suggest that people whose personal space has been violated do not simply escape from the violator; they also impute to the violator certain personality characteristics that are not conducive to later social interaction. They also suggest that people whose personal space has been violated tend to be less likely to help not only the individual who violated their space but others as well.

The studies cited so far dealt with personal-space zones of individuals. Researchers have also attempted to apply personal-space concepts to boundaries of larger social units. Lyman and Scott (1967) define social space as an interaction territory and suggest that every interaction territory "implicitly makes the claim of boundary maintenance for the duration of the interaction" (p. 240). The concept of a social-space boundary provides a useful model for describing the relations between a small group and its social environment. It has been found that the strength with which members of a group protect a social space varies with the sex of the group (Knowles, 1972) and that the degree of protection of a social unit from outside penetration depends on the size of the group, the status of the members (Knowles, 1973), the sex composition of the group, the degree of group interaction (Cheyne & Efran, 1972), and the distance maintained between group members (Efran & Cheyne, 1973). Knowles, Kreuser, Haas, Hyde, and Shuchart (1976) also found that pedestrians walked farther away from groups than from individuals and that they walked farther away from individuals than from an empty bench. The closest pedestrian stayed farther away from a group of four than from a group of two or three persons.

Findings on personal space and interaction distance may eventually be linked with effects of overcrowding, since under conditions of crowding the probability of a personal-space violation as well as other nonviolent dominance-related confrontations increases. Efran and Cheyne (1974) suggest that the cumulative reaction to nonviolent, perhaps even individually trivial, encounters may be a critical factor mediating the negative effects of crowding. This contention is supported by their own findings.

As we have pointed out, there is a considerable amount of research on personal space, and we have only briefly surveyed some of the more relevant findings. Anyone who wishes to pursue this topic in depth should read Sommer's (1969) book on personal space or Altman's (1975) thorough review of the area in his book dealing with the environment and social behavior.

Territorial Behavior

There is a considerable body of literature on territoriality in animals, but until recently there has been relatively little interest in this phenomenon in humans. Studies with animals have shown that territorial behavior is complex, that it has a wide range of functions, and that it is demonstrated in a variety of ways. Although it is an interesting exercise to use the data from these animal studies to speculate about territorial behavior at the human level, it is only speculation. The available information on human territoriality is scarce.

However, interest in this topic is growing, and we will probably see more empirical research on territoriality with humans in the future. There are several reasons for this increased interest. We have already pointed out that territorial behavior is a relevant topic for environmental psychologists who wish to obtain a better understanding of the relationships between the physical environment and human social behavior. The interest of behavioral scientists in this area is evidenced in the reviews of human territoriality that have appeared recently (Altman, 1975; Edney, 1974, 1976). Considerable interest in this topic has been generated in laymen and scientists alike by Ardrey (1966, 1970), Lorenz (1966), and other popular writers who have raised questions regarding the origin of certain types of human social behavior, including aggression and territoriality. These writers suggest that these behaviors have a genetic or instinctive basis, although the environment does have some influence. This idea, of course, is in sharp contrast to the views held by most behavioral scientists; they feel that social behavior is primarily a learned behavior and very much dependent upon environmental and cultural influences.

Although the issue of whether territorial behavior is based primarily on genetics or is learned is interesting and provocative, it is not particularly relevant to our discussion. Instead, we will turn our attention to defining the concept of territoriality and to some of the research that has been conducted in the area.

A Problem of Definition

As so often seems to be the case with terms used in psychology, there is no commonly accepted definition of the concept of territoriality. However, as we shall see, most of the numerous definitions do have some points in common.

In their analyses of territorial behavior, Edney (1974) and Altman (1975) list a number of definitions that have been used by writers concerned with this type of behavior in both animals and humans. Edney suggests that most definitions fall into one of three groups. In one group are the definitions that stress the importance of active defense of a given area. Thus, territorial behavior may be defined as simply the defense of a given space or object. Definitions falling into the second group also refer to defense but recognize that there are other characteristics of territoriality. For example, Brower (1965) defines territoriality as a "tendency on the part of organisms to establish boundaries around their physical confines, to lay claim to the space or territory within these boundaries, and to defend it against outsiders" (p. 9). The third class of definitions avoids the use of the term *defense*. A definition falling in this group is that territoriality involves exclusive use of objects or areas by individuals or groups.

Altman (1975) suggests that these definitions have several common themes: (1) The definitions nearly always refer to geographical areas. (2) They suggest various needs that are served by territorial behavior, such as sex, food gathering, and so forth. (3) They tend to imply ownership of an area and involve personalization by means of markers, such as fences or signs. (4) They refer to the domain of either individuals or groups. (5) Most are concerned with territorial intrusion or defense.

It should be obvious that any definition of territoriality including all the features just listed would be a formidable one, and we are not prepared to offer such a definition. Perhaps for our purposes the best definition is a statement made by Edney (1974): "Human territoriality can conveniently be characterized with a catchall description as a set of behaviors that a person (or persons) displays in relation to a physical environment that he terms 'his,' and that he (or he with others) uses more or less exclusively over time" (p. 959).

Other definitions of territoriality will emphasize one or another of the behaviors encompassed in this statement and, consequently, will differ from this and from one another. Anyone wishing to pursue this topic further should read the material on territoriality by Altman (1975) and Edney (1974, 1976).

Research on Human Territorial Behavior

Although sociologists have long been interested in territoriality and its role in the social structure of neighborhood gangs and groups, the analyses of these investigators were frequently nonsystematic descriptions and did little to provide a theoretical framework for empirical studies. Consequently, empirical research on human territorial behavior is scarce, and most of what is available has been published quite recently. Also, as pointed out by Altman (1975), only a few topics have been selected for investigation. According to Altman, these topics include:

> (1) studies of how territorial markers are used and the effects of types of markers on potential intruders, (2) analyses of the relationship between the dominance, power, or status hierarchy of groups and members' use of territories, and (3) studies that investigate the general role of territories in stabilizing social systems and smoothing their operations [pp. 128–129].

Sommer (1969) reports several studies he conducted on the use of markers—in this case territorial markers used to reserve seats in a library while the occupants were away. He found that under low-density conditions—that is, when relatively few people were using the library—almost any marker was effective. "In 22 trials with markers ranging from notebooks to old newspapers, the territory was invaded only three times—twice when an old newspaper was used and once when a paperback book was left on the table" (p. 53). Sommer points out, however, that the object must be perceived as a marker and not simply as litter and that this requires "the item to have either symbolic meaning as a territorial marker—a 'Keep Out' or 'Reserved' sign—or some intrinsic value—a coat, purse, or other object that the owner would not discard without cause" (p. 53). Personal markers, such as a sweater or jacket, keep intruders away more effectively than impersonal markers. There are interesting exceptions, however. In a study by Hoppe (1970) in bars, it was found that a half-glass of beer reserved a place better than a jacket.

In a follow-up on Sommer's study, the effectiveness of markers under high-density conditions was investigated in a study hall. The investigator arrived at the study hall early, placed his markers, and then observed from another table. Sommer reports: "All the control (unmarked) areas were occupied well before the two-hour sessions had finished, the average time before occupancy being 20 minutes. Each of the markers delayed occupation, although some were more potent than others" (p. 53). Similarly, Sommers reports another study in which markers were left at empty tables in a university soda fountain. The markers (a wrapped sandwich, paperback books, or a sweater) resulted in a tendency for people to avoid the marked tables and sit at nearby unmarked ones.

There have been a few other investigations dealing with the role of markers in human territorial behavior. Edney (1972) compared residents of homes with distinctive territorial markers, such as signs, hedges, or fences, with residents of homes that did not have these types of markers. Residents of the houses with distinctive territorial markings tended to be longer-term occupants than those with less distinctive markings. It was hypothesized, based on other measures, that residents of houses with the distinctive markings had a stronger commitment to the place and were more sensitive to territorial intrusions than the residents with less elaborate marking systems. Edney and Jordan-Edney (1974) studied the territorial behavior of groups on beaches and found that the territories (marked spaces surrounding the groups) varied in size and shape as a function of the sex makeup of the group and the length of time the group was on the beach. Larger groups had more markers and mixed-sex groups had more markers the longer they stayed on the beach. These as well as several other studies suggest that markers are important factors in human territorial behavior. They are employed to label and define a territory and tend to be recognized and honored by others. (See Figure 6-1.)

Data from animal studies often show that there is a strong relationship between dominance and territoriality, with the dominant animal of a group establishing control over the area it wants. This relationship is not as clear when we consider human territorial behavior. There are several methodological difficulties involved in attempting to study the relationship between dominance and territoriality with humans. In the first place, it is not always a simple matter to determine which member of a group is dominant. Typically, the researcher must rely on various rating scales that do not always have a high degree of validity. Also, measuring territorial behavior in such a fashion that one can relate it to dominance can be difficult.

The results of these investigations have been somewhat ambiguous. Some studies have shown no relationships, some have suggested that there is a positive relationship, with dominant individuals showing more territorial behavior, and still other studies have found negative relationships. In general, however, research on the relationship between dominance and territoriality in humans indicates that dominant people tend to have territories to a greater extent than do less dominant individuals but that this relationship is very dependent upon situational factors.

The third class of studies on human territorial behavior are those that deal with the role of territories in stabilizing social systems. As Altman (1975) points out, most research on territoriality, whether it deals with markers or the relationship between dominance and territorial behavior, supports the view that this type of behavior helps to stabilize social systems. Edney (1976), in discussing the functional properties of human territoriality, stresses the importance of territoriality as an organizer in human life and behavior and gives examples of how disorganized and unstable our social systems would be without it. He states:

Figure 6-1. A variety of methods are used to mark territories and ensure privacy. (Bottom left photo by Lars Larmon.)

> . . . life without territory would be largely characterized by aggregates of unrelated, inefficient, and elementary responses. Naturally, social and community life would also suffer. With collections of milling individuals unattached to particular personal places, it would be difficult, first, to find any specific person, and equally difficult to avoid a person [p. 35].

Several investigators, using somewhat different approaches, have examined the notion that territories contribute to a more stable social system. Altman and Haythorn (1967) and Altman, Taylor, and Wheeler (1971), using U.S. Navy volunteers, placed pairs of strangers in socially isolated and confined quarters for a number of days. The quarters were designed to simulate an undersea environment. Territorial behavior, together with a variety of other behaviors, was measured. Although the design of these studies was quite complex and a number of behavioral measures were obtained, one of the findings was that "compatible" or "successful" pairs established territories early and only relaxed their territorial behavior later in their association. These pairs were considered to have a higher level of social stability than other pairs. Other studies (O'Neill & Paluck, 1973; Paluck & Esser, 1971), using retarded boys as subjects, found that established territories resulted in less aggressive behavior and helped the boys exert some control over their lives.

In Chapter 3 we discussed Newman's (1973a, 1973b, 1973c) study of crime in low-cost urban housing developments. Crime rates were highest in the absence of "defensible space," which, in turn, was determined in part by the existence of territories. This is an example of social instability in a situation where territories are absent, and it lends further support to the concept that territoriality serves an important function in helping maintain stability in social systems.

DENSITY STUDIES WITH ANIMALS

We have discussed a number of studies dealing with the relationships between human social behavior and the environment. We have seen that our understanding of these relationships is growing but that we have a long way to go. Some investigators feel that in order better to understand human behavior in, for example, high-density situations, we should first investigate this type of behavior in simpler organisms. There have been a number of animal studies conducted in this area, and more are being reported continually in the literature. Because many investigators in environmental psychology consider these types of investigations to be important, we will discuss in some detail population-density research with animals.

As we have seen in this chapter, there are difficulties involved in designing investigations dealing with the effects of density on humans. In most instances it is simpler to study the effects of density using various types of animals, particularly rodents, as subjects. Consequently, a substantial number of investigations have been conducted on the effects of density on animals' behavior and physiological responses. Keeping in mind that rodents are far from perfect models of humans, so that generalizations from rodents to people must be made with a great deal of caution, let us consider some of the findings from animal studies.

There is considerable evidence that the population size of many mammalian species, especially rodents, is self-limiting. Once a particular population density is reached, the animals' reproductive capabilities are modified to the extent that the population either remains stable or decreases. Much of the population-density research on animals has been designed to explain why this self-limiting phenomenon occurs.

One popular explanation is based on the concept of social stress. It is generally agreed that as population density increases, the animals are subjected to more and more contact with other animals and that at some point these social contacts become stressful. Thus, the high-density condition is considered a stressor that creates various behavioral and physical changes in the animals.

These reactions may be dramatic and easily observable or subtle and observable only under carefully controlled conditions. An example of a dramatic reaction associated with high densities is the mass migration of lemmings. However, the behavior of animals subjected to high densities may also involve more aggressive behavior than normal, various forms of "aberrant" sexual behavior, the devouring of young by their mothers, and other types of behavior that, for the animals involved, can be considered unusual or abnormal. Physical changes also occur, with various internal organs modified and endocrine functions disturbed. Thus, under stressful conditions the adrenal glands enlarge and are hyperactive, as is the pituitary gland, while the gonads may atrophy and become hypoactive. In discussing the pituitary/adrenal/gonadal effects of stressors, Thiessen and Rodgers (1961) point out:

> If population density were a stressor, it would be inversely related to gonadal activity and therefore to reproductive behavior, as well as to other factors affecting survival. Such relationships could account for the apparently self-limiting nature of density of population and would help to account for the triphasic population cycle. Under conditions of low density of population and in otherwise favorable circumstances, gonadal and reproductive activity would be high, resulting in an expanding population. The increasing population density, acting as an increasing stressor, would eventually reduce reproduction to the point that deaths would match births. The population would reach equilibrium at that point and would enter the second phase of the population cycle. Such stability would be maintained until the population was subjected to an additional stressor, such as increased daylight or increased cold occurring with seasonal change. The additional stressor could destroy the equilibrium

and precipitate a more or less rapid decline of population, partially by its effects on reproduction rate and partially by other lethal effects of the increased stress [pp. 441–442].

We will not attempt to summarize all the studies in this area. Rather, we will describe several investigations that are representative of the approaches used by researchers studying the effects of increased population densities on animals. In general, these studies are either field studies, in which the investigator attempts to study the animals under natural or nearly natural conditions, or laboratory studies, in which the animals are studied under carefully controlled conditions.

Field Studies

At one time it was customary to explain population changes among small mammals as the result of cycles in the environment—temperature and rainfall, predator populations, or disease cycles, for example—or of available food and shelter. Although these may be important factors in some instances, a study by Calhoun (1952) showed that other aspects of the environment may be even more important in limiting population. In this study Calhoun observed rats in a 10,000-square-foot pen for 28 months. During this time the colony grew from a few individuals to about 150 and then leveled off at this number. Of particular interest in this study was that the population remained at this level even though Calhoun estimated that there was enough food as well as space for several thousand rats. According to the observed reproductive rate, at least 5000 adult rats might have been expected. However, the population remained at about 150 because of the extremely high infant-mortality rate. Even with only 150 adults in the pen, stress from social interaction led to such a disruption of maternal behavior that most of the young rats did not survive. Calhoun states:

> As the population increased in numbers there was an increase in frequency, intensity, and complexity of behavior adjustments necessitated among and between groups of rats. This forced more and more rats to be characterized by social instability with the accompanying result of lowering the biotic potential to the point where there was a balance between natality and mortality—all this in the continued presence of a superabundance of food and unused space available for harborage [p. 141].

Although Calhoun does not report any physical changes in the rats as their population reached its peak of about 150, other studies have shown that there is a definite relationship between population density and adrenal weight in natural populations of Norway rats. Christian and Davis (1956), for example, studied rats from 21 Baltimore city blocks. These researchers pointed out that "each city block is effectively an island and its rats form a discrete population unit since immigration and emigration of rats is negligible or absent" (p. 476). In all the blocks studied, ample food was available from garbage cans, and there was adequate harborage on each block.

At the start of the investigation, considerable information from previous studies was available on the population characteristics of the various blocks. These data and data from live trappings allowed the investigators to assign each of the blocks to a particular population-cycle stage. These stages, which are illustrated in Figure 6-2, were labeled the low stationary stage, the low increasing stage, the high increasing stage, the high stationary stage, and the decreasing stage. Thus, if a longitudinal study had been conducted on a single block, it would be expected that the rat population in that block would proceed through each of the stages shown in Figure 6-2. In the Christian and Davis study, however, a number of blocks were sampled, and it was determined whether rats in a particular block were at the low stationary stage, the low increasing stage, or one of the other stages.

Rats from all the blocks were trapped and killed, and the weights of a number of organs were determined. Although the weight of the adrenal gland

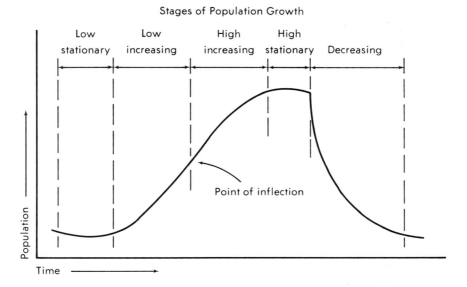

Figure 6-2. Hypothetical growth curve. In the Christian and Davis study, each population of rats was placed in one of the five population stages at the time of collection of each sample. From Christian, J. J., & Davis, D. E. The relationship between adrenal weights and population status of urban Norway rats. *Journal of Mammalogy,* 1956, *37,* 475–486. Reproduced by permission of the *Journal of Mammalogy.*

was of primary interest, the weights of the thymus, thyroid, and pituitary glands were also obtained. No changes were found in the weights of the thymus, pituitary, and thyroid glands. However, a progressive increase was found in the adrenal-gland weights, starting with the low increasing population, progressing through the high increasing and high stationary stages, and ending with an overall 18% increase in adrenal weights in the decreasing population. To the extent that adrenal weight correlates with adrenal activity, the results of this investigation indicate that stress increases as the population cycle progresses. Since ample food supplies were available, it appears that social factors rather than purely biological factors were of primary importance in determining the differences in adrenal-gland weights.

A number of other field studies have found population density to be associated with changes in adrenal weights and with other physiological indexes assumed to reflect stress. In all these studies the absence of food shortages and other environmental stressors suggests that social stressors brought about by a high population density were responsible for the stress reactions.

Laboratory Studies

Laboratory studies, in which the population density can be carefully controlled and in which extraneous variables that might serve as stressors can be either eliminated or controlled, have supported the field findings that high density serves as a stressor. In these investigations adrenal glands have been found to enlarge as density increased. Changes in other organs have also been noted. One of the studies demonstrating the relationship between population size and adrenal-gland size is that of Christian (1955). He placed weanling mice in groups of 1, 4, 6, 8, 16, and 32 for a period of one week. The animals were then killed and their adrenal glands weighed. The adrenal weights showed a linear relationship to the logarithm of the population size in all cases except the groups of 32 mice, in which the adrenal weights declined. Initially, Christian interpreted this finding to mean a "social structure deterioration" at this group size that represented some decrease in stress. However, later work by Christian showed that the decrease in adrenal weight at this population level was due to a loss in the lipid content of the cortical cells of the gland, which indicates intense activation of the adrenocortex. Thus, the trend of increased adrenal activity with increased population density held for all the limits tested.

Actually, as pointed out by Brain (1975), changes in adrenal weights as a function of density will also depend upon the sex of the animals involved. It appears that male mice that are isolated have lower relative adrenal weights than grouped male mice; isolated female mice, on the other hand, have higher relative adrenal weights. There is some evidence, however, that adrenal hypertrophy in isolated female mice is the result of increased estrogen levels, not stress.

Physiological changes reflecting a stress reaction in the animal undoubtedly take place when population density reaches a certain level. However, as we have indicated, stress reactions may also be reflected by changes in behavior. Although there is considerably more research on the physical types of stress reactions resulting from high population density, a classic study by Calhoun (1962) reveals a good deal about the behavioral changes that may be associated with this type of stressor.

Calhoun partitioned a room measuring 10 by 14 feet into four pens, as shown in Figure 6-3. Each of the pens was a complete dwelling unit for rats and included a water bottle, a food hopper, and an elevated artificial burrow reached by a spiral staircase. The pens were separated by electrified partitions that had ramps built over them, so that the rats had access to all the pens. The behavior of the rats was observed through a window in the ceiling of the room. The rat population was held constant at 80 rats by leaving in the pens only enough infant rats to replace the older ones that died.

As can be seen in Figure 6-3, there was no ramp between pens 1 and 4.

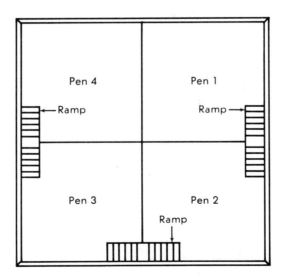

Figure 6-3. A top view of the arrangement used by Calhoun to study overcrowding in rats. Each pen contained food hoppers, water bottles, and living quarters. Note that ramps connect all pens but 1 and 4. From Heimstra, N. W., & McDonald, A. L., *Psychology and contemporary problems.* Monterey, Calif.: Brooks/Cole, 1973.

These pens were reached by only one ramp each, while pens 2 and 3 were reached by two ramps each. Thus, because of the number of ramps entering the pens, numbers 1 and 4 could be considered end pens and 2 and 3 middle pens. Because of the number of ramps available and for other reasons, pens 2 and 3 had higher population densities than pens 1 and 4. The female members of the population tended to distribute themselves about equally in the four pens, while the males were concentrated in pens 2 and 3. Pens 1 and 4 each contained a dominant male that would tolerate only a few other males that respected his dominance. The collection of animals in unusually large numbers, as happened in pens 2 and 3, is called a *behavioral sink*. As Calhoun points out, "The unhealthy connotations of the term are not accidental: a behavioral sink does act to aggravate all forms of pathology that can be found within a group" (p. 144).

Bizarre forms of behavior began to develop quite rapidly, particularly among the animals in the behavioral sinks. The behavior of both the male and the female rats was affected. The females became less adept at building nests and eventually stopped building them altogether. Moreover, rather than transporting their pups from one place to another, which is normal behavior, the females simply picked pups up and dropped them at different places in the pen. During estrous periods the female rats were almost continually pursued by packs of males. There was a very high rate of mortality among these females during pregnancy and parturition.

A variety of different types of behavior was demonstrated by the male rats. The aggressive, dominant males were the most normal, but sometimes even these animals would go berserk and attack females, juveniles, and submissive males. Some of the nondominant males displayed homosexual behavior because they could not discriminate between appropriate and inappropriate sex partners. Other males became completely passive and moved through the pens ignoring other rats and being ignored in turn. Though they were fat and sleek with no scars, their social disorientation was virtually complete.

Possibly the strangest type of behavior was demonstrated by the male rats Calhoun called probers. These rats, which always lived in the middle pens, were hyperactive and hypersexual. They were always on the alert for an estrous female, and if they could not find one in their own pen, they would lie in wait for a female on the top of a ramp leading to another pen. These animals were also homosexual, and some were cannibalistic.

Marsden (1972) describes another study conducted in Calhoun's laboratory that is somewhat similar to the earlier study. In this investigation eight mice were introduced into what Marsden, basing his judgment on food supplies and living accommodations, describes as a "potential mouse utopia." Four of the mice were males and four females. The utopia was closely observed as the mouse population increased, exceeded what was considered to be the optimal population, and approached the maximum. As this happened,

> Processes evolved that resulted in the emergence of proportionally more and more divergent types of animals, animals deviating strongly from the ideal of how a normal mouse should behave—that is, a male being occupier and defender of his personal space and the procreator of his species and a female bearer and rearer of healthy young [p. 9].

The abnormal behavior patterns were first seen in male mice. Males that had been ejected from their usual living quarters now lived on the open floor in large groups of similar individuals. They moved to food and water but then returned to their groups. Normal mouse behavior disappeared, and they withdrew almost completely from normal social interactions.

The grouped withdrawn males on the floor were the first deviants to emerge as the population density increased. A second type appeared shortly afterward. These were solitary withdrawn males that lived alone on the floor at the base of food hoppers or on top of them. There was also a third type of deviant males, which Marsden called the Beautiful Ones, since they were fat, sleek, and well groomed and had few if any wounds. They lived in the quarters that were available but did not participate in sex activities or compete for territory. These mice actually appeared to be less involved in social activities than either the grouped or the solitary withdrawns. Apparently this type was unstressed; tests of adrenal enzymes showed that the Beautiful Ones had a lower level of the enzyme than did the withdrawn mice.

The population of mice reached a maximum of about 2000, which was about half of the theoretical maximum but well above what was considered to be the optimal number. When the number of mice reached about 2000, the population began to decrease steadily. Eventually, all inhabitants of the mouse utopia died.

It is apparent from these studies and several others we have not discussed that social pressure brought about by high population density will result in drastic behavior changes as well as in stress reactions manifested by physiological changes in the animal.

Combinations of Stressors

In laboratory studies as well as in many field studies, researchers try to eliminate or control variables other than the independent variable that might affect the subjects. Although such efforts are a necessary experimental procedure, they remove the studies even further from the real world, in which numerous variables interact and affect the organism. Thus, we know that high population density is a stressor and causes a variety of reactions. What happens, however, in high-population-density situations when additional stressors are added?

Relatively little research has been conducted on the effects of population density in combination with other stressors. However, to illustrate the dramatic effects that combinations of stressors can have, let us briefly consider research in which social stressors associated with population density are combined with chemical stressors.

Amphetamine sulfate is a central-nervous-system stimulant that a significant number of persons use for its mood-changing characteristics. In addition to this illicit use, the drug has become widely used for treating certain types of behavioral disorders in children. When administered to a research subject, such as a mouse or a rat, it will generally result in hyperactivity and other behavior changes.

A number of years ago amphetamine was found to be much more lethal to mice placed together in groups of three or four than to isolated animals. For example, an LD 50 (lethal dose for 50% of the subjects) may be about 125 mg/kg for mice that are treated with the drug and placed in isolation. However, the LD 50 for mice treated and placed in groups is only about 10 mg/kg.

If we injected mice with about 50 mg/kg of amphetamine and placed them in isolation, we would observe a number of behavioral effects. Most of the mice would be hyperactive; some would develop strange behavior patterns, such as biting the wire of the cages or moving their heads rapidly back and forth. In general, we would be able to see that these mice behave differently from untreated mice. Very few would die, however. On the other hand, if we were to give a number of mice 50 mg/kg doses and then place them in groups of four in small cages, the behavioral changes shown by these mice in comparison to nontreated controls would be startling. Almost immediately the mice would begin to ricochet around their cages at a tremendous speed. Occasionally, when mice ran into one another, they would adopt a defensive posture by standing on their hind legs and holding their front legs in a boxing position. Almost at once the running would be resumed. Within a few minutes all the amphetamine-treated mice in the group condition would go into convulsions and die.

The lethality of this combination of population density and the amphetamine can even be increased by adding other stressors. For example, mice treated with amphetamine and placed in groups will die at an even lower dosage level when heat stress in the form of a hot testing room is added. Other variables decrease the lethality. A study by Mast and Heimstra (1962) showed, for example, that prior social experience will modify the death rate of amphetamine-treated mice placed in group conditions. Mice that had been reared in group conditions had a lower mortality rate after drug treatment than did mice reared in isolation. Obviously, then, many factors will modify the stress effects of population density.

Implications of Animal Studies for Humans

It is tempting, of course, to make, on the basis of the findings of density studies with animals, dire predictions about the eventual fate of humans if population pressures become too great. As we have pointed out, however, the rodent is far from a perfect model of the human, and any generalizations from findings of animal studies to human behavior must be made with great caution. Clough (1965) points out:

> As might be expected, the ideas devised to explain animal cycles—especially the finding that life in crowded conditions can have profound physiological effects—are now being used to discuss human population problems. But, in my view, there are too many basic differences to justify much of this speculation. For one thing, historically, human populations have shown only a steadily increasing growth over thousands of years—or no significant change in the case of some isolated peoples. There has never been the regular, short-term rise and fall seen in the rodent populations. For another difference, although it is probably true that humans crowded into urban centers are plagued by certain mental and physical diseases of civilization, their birth rates are not greatly inhibited (if at all) nor their mortality rates increased. In fact, the birth rates are comparatively high among the people who live with the poorest conditions of nutrition, housing, and, perhaps, even emotional and mental hardships [pp. 204–205].

Recently, several articles have been written reviewing the studies conducted with animals and discussing the implications for humans (Brain, 1975; Lloyd, 1975). Although both Brain and Lloyd are cautious about generalizations from animal studies, they raise some interesting points. For example, Lloyd states: "Animal studies are a good point of departure and can provide us with much valuable information and important insights useful in formulating questions and designing experiments to study similar phenomena in man" (p. 15). He also says:

> While interpolations from studies of animals to man are always fraught with hazards, it is possible that an overly rigid · concern about being anthropomorphic may be as counter-productive and misleading as are oversimplistic interpolations. The fact is that man is a biological system subject to biological laws just as are other species [p. 14].

Brain, while stressing the limitations of the use of rodent studies in attempting to understand the effects of crowding in human societies, discusses what he feels are areas of relevance. Studies with rodents enable us to develop techniques that are applicable to humans and indicate relationships among variables that can be studied with humans. Also, they provide us with an idea of the complex nature of the variables involved in population studies, even with "simple" animals such as rodents. Thus, these studies "serve as a warning to those who would attempt to produce simplistic statements relating physiology, behavior, and stress in our species" (p. 26).

CHAPTER 7

THE NATURAL ENVIRONMENT AND BEHAVIOR

In Chapter 1 it was pointed out that the physical environment consists of the built environment and the natural environment. In the other chapters we have been concerned with the built environment and with the relationships between this type of environment and human behavior. Although much of the research in environmental psychology has been concerned with the built environment and its effects on behavior, some researchers have been interested in the relationship between the natural environment and behavior. In this chapter we will discuss some of the theories and research on this relationship.

It would be convenient to think of the natural environment as the nonbuilt environment, but doing so would result in a more restricted definition than we have in mind. As used in this chapter, the term *natural environment* means not only geographic regions and wilderness areas, which, essentially, are natural areas and parks, but also large and small recreation areas, which usually have many man-made features. These recreation areas, however, are simulated natural environments in that they are built to give people some contact with trees, open space, streams, and so forth, which are viewed as components of the natural environment. Spending an hour or two in an urban park with its ponds and trees means, for many city dwellers, contact with the natural environment in contrast to the built environment of buildings, streets, automobiles, and so on. This is the case even if the pond is man-made and the trees were carefully planted in orderly rows.

People interact with the natural environment in many ways and at many levels. (See Figure 7-1.) In general, however, we can think of these interactions as falling into two categories: *temporary* interactions and *permanent* interactions. For example, for most people, a visit to a national park or wilderness area, or to a regional park or recreation area, would involve a temporary interaction; for park rangers and other persons associated with these areas, a more permanent interaction would be involved. As we shall see, these temporary interactions are actively sought by many individuals and are

Figure 7-1. The ranchers herding horses have a different type of interaction with the natural environment shown in this photograph than the hunters who hunt mule deer here in the fall or the occasional fishermen who take bass out of the stock dam. (Photo courtesy of the South Dakota Department of Highways, Pierre, South Dakota.)

thought to give them satisfaction or pleasure. We shall also see, however, that the motivation underlying this pursuit of the natural environment by millions of persons annually is not clearly understood and may be quite complex.

We all interact with the natural environment on a more permanent basis, although the nature and intensity of this interaction vary according to individual circumstance. We live in geographical regions that may be characterized by extreme heat or cold, by droughts or frequent floods, by tornadoes, hurricanes, or earthquakes, or by combinations of these. Each region also has distinctive terrain features, such as mountains, plains, or deserts. Although the relationships between these terrain and climatic features and behavior have not been clearly demonstrated, many environmental psychologists assume that such relationships do exist. We will discuss these permanent interactions in detail later in the chapter. At this point we will consider one of the most important of the temporary types of interactions—that encountered in outdoor recreation.

OUTDOOR RECREATION

Only a few years ago, articles on the psychological aspects of outdoor recreation were relatively rare. However, interest has recently been increasing in the motivations for participating in outdoor recreation and the satisfaction associated with it. This increased attention is probably due to two primary factors. The first is that certain types of outdoor-recreation facilities, such as national parks and wilderness areas, have in many instances already reached the saturation point in numbers of users, yet user demand continues to increase. Because the parks and wilderness areas are in limited supply and are not reproducible, the management system must decide how to cope with the demand. At the one extreme the management can let the use continue unabated; at the other they can severely restrict the use of the areas. Neither option is feasible, so managerial action somewhere between these extremes is required. To make these decisions, the management must have considerable information on the characteristics of the users, including their motivations for coming to the area, their perceived requirements of an area, and the types of interactions associated with a particular area that produce maximum user satisfaction. Although researchers have been attempting to gather information about these kinds of user characteristics, much more needs to be known before decisions about managing the park and wilderness areas can be made with any real confidence.

The other reason for the increased interest in behavior and outdoor recreation is the steadily growing amount of leisure time available to many segments of our society. Already some organizations have instituted the four-day work week, and a shorter work week has become an important negotiation point in many labor contracts. Although total leisure time might increase in various other ways (lowering the retirement age, for example), millions of people now appear to have more leisure time than ever before and may have even more in the near future.

There is a close relationship, of course, between leisure and recreation, whether indoor or outdoor. As leisure time increases, those who prefer some form of outdoor recreation will increase the demands on existing facilities, and new ones of many kinds will have to be constructed. Some research on the behavior of the users of these facilities is being conducted that will hopefully provide useful information to the managers of existing outdoor-recreation areas and the designers of new ones.

Categories of Outdoor Recreation

The range of outdoor-recreation activities is, of course, wide, and they take place in a number of different areas. One of the schemes for classifying these areas is that of Clawson (1966):

At one extreme are the user-oriented areas: close to where people live, suitable for use after school and after work, individually often rather small and not too demanding as to physical characteristics, ready location is their prime requirement. Farther out lie the intermediate use areas: designed primarily for day-long recreation use, generally within an hour's travel time of most users, on the best sites available, they present much more flexibility in location and in resource qualities required. At the other extreme are the resource-based areas, whose superb and unusual physical or historical characteristics make them desirable in spite of a frequently inconvenient location for most users. The first require or are best suited to daily leisure, the second to weekend leisure, and the third to vacation time [p. 253].

In this chapter we will be primarily concerned with the last type of areas, those that Clawson categorizes as resource based. These include the national parks and wilderness regions, which serve as an important source of interactions with the natural environment for millions of people each year. However, as we shall see, the other types of areas are also important; for many people, user-oriented and intermediate-use areas are the primary source of temporary interaction with the natural environment.

Studying Outdoor Recreation

Much of the research on the behavior of users of outdoor-recreation areas and facilities has been applied research—that is, research designed to answer specific real-world questions. Typically, the questions were raised by management personnel confronted with the need to make decisions about present and future use of outdoor-recreation areas.

Some of the information required is straightforward and not particularly difficult to obtain. For example, the behavior of users of the various types of recreational areas can be observed and data obtained on the use of such facilities as campsites, trails, and lakes. Users can be questioned about what they did or did not do during a visit to a recreational area, and a relatively accurate idea of the overt-behavior patterns of the typical user can be obtained. Other types of needed data, however, are not so easily collected. For instance, management personnel are interested in what factors associated with the user and the environment are most important in determining whether the outdoor-recreation experience is satisfactory or unsatisfactory. Thus, several investigations have been conducted to determine the characteristics of wilderness areas that are considered to be critical aspects of the "wilderness experience." In this type of study, the researcher must isolate various affective states of the users—moods and feelings, attitudes, aesthetic experiences, and so forth—and relate them to the physical characteristics of the wilderness area.

A common research method used in this type of study is to interview or give questionnaires to the users of an outdoor-recreation area either while they are there or shortly after they leave. Although the survey instruments vary depending upon the objectives of the study, many are designed to elicit the attitudes or feelings of the respondents about their recreation experience. Other techniques have also been used with some degree of success. For example, Craik (1972) developed a landscape adjective check list that was used by subjects to describe a large number of different landscape scenes. Other investigators have used various types of representations of an area, such as a map (Lucas, 1964), in attempting to determine users' perceived requirements of a wilderness area. Lane, Byrd, and Brantly (1975) evaluated recreational sites by presenting color slides of various sites to various groups and having the individuals score each site on a number of dimensions.

As the demand for recreation services and facilities has increased, new approaches to studying recreation behavior have also been developed. For example, Ditton, Goodale, and Johnson (1975) used a sophisticated statistical technique called cluster analysis to study participation in water-based recreation. With this technique the researchers were able to identify types, or clusters, of individuals on the basis of not only participation in eight types of water-based recreational activities but also several predictor variables, such as age, sex, urban or rural locale, and so on. Although their study is far too complex to describe in detail here, it is a promising approach to better understanding recreation behavior.

Where do we stand now on recreation or leisure research? Where do we go in the future? A study by Crandall and Lewko (1976) attempted to answer these questions. They sent questionnaires to a large number of individuals. They included members of recreation departments in universities, heads of sociology and psychology departments at a number of institutions, who were asked to circulate the questionnaires, and authors of articles appearing in several journals. More than 1200 questionnaires were sent out. Of these, 371 responses were received.

Items dealing with current research trends showed that the major area of research interest was general leisure behavior. A more detailed breakdown showed that the seven areas of research most commonly listed under this general heading were (1) conceptual/historical; (2) outdoor recreation; (3) sociology of leisure; (4) administration, planning, and management; (5) sports competition and games; (6) leisure lifestyles, values, and attitudes; and (7) psychology of leisure.

Opinions on what should constitute future leisure research varied, but content analysis revealed 21 suggested areas of future research. The area that tended to dominate had to do with the need to understand better the antecedents and consequences of leisure behavior. Other areas listed included research on resource planning and management; methodology, measurement, and analysis; sociology of leisure; theory building; and leisure and the elderly.

NATIONAL PARKS AND WILDERNESS AREAS

One of the major sources of temporary interactions between people and the natural environment are the national parks and wilderness areas. Annually, millions of persons visit these areas and engage in a variety of activities—fishing, backpacking, camping, hiking, horseback riding, and many others. Each year the number of persons visiting these areas increases substantially, and many parks and wilderness areas have already reached the saturation point. The problem promises to become even more critical. Since World War II the use of wilderness areas has increased about 10% per year, and there is no reason to expect that this growth rate will decrease. Indeed, Stankey (1972) points out that it may even increase:

> Simple projections do not tell the whole story. Wilderness users tend to be disproportionately drawn from higher-income groups, professional and technical occupational categories, urban areas, and the college and postgraduate ranks. Moreover, these characteristics apply to a steadily increasing proportion of the population. If indeed some causal relationship exists between any or all of these variables and wilderness use, then the possibility of future increases in wilderness use is further enhanced [p. 90].

Because of the tremendous increase in the use of national parks and wilderness areas, the persons responsible for their management have been faced with a number of crucial decisions. The key issues revolve around the question of how much change can be made in these areas to accommodate more visitors without changing the "wilderness experience" they seek. Management's need for more information on which to base decisions has led to research on the characteristics of the users of the areas, the characteristics of the natural environment that are important to the users, and the interactions between people and the natural environment that occur in these areas. In this section we will discuss some of this research.

Characteristics of the Users

Surveys show that people in every socioeconomic class and occupation visit national parks and wilderness areas. However, as already pointed out, the users tend to be atypical socioeconomically when compared with the population as a whole. A disproportionate percentage of the users have a college or postgraduate degree, belong to one of the professions, and have an above-average income. Consider, for example, the results of a survey conducted at Yellowstone National Park by McDonald and Clark (1968). Nearly 3000 visitors were given questionnaires at different points in the park. Although the questionnaires were designed to obtain data about the users' reactions to the park, data were also obtained on the visitors' occupations and education. Some of the 57 occupations identified are shown in Table 7-1. Note that, although there were fluctuations across the summer, teachers and students made up a fairly large segment of the visitor population. Of all the visitors interviewed, 68% had at least some college education, a finding implied by the occupations listed in the table. This percentage of college educated is, of course, much higher than that found in the general population. McDonald and Clark's finding is similar to that of Gilligan (1962), who reports that about 80% of all visitors to a wilderness area had a college education and that 27% of these even had some postgraduate training. Recent surveys indicate that these statistics are still reasonably accurate.

Table 7-1. Percentage of visitors' occupations by month

Occupation	June	July	August
Teacher	7.88	6.07	7.97
Student	5.76	2.80	7.97
Labor	6.97	7.48	5.18
Engineering	5.45	6.54	7.17
Business	9.09	9.81	8.37
Military/government	5.76	3.74	7.17
Agriculture	3.33	3.27	5.18
Retired	6.67	5.14	4.38

Obtaining information about the occupations and educational backgrounds of park and wilderness users is, of course, relatively simple. Information on other characteristics, however, is more important for management decisions and is more difficult to obtain. For example, "wilderness" is largely a function of human perception, and management must know the factors associated with a given area that cause it to be perceived as wilderness. Similarly, the relationship between various physical characteristics of an area and the affective states of its users needs to be determined. What motivates so many people to visit these areas? Why are some areas so much more popular than others? What do the recreational "purists" look for in an area in contrast to the ordinary users? Answers to these and many other questions are needed for proper management of parks and wilderness regions. Unfortunately, some of the questions are difficult to answer. Take, for example, the question of why people visit these areas.

Motivations of the Users

We know that each year many millions of people visit national parks and wilderness areas and that this number increases each year. We also know a good deal about the characteristics of these visitors—where they come from, their age, education, occupation, and so forth. What is not nearly so clear, however, is why they come to the parks and wilderness areas. Generally, when asked why they came to a particular area, a majority of the visitors give such reasons as wanting to get away from the city, seeking peace and tranquility, seeking a change in the everyday routine, and getting away from it all. Although replies such as these may partly answer the question of why they visit the park or wilderness area, the reasons for the need to "get away from it all" have not been systematically studied. Driver (1972) suggests that environmental stress encountered in urban areas may create needs of this sort and that recreation in parks and similar areas may serve as a means of coping with environmental stress.

The concept of environmental stress was discussed earlier and will not be considered to any extent here. Briefly, a number of features associated with urban living are stressful, and increasing numbers of people are exposed to these stresses each year. In the literature dealing with stress and behavior, the theme of temporary escape as a mechanism for coping with stress is pervasive. Driver is suggesting that recreation areas provide temporary means of escaping from the stress encountered in everyday urban living and that these escapes enable people to recover somewhat from the effects of the stress.

The view that outdoor recreation has stress-mediating value raises an interesting question, however. If outdoor recreation serves as a temporary escape from the stresses of city living, what will happen as the stresses encountered in the recreation areas become more pronounced? For example, one source of stress usually associated with city living is high population density, which results in the experience of overcrowding. High population density as a source of stress was previously discussed, as was the concept of overcrowding. As we have seen, the experience of being crowded is greatly dependent upon situational variables; a person who does not experience overcrowding on a city street may experience it when forced to share a campsite in a national park or when encountering another backpacker on a wilderness trail. Traffic jams in national parks and crowded campgrounds may be a more significant source of stress than the stresses associated with the city. More and more visitors are complaining about the congestion in recreation areas, and, although management is trying to alleviate this condition, the task is difficult if not impossible. If visiting recreation areas becomes a matter of escaping from one stress-provoking condition to another condition that is equally stressful, the popularity of the parks and wilderness regions may decline.

In addition to suggesting that recreation areas serve as a means for escaping from stress, Driver suggests some other reasons that people visit these areas. He states:

> Recreational engagements provide interesting and sometimes the only opportunities for the gratification of other human needs. These would include the following: to develop, maintain, or protect a self-image (this need seems particularly true for the elderly who select types of recreation that protect or enhance their "age" image); to retain and develop social identities or more simply just to affiliate; to gain esteem, including the reduction of status incongruity; to display, apply, and develop skills or to achieve; to exercise power, for example, in motorboating, snowmobiling, or hunting; to satisfy exploratory and curiosity drives; to engage in creative self-fulfillment; or to achieve some satisfactory degree of closure on or mastery of other problem-need states of the individual [p. 237].

The above represents a substantial list of needs that may be fulfilled by a visit to a national park or wilderness area. As we have emphasized, however, just why people visit these areas in such large numbers remains something of a mystery. Although research aimed at uncovering the motivations of users presents the investigator with a number of problems, it is an important area that requires a good deal more systematic study before we have a satisfactory answer.

Perceived Requirements of Parks and Wilderness Areas

Just what do people look for or expect when they visit a national park or wilderness area? What features serve as sources of satisfaction, and what features do visitors find unsatisfactory? In other words, what do visitors perceive as requirements of an area in order for them to feel satisfaction about their interactions with the natural environment? Answers to these questions are of considerable importance to management personnel in making decisions about providing a particular type of recreation experience.

A number of studies have been conducted to answer these questions. One of the most comprehensive investigations was carried out by Stankey (1972), who examined the attitudes of wilderness users toward features of the areas that were considered important. He interviewed more than 600 visitors to four wilderness areas, the Bob Marshall Wilderness in Montana, the Bridger Wilderness in Wyoming, the High Uintas Primitive Area in Utah, and the Boundary Waters Canoe Area in Minnesota.

Each respondent was asked to rate 14 items or statements, *in the context of wilderness,* on a five-point scale ranging from "very undesirable" to "very desirable." For example, the item "solitude—not seeing many other people except those in your own party" might be rated "very desirable" and would be given a score of 5 on the scale. The responses were scored so that an individual with very strong purist attitudes toward the wilderness would score high and persons with less strong attitudes would score lower. The possible range of total scores was between 70 and 14. On the basis of their scores, the respondents were classified into four groups: strong purists, moderate purists, neutralists, and nonpurists. Although comparisons were made between the responses of the various groups, Stankey considered the strong purists (scores between 60 and 70 on the scale) to be the users most relevant for wilderness-management decisions. We cannot summarize all the findings of this study. Instead, we will consider in some detail one of the more important perceived wilderness attributes indicated by the users—the attribute of solitude.

When the respondents were asked about the importance of solitude as a feature of the wilderness, 82% of the overall sample responded in a positive fashion, while 96% of the purists thought it a highly desirable feature. Thus, this characteristic of the wilderness would seem to be very important to the users. The attitude toward solitude is, however, more complex than one might think. In a detailed analysis of factors important in generating the feeling of solitude, Stankey points out that, if people truly desire solitude, one might expect to find them traveling alone in the wilderness. However, in the study only 2% of the respondents were traveling by themselves. Solitude, even in the mind of the purist, apparently involves a situation in which contacts with *other* groups are minimal; interaction with members of one's own party does not infringe upon the feeling of solitude. (Actually, for many people, social interaction with members of other groups around a campfire or in other circumstances also seems to be an important and positive part of the wilderness experience, although only about one in ten of the purists thought social interaction an integral part of the experience.)

The visitors were asked whether they would be bothered by (1) meeting many people on the trail and (2) meeting no one all day. About 25% of the respondents other than the purists indicated that they enjoyed encountering others on the trail, but only 10% of the purists felt this way. About three out of four of the purists stated that they would enjoy meeting no one all day, whereas only 3% of the purists indicated that this would bother them.

Few or no encounters thus seems to be an important dimension of the wilderness experience for purists. However, other factors associated with solitude are as important as frequency of encounters. For example, Lucas (1964) found that canoeists felt their solitude more threatened when they encountered a single motorboat than they did when they encountered several other canoes. Wilderness users are also typically more disturbed by large groups of people than by small ones. The location of the encounter is another important variable. For example, both the purists and the nonpurists seem to prefer trail encounters to encounters in the vicinity of their camps; the majority of both groups agree that the wilderness campsite should provide complete solitude. When the respondents in Stankey's study were asked to consider a situation in which several other parties arrived after camp had been set up, most purists indicated that they would be disturbed. A number stated that they would attempt to find another campsite or would cut their visit short.

Another aspect of solitude, which does not actually involve encounters but is also important, is the evidence of previous use of a wilderness area by other visitors. Two obvious indications of previous use are litter and campsite deterioration. It is not surprising that the purists in Stankey's study expressed strong dissatisfaction with campsites that showed wear and tear and with finding litter in the wilderness.

In a somewhat similar study by Shafer and Mietz (1972), five phrases or statements were selected that were thought to represent what an individual enjoys most about a wilderness experience. The statements described the qualities of a recreational experience—physical, emotional, aesthetic, educational, and social. Thus, a physical experience involved the opportunity for physical exercise that stimulated the body, an emotional experience was identified by such physical reactions as the thrill of experiencing new sensations and exploring wild regions, and so forth.

Each of the five statements about wilderness values was printed on a separate card, and the cards were arranged in sets of two into all possible combinations, for a total of ten sets. A total of 76 hikers from two wilderness areas were asked to select the statement in each set describing the value that was important to them. The results showed that aesthetic experiences were most important, with emotional experiences a close second. These were about ten times more important than social values, which came last. Physical experiences were third, while educational experiences were fourth.

The results of this study suggest that the most critical perceived attributes of a wilderness area are those that result in aesthetic experiences. Although it is difficult to distinguish between aesthetic experience and emotional experience (both of which rate high as requirements), it has been suggested that, at least in the wilderness context, emotional experiences are identified by physical reactions, while aesthetic experiences are more related to mental appreciation. Obviously, these experiences are closely allied and may occur during the same recreational activity. Thus, one may have an emotional experience when a rainbow trout strikes and simultaneously derive aesthetic satisfaction from the surroundings.

Very little is known about the characteristics of a natural environment that result in an aesthetic response. Litton (1972) attempted to define the aesthetic dimensions of the landscape and to establish appropriate "aesthetic criteria." He considers unity, vividness, and variety to be basic criteria and emphasizes that these are not discrete but overlap. According to Litton, "*unity* is that quality of wholeness in which all parts cohere, not merely as an assembly but as a single harmonious unit" (p. 284), while *"vividness* is that quality in the landscape which gives distinction and makes it visually striking" (p. 285). *"Variety,* in simple form, can be defined as an index to how many different objects and relationships are found in a landscape" (p. 286). Craik (1972) appraised the objectivity of these dimensions by developing rating scales and having subjects rate various landscapes. He concluded, "The results of this appraisal of the objectivity of a system of landscape dimensions are encouraging" (p. 306). The importance of the aesthetic experience for the wilderness user would seem to justify considerably more research on it.

Other factors involved in determining whether an area is perceived as wilderness were examined in studies by Muriam and Amons (1968) and Lucas (1964). In the former study 108 subjects were interviewed in three wilderness areas of Montana that differed considerably in isolation and access. The researchers identified among the subjects basically two types of temporary users—one group consisting of hikers and horseback riders and the second consisting of roadside campers. When asked to define what they considered wilderness, the hikers and riders included such criteria as undeveloped natural country, difficulty of access, few people, and the absence of improvements brought about by civilization. The hikers interviewed in the largest, most accessible area (Glacier National Park) were quite specific in stating that people had to be at least 3 miles from the nearest road or guided nature tour to consider themselves in the wilderness. To the campers, the wilderness began at the edge of the campground.

In the Lucas study, users of a wilderness area in northern Minnesota were surveyed. Upon leaving the area, the respondents were shown a map of it and were asked to indicate where they had been and where they would draw the boundary between wilderness and nonwilderness on the map. Generally, the users who engaged in the more purist activities (canoeing, for example) indicated a much smaller area than did the more casual users (the motor-boaters and weekend campers, for example).

Implications of Perceived Requirements for Management Personnel

We have seen that several characteristics of a park or wilderness area are important in determining whether the area is perceived as wilderness by the users. One example of such a feature is perceived solitude. In Stankey's study, solitude was rated very high by both the purists and the nonpurists. Similarly, in the Shafer and Mietz study, the respondents rated social experience lowest as a wilderness value. Indirect evidence of high usage of an area, such as litter and deteriorated campsites, also tends to result in dissatisfaction.

These findings have important implications for management personnel.

It is apparent that the desired wilderness environment would involve low usage. Possibly, through design, schedules of use, and other modifications, the total use of some wilderness areas can be maintained at present levels and most users can be given at least a satisfactory experience of solitude. However, in all likelihood, use limitations will eventually have to be imposed in many parks to maintain a satisfactory recreational experience for those who do use the areas. Some would argue that the problem of maintaining a feeling of solitude is not so serious as it appears to be because the perception of solitude will change as the population increases. Stankey points out:

> A standard argument for not using visitor attitudes as a means of formulating wilderness management strategies is that public attitudes as to what constitutes solitude, the pristine, or the natural will become less discriminating as population rises, urban densities increase, and so forth.
> The idea that attitudes about what is "pure wilderness" will weaken in the future might be a classic example of a self-fulfilling prophecy. If we orient wilderness management along a line designed to accommodate gradually less-demanding tastes, we will almost certainly attract a clientele that, in time, will hold a less demanding concept of wilderness [pp. 113–114].

Many other features of wilderness areas, of course, seem to contribute to the overall satisfaction of the users and so are important to consider in management decisions. For example, the absence of man-made features (except for trails) seems to be an important factor. If an area has roads and trails, many users feel that these should be restricted to backpackers or to horseback riders, with no motorized vehicles permitted. Many other such requirements of the physical aspects of an area appear to be important to users. Even the size of the area is important; if an area is not large enough (even though it meets most of the other requirements), it is not as satisfactory as a larger area. Requirements also depend upon the type of wilderness area involved. Thus, in areas where the most important activity centers around water, the purists use canoes and, if they had their way, would ban all motorboat activity. Obviously, just what features of an area contribute most to an aesthetic or emotional experience depend upon the personal characteristics of the individual using the area.

Nonetheless, some specific features found to be aesthetically satisfying were determined by Shafer and Mietz in their interviews with hikers in the two wilderness areas they surveyed (see Figure 7-2). The hikers felt that the most scenic enjoyment was obtained from trails that

> (1) include large rock outcrops where the hikers can observe the surrounding landscape; (2) go through natural openings in forest stands where there is variability in lighting, color, temperature, and the distance one can see through the forest; and (3) follow stream courses whenever possible so that waterfalls and rushing water are part of the natural beauty along the trail [p. 214].

Figure 7-2. Wilderness hikers have a strong preference for trails that include large rock outcrops, go through natural openings in forest stands, and follow stream courses containing waterfalls and rushing water. The above photo illustrates a location having these kinds of features. (Photo courtesy of the South Dakota Department of Highways, Pierre, South Dakota.)

The hikers also reported that forest stands having a mixture of pine and white birch were more appealing aesthetically than pure stands of pine but that "at other times a pure stand of majestic old culls may be far more desirable. From an aesthetic viewpoint, trails should be located on grades that will prevent erosion from water and heavy use. Overall, the respondents wanted variation in trail scenery more than anything else" (p. 214).

Individual Differences in Perceived Requirements

Clearly, all the studies we have discussed on the preferences of national-park and wilderness users show that the users differ considerably in their perceived requirements of an area. Thus, one type of user may be disturbed by encountering another backpacker on a wilderness trail, while another type of user may welcome the social contact. That users perceive virtually all the features of these areas differently and respond to them differently is obvious from Stankey's study, for he was able to classify users into several different groups according to their responses to items about features of a wilderness area.

Relatively little is known, however, about the basis for differences in perceived requirements of wilderness areas. It is reasonably safe to state that these differences are due to the backgrounds and experiences of the users, but saying so does not tell us very much. For example, what kinds of past experiences are important in determining whether people are purists or nonpurists in their attitudes toward the wilderness? Are personality factors related to perceived requirements of wilderness areas?

One study that supplies some answers was conducted by Cicchetti (1972). Through sophisticated statistical techniques, he attempted to analyze the relationship between the preferences and behavioral patterns of wilderness users and such factors as (1) age, sex, income, and education and (2) childhood residential and recreational experience. Using Stankey's purist score, Cicchetti was able to relate a number of these variables to users' purist scores. The details of this study are too technical to discuss in full, but we will mention some of the relationships he established.

Cicchetti found that the older people were when they first visited a wilderness, the higher were their purist scores. This direct relationship was also true for the variable of education; for each year of education beyond the eighth grade, the purism score increased by about .65 points. It would seem, then, that with greater age and education the individual needs a more pristine or remote wilderness experience. In some cases, relationships between other variables were also found. For example, in the Bridger area male visitors tended to rank higher in purism than did women visitors.

Childhood residence and recreational experiences were also found to affect purism scores. In general, visitors who grew up in a small town or in a rural area had lower purism scores than did visitors who grew up in an urban area. Cicchetti suggests that rural residence leads to the development of a utilitarian view of the wilderness; that is, the trees or other resources of a wilderness area are valuable and should be exploited. The users who said that they had hiked frequently as children scored higher on the purism scale than did the users who had not. Such other types of childhood experiences as camping also had a positive effect on the score.

We have already indicated that solitude appears to be the most important attribute of a wilderness area as perceived by users. In relating some of the above variables to this wilderness value, Cicchetti reports that the results of his study

> seem to indicate that the visitor who is older when he first visits a wilderness, who had considerable auto camping and hiking experience as a child, who has a discriminating view of the wilderness, and who did not grow up in a small town is the one likely to be most upset by congestion. He may even cut short his planned trip and return home [p. 158].

In another investigation Ullrich, Ullrich, Touzeau, Schweitzer, and Braunstein (1975) had different panels rate photographs taken of nine forested areas. The panels were made up of introductory-psychology students from the University of Montana, from the University of Michigan at Flint, from elementary-school and secondary-school teachers taking part in a meeting in Montana, and from Forest Service landscape architects and forest researchers. The panel members rated a total of 105 slides from the various sites on a rating scale from 0 to 9, with 0 indicating most liked and 9 indicating most disliked. Although one might expect that panels made up of members with such different backgrounds would evaluate the aesthetic quality of forest scenes differently, the panels did not differ significantly in their responses.

An obvious source of individual differences in responses to features of the natural environment is, of course, the nature of the interaction with the environment that the users expect or seek. Although this factor has been implicit in our discussion up to this point, its importance cannot be overemphasized. Obviously, if visitors expect to encounter other parties in a wilderness area, they will not be as disturbed as they would be if they did not expect encounters. The users' expectancy, or set, is thus an important determinant of the degree to which they will be satisfied or dissatisfied with their wilderness experience. Similarly, the users' objective in visiting an area will determine to a great extent their satisfaction with the area. Thus, the same user visiting a particular wilderness area on two occasions with two different objectives in mind may be highly satisfied on one visit and highly dissatisfied on the other. Consider, for example, a user who visits an area in the spring for several days of backpacking and then visits the same area in the fall for several days of deer hunting. The user may walk on the identical trails, but the perceived requirements are quite different. While on the spring hike, this person may consider various terrain features from an aesthetic point of view and find them very satisfying; the same features may be viewed as a nuisance during the fall because, for various reasons, they interfere with effective hunting. Similarly, the user may not be bothered by meeting other hikers in the spring, but encountering other hunters in the fall may be annoying. Both trips, however, may be satisfying—the spring trip because of the aesthetic experiences (the primary objective) and the fall trip because of success in bagging a deer. For most hunters, though they may prefer hunting in a natural environment where they can enjoy the scenery, the overwhelming criterion of a satisfying or dissatisfying interaction with the natural environment is whether or not they were successful in obtaining the game they were seeking.

A number of other studies along the same lines as those reported in this section have been conducted. Although the findings of all these studies differ somewhat, depending on the particular wilderness area involved and the purpose of the survey, we do have some idea of users' perceptions of the wilderness. As the use of wilderness areas increases, it will be essential that those responsible for the management of these areas use this information if the perceived requirements of the wilderness users are to be met.

In this section we have concentrated on wilderness areas rather than on national parks. Although the perceived requirements for wilderness areas and national parks differ somewhat, the approaches to studying the requirements are quite similar. Moreover, the motivations for visiting the parks are quite similar to those involved in wilderness use. Consequently, instead of discussing studies focusing on park users' behavior, we will now consider interactions with the natural environment in other kinds of outdoor recreation.

SOME OTHER TEMPORARY INTERACTIONS

Many of the millions of persons who visit national parks and wilderness areas each year, as well as millions of others, engage in numerous other forms of temporary interaction with the natural environment. (See Figure 7-3.) We pointed out earlier that our definition of the natural environment is quite broad and includes a number of environments in which built features are present and may even predominate. Some of these environments can be considered simulated natural environments in that they provide users with what they feel is at least an approximation of some features of natural environments. An example is the elaborate outdoor-recreation facilities that have been developed for residential neighborhoods and communities. For many persons, the recreation opportunities offered by these facilities, such as swimming, golfing, hiking, boating, and tennis, serve as either a primary or the only source of interaction with what they consider a natural environment.

Figure 7-3. There are many forms of temporary interaction with the natural environment. Boating, for example, is a popular form of outdoor recreation for millions of people. (Photo courtesy of the South Dakota Department of Highways, Pierre, South Dakota.)

There are, of course, many recreational activities that allow participants to "get outdoors" and, at least to some extent, temporarily interact with the environment. Some examples are skiing, boating, and snowmobiling; and all of these have increased tremendously in the past few years. Large numbers of people also engage in hunting or fishing, hiking, rock collecting, spelunking, mountain climbing, scuba diving, or simply driving in the country. The last may in fact be an important people/environment interaction that is not generally recognized. As Suholet (1973) points out, the highway can serve as open space and thus provide opportunities for significant interactions with the natural environment (see Figure 7-4). Although at one time highways were designed simply as asphalt or concrete "corridors" from one point to another, with little or no attention paid to environmental considerations, this is no longer the case. For example, in a special report the Highway Research Board (1973) discussed in detail the environmental considerations in the planning, design, and construction of highways. In that report David Jervis (p. 90) discusses pleasure driving—the use of highways and byways for recreational purposes. He points out that data exist indicating that driving for pleasure is the most popular outdoor-recreation activity in the United States and probably will remain among the most popular until at least the year 2000, despite the energy crisis.

Obviously, every highway cannot be constructed in such a fashion that it can serve as a source of "pleasure driving." Economic considerations dictate otherwise. However, as Jervis points out, consideration can be given to planning at least some leisure-driving facilities that would involve scenic corridors, development of complementary facilities, such as trails and picnic sites, documentation of historic or other heritage areas, and control of traffic volume and speed. We are currently seeing more highway development with these considerations kept in mind.

Another important type of outdoor activity generally ignored by those concerned with outdoor recreation is gardening. Vogt (1966) states:

Figure 7-4. One type of interaction with the natural environment enjoyed by millions is simply driving in the country. Although in many areas highways cannot be considered "open space," in other areas, such as that shown here, highways provide an opportunity for people/environment interactions. (Photo courtesy of the South Dakota Department of Highways, Pierre, South Dakota.)

Gardening—conservatively—must involve over twenty million people, a number approaching the numbers of hunters and fishermen combined, exceeding those in attendance at major-league baseball games, and vastly exceeding the numbers of those who own motors and boats and who are such a pampered fraction of outdoor recreationists. In view of the day-to-day relationship of gardening to the way people live and would like to live, and therefore the impact it could—and should—have on the future development of our society, it is to be regretted that gardeners have not been given the consideration they merit in thinking about the future of the American environment [pp. 383–384].

All the above activities and many more are important sources of outdoor recreation. The wilderness purists may scoff at these kinds of natural-environment interactions, but it should be kept in mind that the purists represent only a small percentage of the persons who value and achieve satisfaction from outdoor recreation of one kind or another.

The motivations of the persons enjoying the many kinds of temporary interactions listed above vary tremendously. However, they can be considered the same as the motives for visiting national parks and wilderness areas. Thus, outdoor recreation may serve as a temporary escape from stress. Such outdoor-recreation activities may also fulfill all the needs listed earlier—to develop and maintain a self-image, to develop a social identity, to affiliate, to gain esteem, to develop and apply skills, and so forth. Those interested in a detailed analysis of recreational behavior should read Driver and Tocher (1970), who deal with this issue in great depth.

One motivation for outdoor recreation is not written about a great deal but may be quite important. Many types of outdoor recreation involve the risk of injury or death. It has been frequently pointed out that North American culture has always prized and even rewarded behavior that involves taking risks of one kind or another. Indeed, in our society a man is often defined as someone who has courage or who takes a chance. Thus, many persons may consciously seek outdoor recreation that has a high level of risk to satisfy a social value or need.

As we emphasized earlier, the motivations of users of any outdoor-recreation area, whether it is a wilderness area or a neighborhood park, are complex. Although the motivations involved in outdoor recreation have been subjected to study in recent years, much more remains to be learned before we have a reasonably complete understanding of this kind of behavior.

Perceived Requirements

We have pointed out that users of national parks and wilderness areas (particularly the latter) have some very definite requirements of these areas. To the extent that these perceived requirements are met, the wilderness experience can be considered satisfying. One of the key elements of the satisfactory wilderness experience is solitude. Aesthetic, emotional, and other experiences are also important. As one might expect, perceived requirements are associated with other types of recreation areas as well.

Outdoor-recreation areas were earlier classified as user-oriented areas, intermediate-use areas, and resource-based areas. The first type is best suited to daily leisure, the second to weekend leisure, and the third to vacation time. Thus, accessibility is an important requirement for the first two types but may be an undesirable feature of the resource-based areas, or wilderness areas, where inaccessibility may be considered as contributing to solitude and, consequently, to the satisfaction of the experience. Landscape is typically of less concern to those visiting the user-oriented and intermediate-use areas than to the users of the resource-based areas, where landscape is important for the aesthetic experience. Similarly, those using the first two types of areas expect to encounter a considerable number of built features and facilities, while these are undesirable to users of the wilderness areas.

In other words, the perceived requirements of the types of areas depend greatly upon the objectives of the person using the areas—a point we have emphasized previously. We cannot discuss or even summarize the require-ments associated with the various types of outdoor-recreation areas because of their number and diversity. What the users perceive as requirements of a ski area differ considerably from the requirements of a hiking area, which, in turn, are different from those of a hunting area. However, participants in each type of outdoor recreation establish requirements for an outdoor-recreation experience, and, to the extent that these requirements are met, the experience will be perceived as satisfactory.

The Recreation Experience

In concluding our discussion of temporary interactions with the natural environment, we should point out that we have emphasized only a small part of what can be considered the total recreation experience. Clawson (1966) notes that the outdoor-recreation experience, particularly that involving the resource-based areas, has five distinct phases. The first of these phases Clawson calls the anticipation or planning phase, in which the family or group decides when and where to go, what to do in the area, what to take, and so forth. This phase may involve a number of months, as in the case of planning an extended visit to a national park or wilderness area, or only a few minutes, as in the case of planning to visit a local recreation area. For many persons, this phase, as the name indicates, is a time of pleasant anticipation and is an important part of the recreation experience. Many hours may be spent discussing the proposed trip, buying equipment, perhaps making financial sacrifices so that the family or group can afford the trip, adjusting work schedules, applying for vacation, and so forth. Although the actual interaction with the natural environment may be some time away, the behavior of the participants will already be modified to a considerable extent during the planning phase.

The second phase of the recreation experience is the travel to the site of the recreation. This trip may involve considerable time and money. Many persons find the travel experience itself a pleasurable and satisfying part of the recreation, although others regard it less highly. The third phase is the on-site experience, which we have concentrated on in the preceding pages. The trip back home from the site is the fourth phase of the recreation experience. Although the beginning and end points are usually the same as are involved in travel to the site, the mood and attitudes of the travelers may be quite different during this trip. This aspect of the recreation experience has not been subjected to study, but most readers will agree that their feelings are quite different when returning from an outdoor-recreation area than when traveling to it. In discussing the last phase—recollection—Clawson states: "Recollection is the last, and possibly the most important, phase of the total experience. It is altogether possible that more total satisfactions or values arise here than in all the other phases combined" (p. 254).

Clawson emphasizes that the recreation experience must be considered as a package deal and that the demand for outdoor recreation can be studied meaningfully only in terms of the whole experience. Although we have concentrated on the on-site experience—and most of the available research findings deal with that phase—the other phases are also important. As Clawson points out, "The recreationist will balance up his total satisfaction from the whole experience against its total costs; the dirty restroom will loom as large for some persons as the fine new park museum" (p. 256).

PERMANENT INTERACTIONS WITH THE NATURAL ENVIRONMENT

In the preceding pages we were concerned with a number of kinds of interactions between people and the natural environment. These interactions take place in a wide variety of outdoor-recreation areas, ranging from wilderness regions to local parks and recreational facilities. Although the duration of these interactions may vary from only an hour or so to several weeks or even longer, they can be considered temporary interactions. In this section we will examine more permanent types of interactions that usually involve years or even entire lifetimes.

In previous chapters we dealt in some detail with the relationships between the built environment and behavior. In this context we discussed, as an expanding system, rooms, houses, buildings, institutions, and cities and their effects on behavior. These environments, however, are part of what we will call the geographic environment, which may also influence behavior.

The Geographic Environment and Behavior

By *geographic environment* we mean the natural physical characteristics of a region, such as its geology, climate, and possible natural hazards, such as floods, blizzards, hurricanes, tornadoes, and earthquakes. Psychologists in the past considered the geographic environment to be of little significance as a determinant of behavior, but the growing interest in people/environment relationships has been accompanied by an increase in the attention paid to the geographic environment as a potential influence on behavior.

For many years, anthropologists, historians, geographers, and others have been writing about the influence of physical environmental variables on human activities. These writers, who have been called *environmental determinists,* contend that there are important factors in the geographical environment that affect the customs and character of people exposed to particular environments. Thus, environmental determinists argue that such national traits as bravery, laziness, and superstition may be determined by various geographical factors. This view is in contrast to the view of those who tend to think of people as the active agent in interactions with the natural environment. These theorists minimize the influence of the environment on behavior and, rather than thinking of the environment as shaping the organism, think of the organism as shaping the environment. Many psychologists and social scientists hold this view; members of the design professions are more likely to hold the former view.

The available data do not support the view of the environmental determinists, for relationships between national traits (which are not easily identified) and geographic characteristics are far from firmly established. Perhaps the most convincing data come from anthropological studies, such as those reported by Barry, Child, and Bacon (1959), who found some evidence that the type of subsistence economy determined by geographic environment may have a significant effect upon child-rearing practices. Agricultural societies apparently emphasize the development of such traits as obedience and responsibility. In hunting and fishing societies, on the other hand, personal achievement and self-reliance tend to be stressed.

A great deal of evidence, of course, supports the view that people have a considerable influence upon their physical environment. Their activities can and often do result in temporary and, frequently, permanent damage to the geographical environment. As mentioned previously, people's interactions with the environment can be studied from two points of view. One way is to view behavior as the dependent variable and some aspect of the physical environment as the independent variable. This approach would be the logical way to study such interactions from the point of view of the environmental determinist. However, people/environment interactions can also involve situations in which behavior is the independent variable and changes in the physical environment brought about by the behavior are the dependent variable. This type of interaction is of more concern to conservationists and others who are concerned with the changes that people make in their natural environment. Although environmental psychologists are also concerned with this problem, we have limited our discussion in this text to the situations in which behavior is thought to be influenced by the natural environment.

The Kinds of Behavior Studied

One can easily think of a variety of human activities that are directly or indirectly influenced by the geographical environment in which a person resides. The kinds of clothes that people buy will be determined, to some extent, by the region in which they live, as will the leisure activities in which they engage. Their job, the type of house they desire, and the type of automobile they buy may all be a function of the particular geographic environment involved. Obviously, the environment of a region has a great deal to do with the economy of the region, which, in turn, directly influences the behavior of the residents. Typically, however, these kinds of environment/behavior relationships have been of more interest to economists than to environmental psychologists.

Environmental psychologists have, instead, been chiefly interested in people's perception and comprehension of their geographical environment. The sparse research in this area that has been reported deals, for example, with residents' attitudes toward such natural hazards as floods or earthquakes. Similarly, some studies have dealt with how physical features of regions are perceived by residents of these areas. Researchers have asked, for example: What are the characteristics of a region that influence decisions on residential choice and migration? What characteristics tend to make living in a particular region a satisfactory experience? An unsatisfactory experience?

Obviously, researchers attempting to study the effects of geographic environments on behavior are dealing with an extremely complicated type of independent variable. Although a particular geographic environment may encompass other physical environments, such as buildings and cities, it is still only part of a person's total environment. In other words, it is difficult to use some feature of the geographic environment as an independent variable without having it confounded with a variety of other variables, all of which may influence behavior. These studies are further complicated by the fact that all the persons living in a particular region are not equally exposed to its geographic environment. Some residents are "closer to nature" than others, so that the environment may have a much more profound effect on their behavior.

When we consider the kinds of behavior that may be affected by permanent interactions with the natural environment, it is important to keep in mind that the environment may differentially affect individuals living in a particular region (see Figure 7-5). For example, consider the effect of the natural environment on farmers or ranchers and on city dwellers in the same general geographic region. Both types of individuals are exposed to basically the same climatic conditions but have a very different attitude toward the weather. Though the city dwellers may complain about a long hot spell and having to water their lawns frequently or running up their electric bills because of using their air conditioners, at worst the weather is a source of inconvenience and annoyance. The hot weather, however, may jeopardize the ranchers' or farmers' livestock or crops. The weather in this case is not just an inconvenience; their livelihood may be threatened. As Heimstra and McDonald (1973) point out:

> One of the reported differences in rural-versus-urban lives most referred to by urban people is their amazement at the many references rural people make to the weather. However, the entire rural community in an agricultural economy is dependent on the weather. If there is not enough rain, crops don't grow; if there is too much rain at the time of harvest, crops are lost; if it freezes or if it's too hot, income is lost. This affects not only the farmer but the machinery suppliers, warehouses, agricultural production, grocery stores, banks, realtors, car salesmen, and so forth [p. 315].

The Perception of a Geographic Environment

Persons seeking employment often list on their résumés a regional preference as well as their qualifications and job requirements. Some individuals may indicate a preference for the Southwest, others may state that they are seeking employment in the Northwest or the Great Plains region, while still others may simply state that they would prefer a position in a region where they have access to mountains or to some other feature of the geographic environment. Some individuals will suffer economic loss to live in a specific geographic environment.

Obviously, people's perception of a region is an important factor in determining whether they will establish residence there or, if they already live in the region, whether they will remain there. Residential choice or migration decisions, of course, are typically based on many other variables as well. For most individuals, economic factors are more important than geographic factors, particularly during periods of tight job markets, as in recent years. Thus, one does not see nearly so many regional-preference statements in employment bulletins as was the case some years ago, when a seller's market prevailed. However, if asked, most people would be able to list a number of

Figure 7-5. The geographic environment affects various individuals in different ways. Thus, the rancher whose livelihood is affected by a blizzard will develop attitudes and feelings about the geographic environment different from those of city dwellers who are inconvenienced by the blizzard or of others who find the results of a major storm a source of satisfaction and a means of interacting with the natural environment. (Photos by Don Polovich. Courtesy of the *Rapid City Journal.*)

features of the geographic environment that they perceive as desirable or undesirable.

How people perceive their geographic environment depends on a variety of factors. Degree of dependence upon the environment partly determines a person's attitude toward such environmental features as weather. As we suggested earlier, the manner in which a farmer perceives a given region may be quite different from the manner in which it is perceived by a city dweller. Similarly, a person in the construction industry, where the opportunity to work is often dependent on climatic conditions, is more aware of the environment than the typical office worker. Any person's list, then, of features of the environment perceived as desirable or undesirable will depend to a considerable extent on the direct impact of the geographic environment on that person's activities and means of making a living.

Personal characteristics are also important in determining how the environment is perceived. Aesthetic preferences for mountains, the desert, or some other terrain feature play an important role for many persons, as do attitudes and beliefs. For example, attitudes on overpopulation, industrialization, or pollution can result in satisfaction or dissatisfaction with a particular region.

Numerous factors contribute to a person's satisfaction with a given region and determine whether migration from the region is undertaken or seriously considered (Gibson, 1975; R. A. Hart, 1975). However, in considering the behavioral aspects of migration, an important point must be kept in mind. Wolpert (1966) says of migration:

> Common explanations for these movements revolve around the attractions of new economic and social opportunities, climes, or landscapes and repulsion from areas of limited opportunity or negative milieus. . . . Yet the migration record is filled with cases of reshuffling exchanges between similar environments. Thus deterministic hypotheses based upon economic, climatic, aesthetic, and other causes are only partial and do not correspond to any inherent determinism in migration behavior [p. 92].

Wolpert goes on to discuss a rather complicated model in which migration is viewed as an adjustment to environmental stress. He suggests that "in addition to the push and pull forces which may be latent in the migrational decision, the triggering off of that decision may frequently be associated with a stress impetus" (p. 95).

Considerably more research is required before all the factors associated with geographic-environment satisfaction, residence choice, and migration are understood. However, some studies have been conducted that deal with somewhat more specific aspects of the geographic environment. We will now consider research on the perception of natural hazards associated with various geographic regions.

The Perception of Natural Hazards

As Burton (1972) notes, there appears to be a persistent tendency for people to concentrate in regions subject to various types of natural hazards. He further points out that, despite the recurrence of floods, droughts, earthquakes, and other hazards, people not only occupy these regions in large numbers but also tend to move back into these areas after a disaster has taken place. The hazardous areas are quickly resettled, and new buildings are often more elaborate and expensive than those that were destroyed. Burton states, "The pattern seems to be universal. It occurs in widely different cultures and in relation to a variety of hazard events. How can this behavior be described and what is the explanation for it?" (p. 184). As we shall see, describing and explaining this behavior are difficult tasks and have met with only limited success.

Burton suggests that the tendency of persons to remain in or move back to areas with a high likelihood of natural hazards is due to a complex set of interwoven factors and that this kind of behavior occurs "sometimes as a result of one set of circumstances, sometimes as a result of a quite different set" (p. 185). Analysis of the factors involved indicates that this behavior may be due to one (or a combination) of three primary factors: (1) the comparative economic advantage of hazard areas, (2) the affected individuals' apparent lack of perception of threat or lack of concern, and (3) what Burton refers to as problems of institutional and social rigidities. Although our concern in this chapter is with the second factor, we will briefly mention the other two.

Hazard areas, in many instances, have greater economic advantages for the residents than those offered elsewhere. For example, a flood plain may be more fertile than other areas or may offer advantages for construction of industries or transportation systems. Thus, the opportunity for earning a livelihood may be better in the hazard area than in other regions. Concerning the problem of institutional and social rigidities, Burton suggests that frequently "the institutional arrangements in a society operate to keep people in the same place and to protect existing short-term interests by reinforcing the status quo and by failing to offer means whereby individuals may extricate themselves from an unpleasant situation" (p. 187). For example, in some instances payments are given to victims of a disaster with the stipulation that they rebuild on the same site.

Burton and his co-workers (Barker & Burton, 1969; Burton, 1962, 1965, 1972; Burton & Kates, 1964; Burton, Kates, Mather, & Snead, 1965; Burton, Kates, & White, 1968; Golant & Burton, 1969) and others (Kates, 1962, 1976; Saarinen, 1966) have been primarily concerned with the second factor listed—the apparent lack of perception of threat or lack of concern of individuals living in hazardous regions. These researchers, as well as others, have studied the manner in which people perceive hazard, their awareness of the probable consequences of natural hazards, their attitudes and beliefs about hazards, and the variations in individual responses to natural hazards. We cannot summarize all these investigations, but we will consider several to illustrate the techniques used and the kinds of results obtained.

Kates (1962) investigated the comprehension of flood hazards by residents of flood plains. He interviewed residents of six urban areas on which extensive data on past flooding were available. His interviews revealed a positive relationship between past experience with flooding and both expectation of future flooding and the adoption of protective measures. Nonetheless, many persons who had experienced one or more floods declared that they did not expect future floods. Such expectations are based on attitudes or beliefs. Although some residents believe that floods are in fact repetitive events and will probably occur again, they may feel that for special reasons they will not be struck again. Others do not view floods as repetitive events and feel that circumstances are such that their region will not be flooded again. They may base this expectation on existing or contemplated flood-control programs or on faith in God.

Thus, the interesting feature of studies such as those conducted by Kates is that many persons' comprehension of the flood hazard does not correspond to reality. When a region has been flooded on a regular basis for many years, it would seem logical that most residents would expect future flooding, particularly if no flood-prevention programs have been undertaken. Yet many residents of such a region will, when asked, indicate that they do not expect another flood.

Burton, Kates, and White (1968) studied the responses obtained from many interviews dealing with natural hazards. They found that the responses of residents of hazard areas to questions about their susceptibility to hazards fall into one of two general categories. Some responses can be classified as those that eliminate the hazard, while the other responses can be categorized as those that eliminate the uncertainty. Each of these categories has two subcategories. The responses that fall in the category of eliminating the hazard are broken down into (1) those that deny or denigrate the existence of the hazard ("It can't happen here") and (2) those that deny or denigrate its recurrence ("Lightning never strikes twice in the same spot"). The responses categorized as those that eliminate the uncertainty are broken down into (1) those that make the uncertainty determinate and knowable ("Floods only occur every ten years") and (2) those that transfer the uncertainty to a higher authority ("God will take care of us"). It is apparent that residents of regions susceptible to natural hazards have built up elaborate systems of attitudes and beliefs that, in their own minds, justify their remaining in the hazard areas.

Kates (1976) presents a conceptual model of the environment as hazard.

In this model the environment becomes hazardous only when it interacts with society. In other words, the environment is neutral, and an event becomes a catastrophe only because of people. When they are not present, a natural event such as an earthquake or a flood is not a hazard.

In his model of the environment as hazard, Kates classifies natural events as *intensive* or *pervasive*. The former are intense, brief, sudden, and difficult to predict. Examples are earthquakes and tornadoes. The latter are widespread, diffuse, and of longer duration. Examples are drought and air pollution. Consequences of the events may involve psychological, social, and economic threat as well as injury or death.

Although floods, earthquakes, hurricanes, and similar abrupt and devastating events are obvious examples of natural hazards, Kates's second type of natural events should also be thought of as hazards. Take, for example, droughts. Droughts are, like the other hazards, largely unpredictable and unpreventable. Moreover, large numbers of persons live in areas susceptible to drought, which may adversely affect their livelihoods. The effects of this type of natural hazard on behavior have not been extensively studied, though Saarinen (1966) conducted a comprehensive investigation of the expectations and attitudes of residents of arid regions of the Great Plains. He selected six counties in four states (Nebraska, Oklahoma, Kansas, and Colorado) that were quite similar on a drought index and interviewed a number of persons in each of the six areas. The residents of all the areas tended to underestimate the frequency of drought occurrence. However, the residents of the most arid counties tended to place a higher likelihood on the occurrence of drought in the future and, more specifically, to anticipate a drought in the next year.

To probe the adjustment of the residents to their semiarid environment more deeply, Saarinen administered to his respondents not only the standard cards of the Thematic Apperception Test (TAT) but also several specially designed TAT cards involving pictures of the arid environment. The TAT is a projective test that requires a person to make up a story about each picture in the test set and is designed to reveal to a trained examiner the various drives, needs, and conflicts that make up the subject's personality structure. It is assumed that in making up the story about each picture, the subjects will project their own personality into the situation and reveal aspects of themselves that they might not reveal directly to the interviewer. Analysis of the responses to tests of this type involves a great deal of detail and is beyond the scope of this text. However, Saarinen did find interesting variations among the persons who took his test. Certainly this approach has considerable potential in studies of responses to natural hazards in the environment.

In summary, then, residents of areas subject to natural hazards display what might appear to nonresidents to be some rather strange attitudes and beliefs about their regions. Typically, the threat of future occurrence of the hazard tends to be underestimated based on the statistical probability of the event's recurring. It would seem that the residents construct a rather elaborate system of beliefs and attitudes that, in their own minds, reduces the threat present in the environment. It should be kept in mind, however, that the perception of hazard in the geographic environment is subject to considerable individual variation and that, at least to some extent, the relevance of a natural hazard (in terms of direct impact on an individual) and the expected frequency of occurrence are related to the manner in which the hazard is perceived. (See Figure 7-6.)

THE IMPACT OF PEOPLE ON THE NATURAL ENVIRONMENT

Up to this point in the text we have been primarily concerned with one particular type of people/environment relationship—the effect of the physical environment on behavior. However, behavioral scientists are also interested in the effect of behavior on the environment, since modification of the environment will result in situations that have an effect on some aspect of behavior. For example, when we pollute the environment in some fashion, this pollution will likely affect the behavior of some segment of the population. In this section we will be concerned with some of the ways in which we have modified our physical environment and in some of the behavioral effects.

Pollution and Its Behavioral Effects

For the most part, research on pollution has been conducted by engineers interested in developing techniques that will reduce pollution and by physical and biological scientists interested in the effects of pollutants on the environment and on organisms exposed to the pollutants. Behavioral scientists have been slow in turning their attention to this problem, although the psychological impact of pollution has long been recognized. Now, however, increasing numbers of psychologists, sociologists, and other behavioral scientists are becoming involved in research on pollution. Relatively little research has been conducted on the behavioral effects of pollution. Much of the work that has been done has dealt with attitudes toward pollution and with the effects of pollution on various affective states.

There are, of course, many different kinds of pollution, all of which are capable of eliciting strong negative feelings in various people. (See Figure 7-7.) Some kinds of pollution, because of the obvious threat to health, will bring about a reaction in nearly everyone involved as soon as they are aware that a danger exists. Thus, an accidental release of nerve gas or some other dangerous pollutant would draw an immediate response from persons in the vicinity. For example, when an unusually high bacteria count was found in

Figure 7-6. Perception of the many types of natural hazards depends on a number of factors. Even the same general class of disaster may create different perceptions and feelings. Thus, a flood like the one whose results are shown in the upper photograph, which cost more than 200 lives, will be perceived differently from the flood shown in the lower photograph, where damage was restricted to crop lands and property. (Upper photo courtesy of the *Rapid City Journal.* Lower photo by Lars Larmon.)

Figure 7-7. There are many types and degrees of pollution, and people's reactions to pollution will depend upon the type and degree to which they are exposed. Though a person would probably have a negative reaction when viewing a river covered with soap suds, as in the top photograph, the reaction to thousands of fish killed by a chemical in a river would probably be considerably stronger. (Top photo courtesy of the *Sioux Falls Argus Leader.*)

the drinking water of a large Eastern seaboard resort city, the reaction was immediate and strong.

In this section, however, we will be concerned with what might be termed chronic pollutants, those to which people are exposed for long periods. Most types of air pollution are of this type, as is water pollution. Noise pollution, which was discussed in Chapter 5, has also become a chronic problem in many areas, as has pesticide pollution. These types of pollution generally do not have an immediate and dramatic impact on the individual. Usually, no immediate threat to health is perceived, and the pollution problem is viewed as an annoyance rather than as a physical threat. Many people are not even annoyed and appear quickly to adapt psychologically and biologically to a polluted environment. As will be pointed out later, people's reaction to pollution is a complex psychological phenomenon that is not easily explained.

Air and Water Pollution

National polls and surveys consistently show that a significant percentage of the population express concern over the problem of air and water pollution. In a recent U.S. poll dealing with national priorities, more than 50% of those surveyed named air and water pollution as one of the three most important domestic issues facing the government. One would assume, then, that the majority of persons in our society view pollution as a threat and feel strongly that something should be done about it. As we shall see, this is not the case.

Although virtually no research has been conducted on the effects of pollution on behavior, a number of studies have attempted to determine people's attitudes and feelings toward pollution. Most of these surveys have been conducted in regions where pollution is at a high level and where the attention of the public has been called to its existence by repeated media coverage. Some interesting findings have emerged from these studies.

As was pointed out in Chapter 2, the results obtained from surveys and polls depend to a great extent on how the questions are worded. For example, if surveyors asked their respondents, "Do you think that air pollution is a major health problem?" they could expect to get a very high percentage of positive responses. On the other hand, if the question were worded, "What do you consider to be a major health problem in this locale?" the response would probably be quite different. In fact, one common finding of the public-opinion polls on air pollution is that very few people will *spontaneously* complain about air pollution even if they live in areas with extremely high levels of pollution. In several surveys conducted in areas with serious air-pollution problems, when the respondents were asked whether the area is a healthy place to live, a high percentage said that it was. However, when the respondents in these same areas were asked whether they were bothered by smog, a significant percentage indicated that they were.

Thus, if the survey instrument is worded in a particular fashion, most people will indicate that they consider pollution to be a threat to health at worst and an annoyance at best. One might assume that one effect of pollution on behavior would be the development of a "let's do something about it" attitude on the part of the public. We have seen this development in relatively few individuals; they have been vocal and have been largely responsible for the action programs that have begun. However, most individuals do nothing even though they express concern about pollution when asked. Why?

There are probably a number of reasons for the lack of response in most of the public. Many people lack knowledge about the nature of pollution and have only a vague understanding of its possible ill effects. Although lack of understanding does not mean that intense opinions about pollution cannot be held (in fact, some of the strongest antipollution campaigners appear to know very little about the problem), it is often difficult to combat effectively a problem about which little is known.

Even if individuals do feel strongly that something should be done about pollution, what can they do? Most people have no idea of whom they can complain to or, if they do, may feel that their complaint will do no good. If people perceive their possible role in solving a pollution problem as having no effect, it is likely that no effort will be made. As Maloney and Ward (1973) point out in discussing their research in this area, "most people say they are willing to do a great deal to help curb pollution problems and are fairly emotional about it, but, in fact, they actually do fairly little and know even less" (p. 585).

This problem is illustrated in an article by O'Riordan (1974) dealing with public opinion and environmental quality. He cites a case in which public hearings were held on air-quality standards, people were concerned and attended the hearings, and they made demands but were ignored. The chairman of the commission later indicated that he did not feel the public was "competent" to testify about the standards and that really all the commission wanted from the public was some indication they wanted "pure air." The chairman felt that the public could not "understand what the numbers meant" and that the decisions should be left to the technical people. Obviously, people taking part in a hearing of this type would not feel that their input was of much value.

Actually, the chairman may have had a point. Much of the information available about air pollution as well as other types of pollution is in a highly technical form that relatively few individuals understand. However, some efforts are being made to provide information to the public by means of various types of environmental indexes that summarize complex data in terms that the public can understand. Thomas (1975) reports on the use of such an index (an air-quality index) and the public acceptance and use of it. A significant percentage of the persons who received the air-quality index thought it was a useful device and would serve to increase communication between scientists and the public. Whether methods such as this will be effective in increasing the interactions between the public and environmental decision makers remains to be seen.

Another reason that the public tends to do nothing about pollution problems may be that it will clearly cost something to solve the problems. We have pollution because we depend on a highly complex technology; and any change in the technology that may reduce pollution is bound to result in some drastic changes in our lifestyle. Most people appear to view the fight against pollution within a cost/payoff matrix of some sort. If the payoff appears great and the cost little, there seems to be a tendency to attempt to do something about the pollution problem. Thus, if a pollution source is traced to a particular industry, and closing or modifying the industry will have little economic impact on the region, the attitudes of the people living in the region toward the pollution are likely to be negative. On the other hand, if closing the industry will result in the loss of many jobs and a serious impact on the economy, the attitudes of the people in the region are likely to be quite different. In other words, the cost seems to be considerably greater than the perceived payoff. Though the cost is often measured in financial terms—increased taxes, for example—in some instances the cost may be such that people are involved in a very direct fashion.

The results of various surveys make it seem safe to state that many people are concerned, or at least express concern, about pollution. Though this concern is infrequently translated into action of any type, we do on occasion see forms of behavior that may be motivated by attitudes toward pollution. For example, there have been a number of demonstrations whose stated purposes have been to call attention to pollution problems. Moreover, people are now leaving various areas who say that their primary reason for the move is air pollution or other forms of pollution.

Other forms of behavior may be a direct result of pollution, but they are hard to identify. Obviously, if a high level of pollution results in physical distress of some type, such as burning eyes or difficulty in breathing, associated behavioral changes will occur that can be blamed on the pollution. If a person's agricultural crops or other property is damaged, we can expect some behavior changes. It has become customary for some residents of areas with high air pollution to get away from the smog occasionally for weekends. Thus, pollution may be modifying recreational behavior to some extent, although it is quite probable that if smog were not present, other reasons would exist for getting away.

Possibly the safest conclusion that can be drawn at present on the effects of pollution on behavior is that we do not know how behavior is affected. As pointed out previously, behavioral scientists are just beginning to express an interest in this area, and very few data currently exist upon which to base any conclusions. Though some information is available on attitudes toward pollution and on gross behavioral responses, such as demonstrations and emigration, pollution likely influences behavior in a number of subtle ways. Different approaches to studying the problem will probably have to be used before we can understand these subtle modifications. Laboratory research, in which a particular variable associated with pollution can be studied in some detail while other variables are controlled, may be such an approach.

An example of such a laboratory study is one conducted by Swan (1970), who used as subjects a number of high-school students living in Detroit. The subjects were presented with a series of slides showing various urban environments and were asked to report what environmental problem they observed in each slide. The primary purpose of the study was to assess perceptual awareness of air pollution. To accomplish this objective, each slide series represented a continuum of visible air quality ranging from relatively clean to highly polluted air. The number of slides in the continuum that a subject recognized as showing an air-pollution problem was used as the measure of that student's perceptual awareness of air quality. Swan found that perceptual awareness of air pollution was significantly less for students from low socioeconomic backgrounds. He speculates that such students had less chance to be out of the city and see natural sky colors and had come to accept the brownish-blue polluted atmosphere as normal. This conclusion raises an interesting question that has implications for research. As Swan points out, "it is difficult to determine if people are actually perceptually aware of polluted air in their environment or if they are more likely to base their responses to public opinion surveys on media coverage of the issue" (p. 68). It makes a considerable difference in how we interpret the data from attitude surveys if we know that the responses are based on direct perceptions or on information obtained from the media.

Other types of laboratory studies can contribute important information on the effects of pollution on behavior. Animal studies, for example, have been conducted in which various types of animals are exposed to extremely high levels of air pollution and the effects of this pollution on their behavior and general health determined. It is difficult, of course, to conduct studies of this kind on humans, although it is possible in laboratory situations to study the effects of some aspect of pollution on a person. Thus, in a study reported by Jones (1972), smog was manufactured in the laboratory, and the effects of various components of the smog on the eye were determined. The subjects wore eye masks through which the smog was introduced. The psychophysical method of limits was used, with the subjects being exposed to increasingly stronger concentrations of smog during a series of trials. The point at which a subject indicated eye irritation was considered the threshold for a particular concentration and type of smog. Using this technique, Jones found that the presence of hydrocarbon in smog is the best single predictor of eye irritation and that formaldehyde is close behind.

As indicated, much of the research on the behavioral effects of pollution has been community surveys to determine the percentage of people who are bothered by a particular pollution. Obtaining data of this type is relatively simple, but the data do not tell us much about the behavioral effects of the pollution. If people are in fact bothered, however, it is probably safe to say that their behavior has been modified in some fashion, perhaps in subtle ways that are difficult to measure. We might ask: What changes in lifestyles take place when chronic exposure to pollution is involved? Do social interactions, both within and outside family groups, change in any way? Is a person's affective state modified in any fashion? These questions and many others remain to be answered.

One point has become obvious through the research in this area. If meaningful answers are to be found to questions raised about pollution and behavior, highly sophisticated research techniques will be needed. It is apparent that the behavior/pollution interaction is extremely complex and influenced by many variables. The physical characteristics of the pollutant, the situation in which individuals are exposed to the pollutant, and the characteristics of the individuals themselves all interact in a complex way to determine just what behavioral effects occur. We are far from the point where the effects of a pollutant on behavior can be predicted.

In this section we have been primarily concerned with air pollution. Much of what has been said about this type of pollution is also applicable to the problem of water pollution. Surveys have shown that people are concerned about water pollution, but, as is the case with air pollution, most people are uncertain of what they can do about the problem. There have been strong reactions from some individuals and groups that have led to efforts by the government to do something about the problem. However, very little research has been conducted on the effects of water pollution on behavior.

Littering Behavior

Although we tend to think of pollution in terms of reduced quality of air and water, there is another form of pollution that we encounter in both the built and the natural physical environment. This is the pollution that results from littering. "Litter is trash, discarded or scattered about in disorder over a socially inappropriate area. It is ugly, expensive, widespread, and dangerous" (Robinson, 1976, p. 363). (See Figure 7-8.)

In view of the magnitude of the littering problem and the public

Figure 7-8. Research dealing with littering behavior has shown that it is a complex form of behavior but subject to modification by various approaches. (Photo by Lars Larmon.)

concern expressed about this problem, it is surprising that there is relatively little research dealing with the major variables involved in littering behavior. Robinson (1976), in a review of the available literature on littering behavior, attempts to categorize the studies on the basis of what he considers the personal variables and environmental variables.

Studies on personal variables have shown that age and residence are related to littering behavior. It appears that young people tend to litter more than older people. Persons residing in rural areas are more prone to litter than urban residents, and local residents are less likely to comply with littering regulations than visitors. Investigations of other personal variables have had inconsistent results. For example, there is evidence from one study that males litter more than females, but this finding did not hold up in another study. Similarly, one study found that blue-collar workers litter more than persons in white-collar positions, but another study did not find this to be true.

Some studies have been conducted on level of awareness of and willingness to act against litter. McCool and Merriam (1970) report that campers from local areas were less sensitive toward litter around their camping areas than visitors, that canoers reported seeing more litter than motorboaters, and that people in certain occupations were less sensitive to litter than others. Clark, Hendee, and Campbell (1971) report that only about 14% of the campers in their study believed there was too much litter on the campgrounds, while about 30% of the camp managers thought there was excessive litter. It has also been found that campers who expressed strong negative feelings about litter were more willing to pack out litter left by others than were campers who did not express strong feelings.

We have previously discussed the relationship, or, more appropriately, the lack of relationship, between expressed attitudes and behavior. In a detailed study of littering behavior conducted by Heberlein (1971), one of several factors studied was the relationship between littering attitudes and littering behavior. Essentially, Heberlein found no relationship between the two. In fact, in some instances the more negatively this type of behavior was rated, the more likely a person was to litter.

Studies on environmental variables have explored such questions as whether litter receptacles or litterbags and signs warning against littering modify littering behavior. Such signs and receptacles do appear to have an effect. Several studies have shown that the availability of litter cans will significantly reduce littering, although the effectiveness is determined by factors such as the placement and design of the litter cans and whether the areas involved are clean or dirty initially. As Robinson points out, "It appears more efficient to modify littering responses by manipulating the stimuli to which they are directed than by attempting to change attitudes that may or may not determine the behavior" (p. 375).

Several investigations have been aimed at determining the effectiveness of various motivational techniques in modifying littering behavior. Incentive techniques—for example, giving free movie tickets to children for picking up litter—have generally been effective. Successful incentives with both children and adults have ranged from soft drinks to money. Obviously, although this system may be effective, it is also expensive and probably not feasible on any large scale.

A study by Geller, Witmer, and Orebaugh (1976) examined the effects of instructions on what they called paper-disposal behaviors. In this study, persons entering grocery stores were given handbills listing several items on sale. On some of the handbills, special instructions concerning the disposal of the handbill were given. These instructions stated, "Please don't litter. Please dispose of properly." The instructions were at the bottom of the handbill and circled in red. The eventual disposal place of the handbill was the variable of interest to the investigators. They found that the antilitter message reduced the number of handbills that littered the shelves, counters, and display tables by more than 50%.

In an interesting approach to modifying littering behavior, Baltes and Hayward (1976) evaluated several strategies aimed at reducing littering in a football stadium. Football fans served as subjects. Each subject was provided with a clear plastic litterbag. Four different treatment strategies were employed. Some subjects received bags with a message considered a "positive reinforcer," which stated that the litterbag contained a number and could be turned in after the game for a possible prize. A second strategy, "positive prompting," used this message: "Pitch in! You will be a model for other people. . . ." The third strategy involved "negative prompting"; the message read, "Pitch in! Don't be a litterbug. Others will disapprove. . . ." In the fourth condition, subjects simply received a litterbag with no message. The control subjects received no bags at all. The subjects in each condition were seated in separate sections of the stadium. The dependent variable was simply the weight of litter collected from each section after the game. Baltes and Hayward found that significantly less litter was collected in the sections where the subjects with the litterbags were seated than in the control-group section. There were no significant differences in the effectiveness of the four strategies.

There are a few other studies dealing with littering behavior, but space limitations do not permit a discussion of them. As we have indicated, considering the magnitude of this problem, there is still relatively little research on it. However, theories concerning this type of behavior are beginning to develop (Baltes & Hayward, 1976; Robinson, 1976), and we will probably see more research in the near future.

Energy Development and the Environment

We have briefly discussed the interest of environmental psychologists in the effects of various kinds of pollution. In recent years another type of development has also had a significant effect on the natural environment. As energy has grown scarce, efforts to produce more fossil fuels and to develop new energy sources have resulted in projects that have had a tremendous impact on large numbers of people.

In some instances the production of energy means the construction of huge plants of one type or another. The presence of these plants may greatly modify a community. In other cases, resource extraction, such as coal mining, may disturb significant portions of a land area.

At one time, decisions on whether to go ahead with energy projects were based largely on economic factors. These are still critical elements in the decisions. However, government regulations now require an assessment of the potential environmental impact of these projects before they can be implemented. These environmental impact statements are given serious consideration in the decisions on whether to go ahead.

Psychologists and sociologists have been actively involved in the preparation of impact statements on a variety of projects. Since the specific findings vary from project to project, it would be meaningless to cite them here. Needless to say, however, there are numerous types of behavior that may be modified by energy-related projects. In some cases the modifications may be undesirable; for example, recreation areas may be destroyed. In other situations there may be desirable effects. For example, the energy development may increase local people's standard of living enough for them to indulge in activities that they could not afford before. In some instances, there may be both desirable and undesirable effects. Thus, the development of a large hydroelectric project may destroy a natural river and its accompanying fish and wildlife. On the other hand, it may help create a large lake with entirely new capacities for recreation and other uses. It is the task of the researcher preparing the impact statement to make as comprehensive an estimate as possible of both the desirable and the undesirable effects of the development.

Another aspect of the energy crisis has recently begun to interest behavioral scientists. Together with the concern about the modification of the physical environment by energy-related projects, there is an increasing concern about energy conservation. In an article on the U.S. federal government's relatively recent interest in behavioral aspects of energy conservation, Ferber (1977) points out that, although funds for this type of research are still limited, they are increasing. Studies are now being conducted on the development of psychological strategies for reducing energy consumption in homes, businesses, and so forth. With the existing energy situation, it is likely that a number of environmental psychologists will be engaged in this type of research in the near future.

The Problem of Urban Sprawl

We hear a great deal about people's impact on the natural environment in the form of pollution and energy-development programs. There is another type of impact that is not as well known to the general public but that is causing increasing concern among state and local governmental officials. This is the problem of urban encroachment on rural areas. (See Figure 7-9.)

In the past decade, millions of acres of rural areas have been converted to residential or industrial use. This urban sprawl has had, in many instances, desirable consequences—for example, inexpensive homes for persons who are able to upgrade their standards of living by moving to these areas—but urban sprawl also has many undesirable results. Schwartz, Hansen, and Foin (1975) point out: "The undesirable consequences attributed to urban sprawl include economically inefficient land use, excessive government service costs, unnecessarily large consumption of fuel and other resources for transportation, unattractive character of development, and the loss of open spaces that provide recreational, aesthetic, and resource conservation benefits" (p. 120).

Figure 7-9. Urban encroachment on rural areas is a growing problem. In this photograph is shown the first house in a development on land that only a short time before had been a cornfield. (Photo by Lars Larmon.)

There has been some research dealing with the motives for moving from the city to the suburbs and the resulting changes in behavior after the move is accomplished. Here, however, our concern is with the impact of urban sprawl on the natural environment. For example, just how much rural land is taken over each year through urban sprawl?

This is a difficult statistic to determine. J. F. Hart (1976), in an article dealing with urban encroachment on rural areas, discusses the wild array of estimates that have been presented—they range from 350,000 to 5 million acres a year—and points out that some of these estimates can be little more than sheer guesswork. After a careful review of the existing data, he concludes, "the evidence of urbanized areas indicates that urban encroachment does not appear to represent a serious immediate threat to the nation's supply of rural land" (p. 11). He later states: "It seems reasonable to conclude that little more than 4 percent of the nation's land area will be urbanized by the year 2000 and that urban encroachment will not remove significant acreages of land from agricultural production within the foreseeable future" (p. 15). Although this conclusion may be reassuring in terms of the broad, overall picture, it offers little satisfaction to the individual whose favorite hiking, bicycling, hunting, or fishing area has recently become a suburb.

REFERENCES

Acking, C. A., & Küller, R. *Factors in the perception of the human environment: Semantic ratings of interiors from colour slides.* Lund, Sweden: Department of Theoretical and Applied Aesthetics, Lund Institute of Technology, 1967.

Acking, C. A., & Küller, R. The perception of an interior as a function of its colour. *Ergonomics,* 1972, *15,* 645–654.

Altman, D., Levine, M., Nadien, M., & Villena, J. *Trust of the stranger in the city and the small town.* Unpublished manuscript, Graduate Center, City University of New York, 1969.

Altman, I. Some perspectives on the study of man–environment phenomena. *Representative Research in Social Psychology,* 1973, *4,* 109–126.

Altman, I. *The environment and social behavior.* Monterey, Calif.: Brooks/Cole, 1975.

Altman, I. Privacy: A conceptual analysis. *Environment and Behavior,* 1976, *8,* 7–29.

Altman, I., & Haythorn, W. W. The ecology of isolated groups. *Behavioral Science,* 1967, *12,* 169–182.

Altman, I., Taylor, D. A., & Wheeler, L. Ecological aspects of group behavior in social isolation. *Journal of Applied Social Psychology,* 1971, *1,* 76–100.

Altman, I., & Vinsel, A. M. Personal space: An analysis of E. T. Hall's proxemics framework. In I. Altman & J. Wohlwill (Eds.), *Human behavior and environment: Advances in theory and research* (Vol. 2). New York: Plenum, 1977.

Antigaglia, M. D., & Cohen, A. Extra-auditory effects of noise as a health hazard. *American Industrial Hygiene Association Journal,* 1970, *31,* 277–281.

Appley, M. H., & Trumbull, R. On the concept of psychological stress. In M. H. Appley & R. Trumbull (Eds.), *Psychological stress.* New York: Appleton-Century-Crofts, 1967.

Ardrey, R. *The territorial imperative.* New York: Atheneum, 1966.

Ardrey, R. *The social contract.* New York: Atheneum, 1970.

Babbie, E. R. *Survey research methods.* Belmont, Calif.: Wadsworth, 1973.

Baltes, M. M., & Hayward, S. C. Application and evaluation of strategies to reduce pollution: Behavior control of littering in a football stadium. *Journal of Applied Psychology,* 1976, *61*(4), 501–506.

Barker, M., & Burton, I. *Differential response to stress in natural and social environments: An application of a modified Rosenzweig Picture-Frustration Test* (Natural Hazard Research Working Paper 5). Toronto: Department of Geography, University of Toronto, 1969.

Barker, R. G. *Ecological psychology.* Stanford, Calif.: Stanford University Press, 1968.

Barry, H. A., Child, I. L., & Bacon, M. K. Relation of child rearing to subsistence economy. *American Anthropologist,* 1959, *61,* 51–64.

Barton, M., Mishkin, D., & Spivack, M. *Behavior patterns related to spatially differentiated areas of psychiatric ward day room* (Environmental Analysis and

Design Research Report Series 5). Cambridge, Mass.: Laboratory of Community Psychiatry, Harvard Medical School, 1971.

Bass, M. H., & Weinstein, M. S. Early development of interpersonal distance in children. *Canadian Journal of Behavioral Science,* 1971, *3*(4), 368–376.

Baum, A., Harpin, R. E., & Valins, S. The role of group phenomena in the experience of crowding. *Environment and Behavior,* 1975, *7*(2), 185–198.

Baum, A., & Valins, S. Residential environments, group size and crowding. *Proceedings of the 81st Annual Convention of the American Psychological Association,* 1973, *8,* 211–212.

Baxter, J. C., & Deanovich, B. S. Anxiety arousing effects of inappropriate crowding. *Journal of Consulting and Clinical Psychology,* 1970, *35,* 174–178.

Beck, R. J., & Wood, D. Cognitive transformation of information from urban geographic fields to mental maps. *Environment and Behavior,* 1976, *8*(2), 199–238.

Becker, F. D. Children's play in multifamily housing. *Environment and Behavior,* 1976, *8*(4), 545–574.

Bell, G., Randall, E., & Roeder, J. *Urban environments and human behavior: An annotated bibliography.* Stroudsburg, Pa.: Dowden, Hutchinson and Ross, 1973.

Bennett, C. A., & Rey, P. What's so hot about red? *Human Factors,* 1972, *14,* 149–154.

Berry, P. C. Effect of colored illumination upon perceived temperature. *Journal of Applied Psychology,* 1961, *45,* 248–250.

Betchel, R. B. An investigation of the movement response to environment. In C. W. Taylor, R. Bailey, & C. H. H. Branch (Eds.), *Second National Conference on Architectural Psychology.* Salt Lake City: University of Utah Press, 1967.

Birren, F. *Light, color, and environment.* Princeton, N.J.: Van Nostrand, 1969.

Black, F. W., & Milroy, E. A. Experience of air conditioning in offices. *Architecture Association Journal,* 1967, *82,* 157–163.

Bornstein, M. H., & Bornstein, H. G. The pace of life. *Nature,* 1976, *259,* 557–558.

Brain, P. Studies on crowding: A critical analysis of the implications of studies on rodents for the human situation. *International Journal of Mental Health,* 1975, *4,* 15–30.

Bronzaft, A. L., & McCarthy, D. P. The effect of elevated train noise on reading ability. *Environment and Behavior,* 1975, *7*(4), 517–527.

Brookes, M. H., & Kaplan, A. The office environment: Space planning and affective behavior. *Human Factors,* 1972, *14,* 373–391.

Brower, S. N. The signs we learn to read. *Landscape,* 1965, *15,* 9–12.

Burton, I. *Types of agricultural occupance of flood plains in the United States* (Department of Geography Research Paper 75). Chicago: University of Chicago Press, 1962.

Burton, I. Flood damage reduction in Canada. *Geographical Bulletin,* 1965, *7,* 161–185.

Burton, I. Cultural and personality variables in the perception of natural hazards. In J. F. Wohlwill & D. H. Carson (Eds.), *Environment and the social sciences: Perspectives and applications.* Washington, D.C.: American Psychological Association, 1972.

Burton, I., & Kates, R. W. The perception of natural hazards in resource management. *Natural Resources Journal,* 1964, *3,* 412–441.

Burton, I., Kates, R. W., Mather, R., Jr., & Snead, R. E. *The shores of megalopolis: Coastal occupance and human adjustments to flood hazard* (Publications in Climatology, 18, No. 3). Elmer, N.J.: Thornthwaite, 1965.

Burton, I., Kates, R. W., & White, G. F. *The human ecology of extreme geophysical events* (Natural Hazard Research Working Paper 1). Toronto: Department of Geography, University of Toronto, 1968.

Calhoun, J. B. The social aspects of population dynamics. *Journal of Mammalogy,* 1952, *33,* 139–159.

Calhoun, J. B. Population density and social pathology. *Scientific American,* 1962, *206,* 139–148.

Canter, D., & Lee, K. H. A non-reactive study of room usage in modern Japanese apartments. In D. Canter & T. Lee (Eds.), *Psychology and the built environment.* New York: Halsted Press, 1974.

Caplow, T., & Forman, R. Neighborhood interaction in a homogeneous community. *American Sociological Review,* 1950, *15,* 357–366.

Carp, F. M., Zawadski, R. T., & Shokrkon, H. Dimensions of urban environmental quality. *Environment and Behavior,* 1976, *8,* 239–264.

Caudill, W. W., Lawyer, F. D., & Bullock, T. A. *A bucket of oil.* Boston: Cahners, 1974.

Chapin, F. S., Jr. *Human activity patterns in the city.* New York: Wiley, 1974.

Cheyne, A. J., & Efran, M. G. The effect of spatial and interpersonal variables on the invasion of group controlled territories. *Sociometry,* 1972, *35,* 477–489.

Child, I. L., Hansen, J. A., & Hornbeck, F. W. Age and sex differences in children's color preferences. *Child Development,* 1968, *39,* 237–247.

Child, I. L., & Iwao, S. Comparison of color preferences in college students of Japan and the United States. *Proceedings of the 77th Annual Convention of the American Psychological Association,* 1969, *4,* 469–470. (Summary)

Choi, S. C., Mirjafari, A., & Weaver, H. B. The concept of crowding: A critical review and proposal of an alternative approach. *Environment and Behavior,* 1976, *8,* 345–362.

Chombart de Lauwe, Y. M. J. *Psychopathologie sociale de l'enfant inadapté.* Paris: Centre National de la Recherche Scientifique, 1959.

Christian, J. J. Effects of population size on the adrenal glands and reproductive organs of male white mice. *American Journal of Physiology,* 1955, *181,* 477–480.

Christian, J. J., & Davis, D. E. The relationship between adrenal weights and population status of urban Norway rats. *Journal of Mammalogy,* 1956, *37,* 475–486.

Cicchetti, C. J. A multivariate statistical analysis of wilderness users in the United States. In J. V. Krutilla (Ed.), *Natural environments: Studies in theoretical and applied analysis.* Baltimore: Johns Hopkins University Press, 1972.

Clark, R. N., Hendee, J. C., & Campbell, F. L. *Depreciative behavior in forest campgrounds.* Washington, D.C.: Forest Service Research Note PNW-161, U.S. Department of Agriculture, 1971.

Clawson, M. Economics and environmental impacts on increasing leisure activities. In F. D. Darling (Ed.), *Future environments of North America.* Garden City, N.Y.: Natural History Press, 1966.

Clough, G. C. Lemmings and population problems. *American Scientist,* 1965, *53,* 199–212.

Cohen, S., Glass, D. C., & Singer, J. E. Apartment noise, auditory discrimination, and reading ability in children. *Journal of Experimental Social Psychology,* 1973, *9,* 407–422.

Cooper, C. The house as a symbol of self. In J. Lang, C. Burnette, W. Moleski, & D. Vachon (Eds.), *Designing for human behavior: Architecture and the behavioral sciences.* Stroudsburg, Pa.: Dowden, Hutchinson and Ross, 1974.

Corbett, J. A. Are suites the answer? *Environment and Behavior,* 1973, *5*(4), 413–420.

Craik, K. H. Environmental psychology. In *New directions in psychology* (Vol. 4). New York: Holt, Rinehart and Winston, 1970.

Craik, K. H. Appraising the objectivity of landscape dimensions. In J. V. Krutilla (Ed.), *Natural environments: Studies in theoretical and applied analysis.* Baltimore: Johns Hopkins University Press, 1972.

Crandall, R., & Lewko, J. Leisure research, present and future: Who, what, where. *Journal of Leisure Research,* 1976, *8*(3), 150–159.

Cuttle, C. The sharpness and the flow of light. In R. Küller (Ed.), *Architectural psychology: Proceedings of the Lund conference.* Stroudsburg, Pa.: Dowden, Hutchinson and Ross, 1973.

Dabbs, J. M., Jr., Fuller, J. P., & Carr, T. S. *Personal space when "cornered": College students and prison inmates.* Paper presented at the 81st Annual Meeting of the American Psychological Association, Montreal, September 1973.

DeLong, A. L. The micro-spatial structure of the older person: Some implications for planning the social and spatial environment. In L. Pastalan & D. H. Carson (Eds.), *Spatial behavior of older people.* Ann Arbor: University of Michigan/ Wayne State University Press, 1970.

Ditton, R. B., Goodale, T. L., & Johnson, P. K. A cluster analysis of activity, frequency, and environment variables to identify water-based recreation types. *Journal of Leisure Research,* 1975, *7*(4), 282–295.

Driver, B. L. Potential contributions of psychology to recreation resource management. In J. F. Wohlwill & D. H. Carson (Eds.), *Environment and the social sciences: Perspectives and applications.* Washington, D.C.: American Psychological Association, 1972.

Driver, B. L., & Tocher, S. R. Toward a behavioral interpretation of planning, with implications for planning. In B. L. Driver (Ed.), *Elements of outdoor recreation planning.* Ann Arbor, Mich.: University Microfilms, 1970.

Eberhard, J. P. Architecture and energy: The need for a new esthetic. *AIA Journal,* 1976, *65*(2), 24–27.

Edney, J. J. Property, possession and permanence: A field study in human territoriality. *Journal of Applied Social Psychology,* 1972, *3*(3), 275–282.

Edney, J. J. Human territoriality. *Psychological Bulletin,* 1974, *81*(12), 959–973.

Edney, J. J. Human territories: Comment on functional properties. *Environment and Behavior,* 1976, *8*(1), 31–47.

Edney, J. J., & Jordan-Edney, N. L. Territorial spacing on a beach. *Sociometry,* 1974, *37*(1), 92–103.

Efran, M. G., & Cheyne, A. J. Shared space: The co-operative control of spatial areas by two interacting individuals. *Canadian Journal of Behavioral Science,* 1973, *5,* 201–210.

Efran, M. G., & Cheyne, A. J. Affective concomitants of the invasion of shared space: Behavioral, physiological, and verbal indicators. *Journal of Personality and Social Psychology,* 1974, *29*(2), 219–226.

Ellingstad, V. S., & Heimstra, N. W. *Methods in the study of human behavior.* Monterey, Calif.: Brooks/Cole, 1974.

Erwin, C. W., Lerner, M., Wilson, N. J., & Wilson, W. P. Some further observations on the photically elicited arousal response. *Electroencephalography and Clinical Neurophysiology,* 1961, *13,* 391–394.

Evans, G. W., & Eichelman, W. Preliminary models of conceptual linkages among proxemic variables. *Environment and Behavior,* 1976, *8*(1), 87–116.

Fanning, D. M. Families in flats. *British Medical Journal,* 1967, *18,* 382–386.

Faris, R., & Dunham, H. W. *Mental disorders in urban areas.* Chicago: Phoenix, 1965. (Originally published, 1939.)

Feldman, A. S., & Tilly, C. The interaction of social and physical space. *American Sociological Review,* 1960, *25,* 877–884.

Feldman, R. E. Response to compatriot and foreigner who seek assistance. *Journal of Personality and Social Psychology,* 1968, *10,* 202–214.

Feller, R. A. Effect of varying corridor illumination on noise level in a residential hall. *Journal of College Personnel,* 1968, *9*(3), 150–152.

Ferber, S. Energy research: Coming in from the cold. *APA Monitor,* 1977, *8*(3), 4–5.

Festinger, L., Schachter, S., & Back, K. *Social pressures in informal groups.* Stanford, Calif.: Stanford University Press, 1950.

Fisher, J. D., & Byrne, D. Too close for comfort: Sex differences in response to invasions of personal space. *Journal of Personality and Social Psychology,* 1975, *32*(1), 15–21.

Fitch, J. M. The aesthetics of function. *Annals of the New York Academy of Sciences,* 1965, *128,* 706–714.

Floyd, W. F., & Ward, J. S. Anthropometric and physiological considerations in school, office and factory seating. *Ergonomics,* 1969, *12*(2), 132–139.

Freedman, J. Population density and human performance and aggressiveness. In A. Damon (Ed.), *Physiological anthropology.* Cambridge, Mass.: Harvard University Press, 1971.

Freedman, J. *Crowding and behavior.* New York: Viking Press, 1975.

Fried, M., & Gleicher, P. Some sources of residential satisfaction in an urban slum. In J. F. Wohlwill & D. H. Carson (Eds.), *Environment and the social sciences: Perspectives and applications.* Washington, D.C.: American Psychological Association, 1972.

Friedman, E. P. Spatial proximity and social interaction in a home for the aged. *Journal of Gerontology,* 1966, *21*(4), 566–570.

Fucigna, J. T. The ergonomics of offices. *Ergonomics,* 1967, *10,* 589–604.

Geller, E. S., Witmer, J. F., & Orebaugh, A. L. Instructions as a determinant of paper-disposal behaviors. *Environment and Behavior,* 1976, *8*(3), 417–439.

Gibson, J. G. The intervening opportunities model of migration: A critique. *Socioeconomic Planning Science,* 1975, *9,* 205–208.

Gilligan, J. P. (Ed.). *Wilderness and recreation* (Study Report 3). Washington, D.C.: Outdoor Recreation Resources Review Commission, 1962.

Glaser, D. Architectural factors in isolation promotion in prisons. In J. F. Wohlwill & D. H. Carson (Eds.), *Environment and the social sciences: Perspectives and applications.* Washington, D.C.: American Psychological Association, 1972.

Glass, D., & Singer, J. *Urban stress.* New York: Academic Press, 1972.

Golant, S., & Burton, I. *The meaning of a hazard—Application of the semantic differential* (Natural Hazard Research Working Paper 7). Toronto: Department of Geography, University of Toronto, 1969.

Goldsmith, F. J., & Hochbaum, G. M. Changing people's behavior toward the environment. *Public Health Reports,* 1975, *90*(3), 231–234.

Goodman, R. F., & Clary, B. B. Community attitudes and action in response to airport noise. *Environment and Behavior,* 1976, *8*(3), 441–470.

Grandjean, E., Hunting, W., Wotzka, G., & Scharer, R. An ergonomic investigation of multipurpose chairs. *Human Factors,* 1973, *15*(3), 247–255.

Grant, M. A. Students' academic performance as influenced by on-campus and off-campus residence (Doctoral dissertation, Oregon State University, 1968). *Dissertation Abstracts International,* 1968, *29,* 4-A. (University Microfilms No. 68-14, 447)

Griffith, W., & Veitch, R. Hot and crowded: Influences of population density and temperature on interpersonal affective behavior. *Journal of Personality and Social Psychology,* 1971, *17,* 92–99.

Gump, P. V., & James, E. V. *Patient behavior in wards of traditional and of modern design.* Topeka, Kan.: Environmental Research Foundation, 1970.

Hall, E. T. *The silent language.* Garden City, N.Y.: Doubleday, 1959.

Hall, E. T. *The hidden dimension.* Garden City, N.Y.: Doubleday, 1966.

Hall, E. T. *Handbook of proxemics research.* Washington, D.C.: Society for the Anthropology of Visual Communications, 1974.

Hall, R., Purcell, A. T., Thorne, R., & Metcalfe, J. Multidimensional scaling analysis of interior, designed spaces. *Environment and Behavior,* 1976, *8*(4), 595–610.

Hallowitz, D. L. The relationship between selected goals of prospective homeowners and their experience in a new suburban housing development. *Dissertation Abstracts International,* 1969, *30,* 2435A–2436A.

Hart, J. F. Urban encroachment on rural areas. *Geographical Review,* 1976, *66*(1), 1–17.

Hart, R. A. Interregional economic migration: Some theoretical considerations (Part 1). *Journal of Regional Science,* 1975, *15*(2), 127–138.

Hay, D. G., & Wantman, M. J. *Selected chronic diseases: Estimates of prevalence and of physicians' service, New York City.* New York: Center for Social Research, Graduate Center, City University of New York, 1969.

Heberlein, T. A. Moral norms, threatened sanctions, and littering behavior (Doctoral dissertation, University of Wisconsin, 1971). (University Microfilms No. 72-2639)

Heimstra, N. W., & Ellingstad, V. S. *Human behavior: A systems approach.* Monterey, Calif.: Brooks/Cole, 1972.

Heimstra, N. W., & McDonald, A. L. *Psychology and contemporary problems.* Monterey, Calif.: Brooks/Cole, 1973.

Helson, H., & Lansford, T. The role of spectral energy of source and background color in the pleasantness of object colors. *Applied Optics,* 1970, *9*(7), 1513–1562.

Highway Research Board, National Research Council. *Environmental considerations in planning, design, and construction* (Special Report 138). Washington, D.C.: National Academy of Sciences, 1973.

Hollingshead, A. B., & Redlich, F. C. *Social class and mental illness.* New York: Wiley, 1958.

Hollingshead, A. B., & Rogler, L. Attitudes towards public housing in Puerto Rico. In L. Duhl (Ed.), *The urban condition.* New York: Basic Books, 1963.

Honikman, B. An investigation of the relationship between construing of the environment and its physical form. In *Environmental design: Research and practice* (3/AR8). Los Angeles: Environmental Design Research Association, 1972.

Hoppe, R. A. *Territorial markers, requested protection and the good neighbor.* Paper presented at the meeting of the Western Psychological Association, Los Angeles, April 1970.

Horowitz, M. J., Duff, D. J., & Stratton, L. O. Personal space and the body-buffer zone. *Archives of General Psychiatry,* 1964, *11,* 651–656.

Howells, L. T., & Becker, S. W. Seating arrangement and leadership emergence. *Journal of Abnormal and Social Psychology,* 1962, *64,* 148–150.

Hudson, R. Images of the retailing environment: An example of the use of the repertory grid methodology. *Environment and Behavior,* 1974, *6*(4), 470–494.

Hurt, N. J. How to keep kids from getting lost in the open school. *Phi Delta Kappan,* 1975, *56*(5), 345–348.

Imamoglu, V. The effect of furniture density on the subjective evaluation of spaciousness and estimation of size of rooms. In R. Küller (Ed.), *Architectural psychology: Proceedings of the Lund conference.* Stroudsburg, Pa.: Dowden, Hutchinson and Ross, 1973.

Isikpinar, E. M., & Velioğlu, S. The therapeutic environment—An attempt at studying the emotional content of architectural space. In R. Küller (Ed.), *Architectural psychology: Proceedings of the Lund conference.* Stroudsburg, Pa.: Dowden, Hutchinson and Ross, 1973.

Ittelson, W. H., & Kilpatrick, F. P. Experiments in perception. *Scientific American,* 1951, *185*, 50–55.

Ittelson, W. H., Proshansky, H. M., & Rivlin, L. G. Bedroom size and social interaction of the psychiatric ward. In J. F. Wohlwill & D. H. Carson (Eds.), *Environment and the social sciences: Perspectives and applications.* Washington, D.C.: American Psychological Association, 1972.

Izumi, K. Architectural considerations in the design of places and facilities for the care and treatment of the mentally ill. *Journal of Schizophrenia,* 1968, *2*(1), 42–52.

Jaco, E. G. *Evaluation of nursing and patient care in a circular and rectangular hospital unit* (final report). St. Paul, Minn.: Hill Family Foundation, 1967.

Johnson, K. E. The office environment people prefer. *AIA Journal,* 1970, *59*(2), 56–58.

Joiner, D. Social ritual and architectural space. In H. M. Proshansky, W. H. Ittelson, & L. G. Rivlin (Eds.), *Environmental psychology: People and their physical settings* (2nd ed.). New York: Holt, Rinehart and Winston, 1976.

Jones, M. H. Pain thresholds for smog components. In J. F. Wohlwill & D. H. Carson (Eds.), *Environment and the social sciences: Perspectives and applications.* Washington, D.C.: American Psychological Association, 1972.

Kaplan, S., & Wendt, J. Preference and the visual environment: Complexity and some alternatives. In *Environmental design: Research and practice* (3/AR8). Los Angeles: Environmental Design Research Association, 1972.

Kates, R. W. *Hazard and choice perception in flood plain management* (Department of Geography Research Paper 78). Chicago: University of Chicago Press, 1962.

Kates, R. W. Experiencing the environment as hazard. In H. M. Proshansky, W. H. Ittelson, & L. G. Rivlin (Eds.), *Environmental psychology: People and their physical settings* (2nd ed.). New York: Holt, Rinehart and Winston, 1976.

Keleman, K. S. Nurse behavior and nursing unit design. *Proceedings of the Symposium on Environmental Effects on Behavior.* Big Sky, Mont.: Environmental Design Group of the Human Factors Society, 1975.

Kelman, H. C. Human use of human subjects: The problem of deception in social psychological experiments. *Psychological Bulletin,* 1967, *67*, 1–11.

Kerlinger, F. N. *Foundations of behavioral research.* New York: Holt, Rinehart and Winston, 1964.

Kinzel, A. F. Body-buffer zone in violent prisoners. *American Journal of Psychiatry,* 1970, *127*(1), 59–64.

Kira, A. *The bathroom* (2nd ed.). New York: Viking Press, 1975.

Knowles, E. S. Boundaries around social space: Dyadic responses to an invader. *Environment and Behavior,* 1972, *4*(4), 437–445.

Knowles, E. S. Boundaries around group interaction: The effect of group size and member status on boundary permeability. *Journal of Personality and Social Psychology,* 1973, *26*(3), 327–331.

Knowles, E. S., Kreuser, B., Haas, S., Hyde, M., & Shuchart, G. E. Group size and the extension of social space boundaries. *Journal of Personality and Social Psychology,* 1976, *33*(5), 647–654.

Konečni, F. J., Libuser, L., Morton, H., and Ebbesen, E. B. Effects of a violation of personal space on escape and helping responses. *Journal of Experimental Social Psychology,* 1975, *11*, 288–299.

Korda, M. *Power: How to get it. How to use it.* New York: Ballantine, 1975.

Koslin, S., Koslin, B., Pargament, R., & Bird, H. Children's social distance constructs: A developmental study. *Proceedings of the 79th Annual Convention of the American Psychological Association,* 1971, *6*(1), 151–152. (Summary)

Kryter, K. D. *The effects of noise on man.* New York: Academic Press, 1970.

Kumove, L. *A preliminary study of the social implication of high density living conditions.* Toronto: Social Planning Council of Metropolitan Toronto, 1966. (Mimeographed)

Kuper, L. (Ed.). *Living in towns.* London: Cresset Press, 1953.

Lane, C. L., Byrd, W. P., & Brantly, H. Evaluation of recreational sites. *Journal of Leisure Research,* 1975, *7*(1), 296–300.

Lantz, H. R. Population density and psychiatric diagnosis. *Sociology and Social Research,* 1953, *37*, 322–327.

Larson, C. T. *The effect of windowless classrooms on elementary school children.* Ann Arbor: Architectural Research Laboratory, University of Michigan, 1965.

Latané, B., & Darley, J. M. Bystander "apathy." *American Scientist,* 1969, *57*(2), 244–268.

Lawton, M. P. Assessment, integration, and environments for older people. *Gerontologist,* 1970, *10*, 38–46.

Lawton, M. P., Nahemow, L., & Teaff, J. Housing characteristics and the well-being of elderly tenants in federally assisted housing. *Journal of Gerontology,* 1975, *30*(5), 601–607.

Lazarus, R. S. *Psychological stress and the coping process.* New York: McGraw-Hill, 1966.

Lewis, O. A poor family moves to a housing project. In H. M. Proshansky, W. H. Ittelson, & L. G. Rivlin (Eds.), *Environmental psychology: Man and his physical setting.* New York: Holt, Rinehart and Winston, 1970.

Liljefors, A. Light planning with minimum energy consumption. In R. Küller (Ed.), *Architectural psychology: Proceedings of the Lund conference.* Stroudsburg, Pa.: Dowden, Hutchinson and Ross, 1973.

Lipman, A. Chairs as territory. *New Society,* 1967, *9*(238), 564–565.

Lipman, A. Building design and social interaction. *Architect's Journal,* 1968, *147*(3), 23–30.

Lippert, S. Travel in nursing units. *Human Factors,* 1971, *13*, 269–282.

Little, K. B. Personal space. *Journal of Experimental Social Psychology,* 1965, *1*, 237–247.

Litton, R. B. Aesthetic dimensions of the landscape. In J. V. Krutilla (Ed.), *Natural environments: Studies in theoretical and applied analysis.* Baltimore: Johns Hopkins University Press, 1972.

Lloyd, J. A. Effects of crowding among animals: Implications for man. *Sociological Symposium: Human Crowding,* 1975, *14*, 6–23.

Lofstedt, B., Ryd, H., & Wyon, D. How classroom temperatures affect performance of school work. *BUILD International,* 1969, *2*(9), 23–24.

Long, B. H., Henderson, E. H., & Ziller, R. C. Developmental changes in the self-concept during middle childhood. *Merrill-Palmer Quarterly,* 1967, *3,* 201–214.

Lorenz, K. *On aggression.* New York: Harcourt Brace Jovanovich, 1966.

Lowin, A., Hottes, J. H., Sandler, B. E., & Bornstein, M. The pace of life and sensitivity to time in urban and rural settings. *Journal of Social Psychology,* 1971, *83,* 247–253.

Lucas, R. C. User concepts of wilderness and their implications for resource management. In *Western resources conference book—New horizons: Issues and methodology.* Boulder: University of Colorado Press, 1964.

Lyman, S. M., & Scott, M. B. Territoriality: A neglected sociological dimension. *Social Problems,* 1967, *15,* 236–249.

Lynch, K. *The image of the city.* Cambridge, Mass.: MIT Press, 1960.

Maloney, M. P., & Ward, M. P. Ecology: Let's hear from the people. *American Psychologist,* 1973, *28,* 583–586.

Mann, L. The social psychology of waiting lines. *American Scientist,* 1970, *58,* 390–398.

Manning, P. *Office design: A study of environment.* Liverpool: Pilkington Research Unit, 1965.

Marsden, H. M. Crowding and animal behavior. In J. F. Wohlwill & D. H. Carson (Eds.), *Environment and the social sciences: Perspectives and applications.* Washington, D.C.: American Psychological Association, 1972.

Martin, G. L., & Heimstra, N. W. The perception of hazard by children. *Journal of Safety Research,* 1973, *5,* 238–246.

Martyniuk, O., Flynn, J. E., Spencer, T. J., & Hendrick, C. Effect of environmental lighting on impression and behavior. In R. Küller (Ed.), *Architectural psychology: Proceedings of the Lund conference.* Stroudsburg, Pa.: Dowden, Hutchinson and Ross, 1973.

Mast, T. M., & Heimstra, N. W. Prior social experience and amphetamine toxicity in mice. *Psychological Reports,* 1962, *11,* 809–812.

Mathews, K. E., Jr., & Canon, L. K. Environmental noise level as a determinant of helping behavior. *Journal of Personality and Social Psychology,* 1975, *32*(4), 571–577.

McCain, G., Cox, V. C., & Paulus, P. B. The relationship between illness complaints and degree of crowding in a prison environment. *Environment and Behavior,* 1976, *8*(2), 283–290.

McCool, S. F., & Merriam, L. C. *Factors associated with littering behavior in the Boundary Waters Canoe Areas* (Science Journal Serial Paper 7357). Minneapolis: Agricultural Experimental Station, University of Minnesota, 1970.

McCormick, E. J. *Human factors engineering* (3rd ed.). New York: McGraw-Hill, 1970.

McCormick, E. J. *Human factors in engineering and design.* New York: McGraw-Hill, 1976.

McDonald, A. L., & Clark, N. *Evaluation of the interpretive program for Yellowstone National Park,* Washington, D.C.: National Park Service, 1968.

McIntyre, D. A., & Griffiths, I. D. The thermal environment: Buildings and people. In D. Canter & T. Lee (Eds.), *Psychology and the built environment.* New York: Halsted Press, 1974.

McKenna, W., & Morgenthau, S. *Urban–rural differences in social interaction: A study of helping behavior.* Unpublished manuscript, Graduate Center, City University of New York, 1969.

McReynolds, P. Reactions to novel and familiar stimuli as a function of schizophrenic withdrawal. *Perceptual and Motor Skills,* 1963, *16,* 847–850.

Mehrabian, A. *Public places and private spaces: The psychology of work, play, and living environments.* New York: Basic Books, 1976.

Mehrabian, A., & Diamond, S. G. Effects of furniture arrangement, props, and personality on social interaction. *Journal of Personality and Social Psychology,* 1971, *20,* 18–30.

Mehrabian, A., & Russell, J. A. *An approach to environmental psychology.* Cambridge, Mass.: MIT Press, 1974.

Mercer, C. *Living in cities.* Baltimore: Penguin, 1975.

Michelson, W. *Man and his urban environment: A sociological approach.* Reading, Mass.: Addison-Wesley, 1970.

Michelson, W. (Ed.). *Behavioral research methods in environmental design.* Stroudsburg, Pa.: Dowden, Hutchinson and Ross, 1975.

Milgram, S. The experience of living in cities. *Science,* 1970, *167*(3924), 1461–1468. (a)

Milgram, S. The experience of living in cities: A psychological analysis. In F. F. Korten, S. W. Cook, & J. I. Lacey (Eds.), *Psychology and the problems of society.* Washington, D.C.: American Psychological Association, 1970. (b)

Milgram, S. A psychological map of New York City. *American Scientist,* 1972, *60*(2), 194–200.

Miller, J. G. Adjusting to overloads of information. In D. McK. Rioch & E. A. Weinstein (Eds.), *Disorders of communication.* Baltimore: Williams & Wilkins, 1964.

Moriarty, B. M. Socioeconomic status and residential location choice. *Environment and Behavior,* 1974, *6*(4), 448–469.

Muriam, L., & Amons, R. Wilderness areas and management in three Montana areas. *Journal of Forestry,* 1968, *66,* 390–395.

Naftalin, A. The urban problem and action research. In F. F. Korten, S. W. Cook, & J. I. Lacey (Eds.), *Psychology and the problems of society.* Washington, D.C.: American Psychological Association, 1970.

Nakshian, J. S. The effects of red and green surroundings on behavior. *Journal of General Psychology,* 1964, *70,* 143–161.

Nemecek, J., & Grandjean, E. Results of an ergonomic investigation of large-space offices. *Human Factors,* 1973, *15,* 111–124.

Newman, O. *Architectural design for crime prevention.* Washington, D.C.: National Institute of Law Enforcement and Criminal Justice, U.S. Department of Justice, 1973. (a)

Newman, O. *Defensible space.* New York: Collier, 1973. (b)

Newman, O. A theory of defensible space. *Intellectual Digest,* 1973, *3*(7), 57–64. (c)

Nowlis, V. Research with the Mood Adjective Check List. In S. S. Tomkins & C. E. Izard (Eds.), *Affect, cognition, and personality.* New York: Springer, 1965.

O'Neill, S. M., & Paluck, R. J. Altering territoriality through reinforcement. *Proceedings of the 81st Annual Convention of the American Psychological Association,* 1973, *8,* 901–902. (Summary)

Onibokun, A. G. Social system correlates of residential satisfaction. *Environment and Behavior,* 1976, *8*(3), 323–344.

O'Riordan, T. Public opinion and environmental quality. In W. R. Derrick Sewell (Ed.), *Environmental quality.* Beverly Hills, Calif.: Sage, 1974.

Osgood, C. E., Suci, G. J., & Tannenbaum, P. H. *The measurement of meaning.* Urbana: University of Illinois Press, 1957.

Osmond, H. Function as the basis of psychiatric ward design. In H. M. Proshansky, W. H. Ittelson, & L. G. Rivlin (Eds.), *Environmental psychology: Man and his physical setting.* New York: Holt, Rinehart and Winston, 1970.

Paluck, R. J., & Esser, A. H. Controlled experimental modification of aggressive behavioral condition of severely retarded boys. *American Journal of Mental Deficiency,* 1971, *76*(1), 23–29.

Parsons, H. M. The bedroom. *Human Factors,* 1972, *14*(5), 421–450.

Paulus, P., Cox, V., McCain, G., & Chandler, J. Some effects of crowding in a prison environment. *Journal of Applied Social Psychology,* 1975, *5*(1), 86–91.

Paulus, P., McCain, G., & Cox, V. A note on the use of prisons as environments for investigation of crowding. *Psychonomic Society,* 1973, *1*(6-A), 427–428.

Porteous, J. D. Design with people: The quality of the urban environment. In W. R. Derrick Sewell (Ed.), *Environmental quality.* Beverly Hills, Calif.: Sage, 1974.

Preiser, W. F. E. An analysis of unobtrusive observations of pedestrian movement and stationary behavior in a shopping mall. In R. Küller (Ed.), *Architectural psychology: Proceedings of the Lund conference.* Stroudsburg, Pa.: Dowden, Hutchinson and Ross, 1973.

Prestemon, D. R. How much does noise bother apartment dwellers? *Architectural Record,* 1968, *143,* 155–156.

Preston, P., & Quesada, A. What does your office say about you? *Supervisory Management,* 1974, *19*(8), 28–34.

Propst, R. L. The Action Office. *Human Factors,* 1966, *8*(4), 299–306.

Proshansky, H. M., Ittelson, W. H., & Rivlin, L. G. (Eds.). *Environmental psychology: Man and his physical setting.* New York: Holt, Rinehart and Winston, 1970.

Proshansky, H. M., Ittelson, W. H., & Rivlin, L. G. (Eds.). *Environmental psychology: People and their physical settings* (2nd ed.). New York: Holt, Rinehart and Winston, 1976.

Pyron, B. Form and diversity in human habitats: Judgmental and attitude responses. *Environment and Behavior,* 1972, *4*(1), 87–120.

Rand, G. Pre-Copernican views of the city. *Architectural Forum,* 1969, *131,* 76–81.

Rapoport, A. Whose meaning in architecture? *Arena-Interbuild,* 1967, *83*(916), 44–46.

Rapoport, A. Toward a redefinition of density. In S. Saegert (Ed.), *Crowding in real environments.* Beverly Hills, Calif.: Sage, 1976.

Raskin, E. *Architecture and people.* Englewood Cliffs, N.J.: Prentice-Hall, 1974.

Reim, B., Glass, D., & Singer, J. Behavioral consequences of exposure to uncontrollable and unpredictable noise. *Journal of Applied Social Psychology,* 1972, *2,* 44–56.

Richardson, E. *The environment of learning.* New York: Weybright and Talley, 1967. Pp. 85–106.

Robinson, S. N. Littering behavior in public places. *Environment and Behavior,* 1976, *8*(3), 363–384.

Ronco, P. G. Human factors applied to hospital patient care. *Human Factors,* 1972, *14,* 461–470.

Rosengren, W. R., & DeVault, S. The sociology of time and space in an obstetrical hospital. In E. Freidson (Ed.), *The hospital in modern society.* New York: Free Press, 1963.

Rozelle, R. M., & Bazer, J. C. Meaning and value in conceptualizing the city. *Journal of the American Institute of Planners,* 1972, *38,* 116–122.

Saarinen, T. F. *Perception of drought hazard on the Great Plains* (Department of Geography Research Paper 106). Chicago: University of Chicago Press, 1966.

Saegert, S. (Ed.). Crowding in real environments. Beverly Hills, Calif.: Sage, 1976.

Saegert, S., Mackintosh, E., & West, S. Two studies of crowding in urban public spaces. In S. Saegert (Ed.), *Crowding in real environments.* Beverly Hills, Calif.: Sage, 1976.

Samuelson, D. J., & Lindauer, M. S. Perception, evaluation, and performance in a neat and messy room by high and low sensation seekers. *Environment and Behavior,* 1976, *8*(2), 291–306.

Sanders, S. G., & Wren, J. P. Open space schools are effective. *Phi Delta Kappan,* 1975, *56*(5), 366.

Schnee, R. G., & Park, J. The open school improves elementary reading scores in Oklahoma City. *Phi Delta Kappan,* 1975, *56*(5), 366.

Schwartz, S. I., Hansen, D. E., & Foin, T. C. Preferential taxation and the control of urban sprawl: An analysis of the California Land Conservation Act. *Journal of Environmental Economics and Management,* 1975, *2*, 120–134.

Selye, H. *The stress of life.* New York: McGraw-Hill, 1976.

Shafer, E. L., Jr., & Mietz, J. Aesthetic and emotional experiences rate high with Northeast wilderness hikers. In J. F. Wohlwill & D. H. Carson (Eds.), *Environment and the social sciences: Perspectives and applications.* Washington, D.C.: American Psychological Association, 1972.

Sherrod, D. R. Crowding, perceived control, and behavioral aftereffects. *Journal of Applied Social Psychology,* 1974, *4*(2), 171–186.

Skinner, B. F. *Science and human behavior.* New York: Macmillan, 1953.

Smith, S., & Haythorn, W. Effects of compatibility, crowding, group size, and leadership seniority on stress, anxiety, hostility, and annoyance in isolated groups. *Journal of Personality and Social Psychology,* 1972, *22*, 67–79.

Sommer, R. Studies in personal space. *Sociometry,* 1959, *22*, 247–260.

Sommer, R. The distances for comfortable conversation: A further study. *Sociometry,* 1962, *25*, 111–116.

Sommer, R. *Personal space: The behavioral basis of design.* Englewood Cliffs, N.J.: Prentice-Hall, 1969.

Sommer, R. *Design awareness.* San Francisco: Rinehart, 1972.

Sommer, R. *Tight spaces: Hard architecture and how to humanize it.* Englewood Cliffs, N.J.: Prentice-Hall, 1974.

Srivastava, R. K., & Peel, T. S. *Human movement as a function of color stimulation.* Topeka, Kan.: Environmental Research Foundation, 1968.

Srole, L. Urbanization and mental health: Some reformulations. *American Scientist,* 1972, *60*, 576–583.

Stankey, G. H. A strategy for the definition and management of wilderness quality. In J. V. Krutilla (Ed.), *Natural environments: Studies in theoretical and applied analysis.* Baltimore: Johns Hopkins University Press, 1972.

Stebbins, R. A. Physical context influences on behavior: The case of classroom disorderliness. *Environment and Behavior,* 1973, *5*(3), 291–314.

Steidl, R. E. Difficulty factors in homemaking tasks: Implications for environmental design. *Human Factors,* 1972, *14*(5), 471–482.

Stokes, S. J. *Student reactions to study facilities with implications for architects and college administrators* (ERIC Document Ed 013 535, EF 000 078). Amherst, Mass.: Committee for the New College, 1960.

Stokols, D. On the distinction between density and crowding: Some implications for future research. *Psychological Review,* 1972, *79*(3), 275–278.

Stokols, D. The experience of crowding in primary and secondary environments. *Environment and Behavior,* 1976, *8*(1), 49–86.

Suholet, D. The highway as open space. *Highway User,* March 1973.

Sundstrom, E., & Altman, I. *Relationships between dominance and territorial behavior: A field study in a youth rehabilitation setting.* Salt Lake City: University of Utah Press, 1972.

Swan, J. Response to air pollution: A study of attitudes and coping strategies of high school youth. *Environment and Behavior,* 1970, *2,* 127–152.

Tagg, S. K. The use of multidimensional scaling type techniques in the structuring of the architectural psychology of places. In R. Küller (Ed.), *Architectural psychology: Proceedings of the Lund conference.* Stroudsburg, Pa.: Dowden, Hutchinson and Ross, 1973.

Tennis, G. H., & Dabbs, J. M., Jr. Sex, setting and personal space: First grade through college. *Sociometry,* 1975, *38*(2), 385–394.

Thiessen, D. D., & Rodgers, D. A. Population density and endocrine function. *Psychological Bulletin,* 1961, *58,* 441–451.

Thomas, W. A. Public acceptance of an air quality index. *Journal of Environmental Education,* 1975, *6*(4), 18–24.

Trites, D. K., Galbraith, F. D., Jr., Sturdavant, M., & Leckwart, J. F. Influence of nursing-unit design on the activities and subjective feelings of nursing personnel. *Environment and Behavior,* 1970, *2*(3), 303–334.

Ullrich, J. R., Ullrich, M. F., Touzeau, R. F., Schweitzer, D. L., & Braunstein, H. M. Aesthetic evaluation of forest scenes in the northern Rockies by different groups of judges. *Proceedings of the Symposium on Environmental Effects on Behavior.* Big Sky, Mont.: Environmental Design Group of the Human Factors Society, 1975.

Valins, S., & Baum, A. Residential group size, social interaction, and crowding. *Environment and Behavior,* 1973, *5*(4), 421–439.

Van Der Ryn, S., & Silverstein, M. *Dorms at Berkeley: An environmental analysis.* Berkeley, Calif.: Center for Planning and Development Research, 1967.

Vogt, W. Population patterns and movements. In F. D. Darling (Ed.), *Future environments of North America.* Garden City, N.Y.: Natural History Press, 1966.

Ward, W. S., & Grant, D. P. Potentials for collaboration between human factors and architecture. *Human Factors Society Bulletin,* 1970, *13*(2), 1–3.

Warner, H. D., & Heimstra, N. W. Effects of intermittent noise on visual search tasks of varying complexity. *Perceptual and Motor Skills,* 1971, *32,* 219–226.

Warner, H. D., & Heimstra, N. W. Effects of noise intensity on visual target-detection performance. *Human Factors,* 1972, *14,* 181–185.

Warner, H. D., & Heimstra, N. W. Target-detection performance as a function of noise intensity and task difficulty. *Perceptual and Motor Skills,* 1973, *36,* 439–442.

Wells, B. W. P. The psycho-social influence of building environment: Sociometric findings in large and small office spaces. *Building Science,* 1965, *1,* 153–165. (a)

Wells, B. W. P. Subjective responses to the lighting installation in a modern office building and their design implications. *Building Science,* 1965, *1,* 153–165. (b)

Whyte, W. H., Jr. *The organization man.* Garden City, N.Y.: Doubleday, 1956.

Wildeblood, P. *Against the law.* New York: Messner, 1959.

Willis, C. L. An empirical study of bathtub and shower accidents. *Proceedings of the Symposium on Environmental Effects on Behavior.* Big Sky, Mont.: Environmental Design Group of the Human Factors Society, 1975.

Wilson, G. D. Arousal properties of red versus green. *Perceptual and Motor Skills,* 1966, *23,* 947–949.

Wohlwill, J. F. The physical environment: A problem for a psychology of stimulation. *Journal of Social Issues,* 1966, *22,* 29–38.

Wohlwill, J. F. The emerging discipline of environmental psychology. *American Psychologist,* 1970, *25*(4), 303–312.

Wolfe, M. Room size, group size, and density: Behavior patterns in a children's psychiatric facility. *Environment and Behavior,* 1975, *7*(2), 199–224.

Wolpert, J. Migration as an adjustment to environmental stress. *Journal of Social Issues,* 1966, *22*, 92–102.

Woodson, W. E., & Conover, D. W. *Human engineering guide for equipment designers.* Berkeley: University of California Press, 1966.

Yancey, W. L. Architecture, interaction, and social control: The case of a large-scale housing project. In J. F. Wohlwill & D. H. Carson (Eds.), *Environment and the social sciences: Perspectives and applications.* Washington, D.C.: American Psychological Association, 1972.

Yoshioka, G. A., & Athanasiou, R. Effect of site plan and social status variables on distance to friends' homes. *Proceedings of the 79th Annual Convention of the American Psychological Association,* 1971, *6*, 273–274. (Summary)

Zehner, R. B. Neighborhood and community satisfaction: A report on new towns and less planned suburbs. In J. F. Wohlwill & D. H. Carson (Eds.), *Environment and the social sciences: Perspectives and applications.* Washington, D.C.: American Psychological Association, 1972.

Zlutnick, S., & Altman I. Crowding and human behavior. In J. F. Wohlwill & D. H. Carson (Eds), *Environment and the social sciences: Perspectives and applications.* Washington, D.C.: American Psychological Association, 1972.

INDEX